No Small Matter

No Small Matter

The Impact of Poverty, Shocks, and Human Capital Investments in Early Childhood Development

Harold Alderman, editor

THE WORLD BANK
Washington, D.C.

ISBN: 978-0-8213-8677-4
eISBN: 978-0-8213-8678-1
DOI: 10.1596/978-0-8213-8677-4

Library of Congress Cataloging-in-Publication Data
No small matter / Harold H. Alderman, editor.

    p. cm. — (Human development perspectives)
   Includes bibliographical references and index.
   ISBN 978-0-8213-8677-4 (alk. paper) — ISBN 978-0-8213-8678-1 (alk. paper)
  1. Cognition in children—Developing countries. 2. Children—Developing countries—Economic conditions. 3. Children—Developing countries—Social conditions. I. Alderman, Harold, 1948-

BF723.C5N58 2011
305.23109172'4—dc22

2010053394

Cover photo: Shehzad Noorani/Drik/Majority World
Cover design: Naylor Design

Contents

Boxes

Figures

Tables

Foreword

The relative lack of attention to early childhood development in many developing countries remains a puzzle—and an opportunity. There is increasing evidence that investments in the nutritional, cognitive, and socioemotional development of young children have high payoffs. Researchers and development practitioners are building on this evidence to raise the topic's profile and bring it to the attention of decision makers.

This volume is an important contribution to these efforts. It thoroughly and carefully reviews the most recent empirical literature linking early childhood development outcomes, poverty, and shocks. In doing so, it brings an added perspective to the debate and makes the case that investments in the first years of life have the potential to be a critical component of poverty reduction strategies. The volume also goes beyond simply documenting the consequences of insufficient or inadequate focus on early childhood and identifies the range of policy options available to policy makers.

The Human Development Perspectives series seeks to present thorough research findings on issues of critical strategic importance for developing countries. At its core is the perspective that investments in human capital are an essential aspect of efforts to promote global development and eradicate poverty. This volume makes it convincingly clear that investing in and protecting the human capital of young children is No Small Matter.

Ariel Fiszbein
Chief Economist for Human Development
Chair, Editorial Board, Human Development Perspectives series
World Bank
Washington, D.C.

Acknowledgments

Many colleagues have contributed to this volume with advice and encouragement. We owe a particular debt of gratitude to Ariel Fiszbein, Elizabeth King, and Wendy Cunningham for initial suggestions in regard to the focus of the endeavor, and to Larry Aber, Emanuela Galasso, Alessandra Marini, and Laura Rawlings for reviews of the manuscript. Moreover, anyone who has worked on early childhood development in low-income settings would not be surprised to hear that Patrice Engle and Sally Grantham-McGregor provided useful advice on the range of programs globally. Peter Lanjouw offered specific insights for chapter 2, and Sinit Mehtsun provided excellent research assistance for chapter 3.

The data on Mozambique reported in chapter 1 would not have been available if not for the efforts of Barbara Bruns, Vitor Pereira, Michelle Perez Maillard, and the staff from the Save the Children office in Mozambique, as well as the Mozambican survey firm Austral-Cowi. Similarly, Norbert Schady, Alison Whyte, Ryan Booth, and staff from the Cambodian survey firm B.N. Consult made the analysis of Cambodia possible.

Contributors

Harold Alderman, Development Research Group, World Bank

Damien de Walque, Development Research Group, World Bank

Deon Filmer, Development Research Group, World Bank

Jed Friedman, Development Research Group, World Bank

Sebastian Martinez, Strategic Planning and Development Effectiveness, Inter-American Development Bank

Sophie Nadeau, Africa Human Development, World Bank

Patrick Premand, Human Development Network, World Bank

Jennifer Sturdy, Human Development Network, World Bank

Emiliana Vegas, Human Development Network, World Bank

Susan Walker, Tropical Medicine Research Institute, The University of the West Indies, Jamaica

Abbreviations

BMI	body mass index
BSID II	Bayley Scales of Infant Development II
CCT	conditional cash transfer
CHW	community health worker
CONAFE	Consejo Nacional de Fomento Educativo (National Council on Education Promotion) [Mexico]
DHS	Demographic and Health Surveys
DQ	developmental quotient
ECD	early childhood development
FFW	Food for Work
GDP	gross domestic product
GNP	gross national product
HAART	highly active antiretroviral treatment
HLBW	high low birth weight
HOME	Home Observation for Measurement of the Environment
IES	Impact of Event Scale
IMR	infant mortality rate
LAMI	low- and middle-income countries
LBW	low birth weight
MDI	mental development index
MMPI	Minnesota Multiphasic Personality Inventory-2
NBW	normal birth weight
NGO	nongovernmental organization
OECD	Organisation for Economic Co-operation and Development

OR	odds ratio
PDI	psychomotor development index
PIDI	Proyecto Integral de Desarrollo Infantil (Integrated Child Development Program) [Brazil]
PPVT	Peabody Picture Vocabulary Test
PTSD	posttraumatic stress disorder
SD	standard deviation
SE	standard error
SES	socioeconomic strata *or* stratus
TVIP	Test de Vocabulario en Imagenes Peabody (Peabody Picture Vocabulary Test)
UNICEF	United Nations Children's Fund
VLBW	very low birth weight
WAZ	weight-for-age *z*-score
WHO	World Health Organization

Introduction

Harold Alderman

There is growing recognition of the importance of early child development (ECD) in establishing the foundation for lifelong learning. Most people involved in basic education, for example, are likely to be aware of the arguments that the Nobel laureate James Heckman and his colleagues have made that champion ECD as the most cost-effective form of human capital investment compared with primary education or any subsequent schooling.[1] The evidence for assessing the cost-effectiveness of such programs, however, is dominated by a few longitudinal studies of interventions with young children in relatively prosperous countries. Only comparatively recently has similar evidence been assembled from developing countries. Still, a fair share of this knowledge generation for ECD fits in the category of "watch this space."

Early childhood development is taken in this volume as the period from when a child is conceived to when that child is six years of age (0–6). Three types of outcomes in early childhood are critical for future development in life: (1) physical growth and well-being, (2) cognitive development, and (3) socioemotional development. ECD policies and programs can directly affect these outcomes and therefore benefit both individuals and societies.[2]

To be sure, numerous thorough and current reviews examine the evidence of the impact of ECD programs on cognitive development from low- and middle-income settings. For example, a series of papers in the *Lancet* in 2007 (Engle and others 2007; Grantham-McGregor and others 2007; Walker and others 2007) assessed the lost development potential due to missed opportunities for early child health and child stimulation and identified promising programs that might be scaled up. Nores and Barnett (2010) added to the evidence base by undertaking a meta-analysis using 38 comparisons from 30 interventions performed in countries other than the United States and confirmed that strong evidence can be found on the cognitive and behavioral benefits from these interventions. Addressing a different audience, Naudeau and others (2010) summarize much of this evidence in a pragmatic guide for policy makers and practitioners.

However, another perspective on the interdisciplinary nature of ECD programs, although implicit in many approaches to ECD, is less prominent in discussions. This approach looks at the contribution of ECD programs to poverty reduction. Thus, the present volume focuses on ECD programs from the dual perspective of equity and efficiency with essays on cognitive development in low-income settings. This set of essays collectively covers the challenges that poverty and economic shocks pose to a child's development and the possible interventions that can be used to mitigate these challenges at scale.

That economic endowments contribute to child development is commonly noted in the literature. Less discussion, however, surrounds the degree to which economic shocks serve as an obstacle to a child's reaching his or her potential. Studies using methodologies ranging from laboratory research on animals to analysis of twentieth-century famines and epidemics confirm that maternal health can have a strong impact on the life of a child whose gestation corresponds to the period of an economic shock. Similarly, it is well established that a drought or similar shocks experienced in a child's first two years of life will still be manifested in that child's nutritional status when he or she is an adult. A few of these studies further confirm that the nutritional shocks are accompanied by economic consequences as well, but the pathways in terms of cognitive and socioemotional development that contribute to these consequences are often inferred rather than elucidated. By explicating these pathways from economic shocks and poverty to child development, these essays aim to contribute to the evidence base for programs that mitigate their consequences.

As such, this volume balances the intrinsic value of promoting children with the instrumental value of such investment in terms of economic outcomes: That is, the theme of this book bridges the rights approach to ECD, which argues that investing in children is the right thing to do, and an approach that argues it is also the smart thing to do.

That such a set of essays is needed may puzzle many readers. The critical period of brain development is well documented in the biological literature (Shonkoff and Phillips 2000). Similarly, the economic returns are documented in various papers, including the aforementioned papers by Heckman and various coauthors. The point is also made for developing country settings in two cross-sectorial reviews that had the evidence on a wide range of interventions presented by specialists in their respective fields and then asked a panel of leading economists to rank these economic returns (Lomborg 2004, 2009). The 2004 panel of eight economists included three Nobel laureates; another panel member received the prize subsequently. The panel assembled in 2008 included five laureates among its eight members. Both panels ranked programs to address malnutrition among those people with the highest rates of economic returns. A substantial share of the estimated returns to nutrition programs in these studies was attributed to cognitive development and can be considered a fair indication of the returns to similar programs in ECD (which were not included in these comparisons). Similarly, Engle and others (2007) illustrate the substantial magnitude of economic returns to ECD investments.

It is hard, however, to identify investment priorities—either between sectors or with the education field—shifting on the basis of such studies of rates of return for early child investments: That is, few budgets are reallocated after a finance minister has had a conversion on the road to Davos. Thus, the papers in this volume seek to make two aspects of the returns to ECD programs and the public rationale for such investments more apparent. The first theme addresses equity directly. Societies, at least in their public rhetoric, generally agree that an equity weight for income gains that accrue to the poor such that a dollar transferred to a poor household or earned by a poor household has a higher value in assessing national priorities than a similar dollar amount for the average household. To an even greater degree, societies value equity of opportunity. Thus, to the degree that ECD investments assist low-income households to participate in overall economic growth, an additional justification exists for the core argument that ECD is a priority component of an economc growth strategy. The essays in this volume present robust evidence that the failure of low-income children to develop to their full cognitive and emotional capacity is a major obstacle to their economic well-being, as well as to their contributions to future economic growth. This is illustrated both by the risk factors that are associated with limited household wealth and by the evidence on the heterogeneity of the overall impacts of ECD investments.

The second theme is a form of a "second best" argument. For various reasons, virtually all governments invest a large share of their public spending on education. Whatever reasons they may have to motivate such public investments in what is largely a private good—and elucidating the market failures and externalities that may underlie such decisions is an intriguing, albeit tangential, topic—any investment that increases the efficiency of these expenditures improves the allocation of public resources. As discussed in the essays in this volume, ECD programs achieve such an improvement in the rates of return to subsequent schooling investments.

The opening chapter in this volume, "Cognitive Development among Young Children in Low-Income Countries" by Sophie Naudeau, Sebastian

Martinez, Patrick Premand, and Deon Filmer, presents the key evidence that low levels of cognitive development in early childhood strongly correlate with low socioeconomic status (as measured by wealth and parental education) as well as malnutrition. Moreover, these developmental delays in early childhood begin early in life and accumulate quickly over time for the poorest children in a range of low-income settings. This chapter includes some of the most recent data available on how such delays accumulate among poor children across countries as diverse as Cambodia, Ecuador, Nicaragua, Madagascar, and Mozambique.

These early developmental shortfalls contribute substantially to the intergenerational transmission of poverty through reduced employability, productivity, and overall well-being later in life. Thus, Naudeau and colleagues conclude that in the absence of ECD interventions, poor children are likely to "play catch-up" for the rest of their lives. Conversely, policies and interventions—including center-based ECD programs, home-based programs designed to promote behavior changes among parents or caregivers, and conditional cash transfers for families with young children—are likely to improve children's cognitive and overall development outcomes.

The following chapter, "The Influence of Economic Crisis on Early Childhood Development: A Review of Pathways and Measured Impact" by Jed Friedman and Jennifer Sturdy, investigates how aggregate shocks—a main contributor to transitory poverty—have long-term consequences for children. Economic crises—stemming from financial downturns, macroeconomic contractions, or adverse weather events—are an unfortunately recurrent component in the economic development landscape. Although the costs from such crises are widespread, society's youngest members may be particularly vulnerable. This chapter reviews the evidence from a variety of literatures including economics, nutrition, and psychology. Recent studies that have identified how crises and other covariate shocks affect the likelihood of infant survival are reviewed in this chapter, which concludes with a discussion of available policy responses, including ex ante safety nets that are likely to mitigate the detrimental impacts of crises on ECD.

Beyond mortality, Friedman and Sturdy find few direct results that link crises directly with ECD. However, numerous studies suggest that economic crises have potentially severe negative impacts on both nutritional and environmental pathways for ECD as well as subsequent life opportunities. Evidence is also at hand that a crisis directly affects infant mortality, at least in low-income countries. Evidence for middle-income countries is more mixed with regard to mortality, and other evidence suggests that mortality effects are greater for more vulnerable populations. The chapter concludes with a discussion of available policy responses. Even though public spending that is relevant for protecting children is often threatened during crisis periods, some countries have successfully navigated this challenge, often with coordinated donor support. Friedman and Sturdy also find data that suggest that policy interventions directed at the demand side can be useful in mitigating the effects of an economic crisis, especially if they are already in place at the outset of the crisis or can be rapidly established.

Chapter 3, "Conflicts, Epidemics, and Orphanhood: The Impact of Extreme Events on the Health and Educational Achievements of Children" by Damien de Walque, deals with a different, yet pervasive, set of shocks that can color a child's entire life's trajectory. Conflicts and epidemics, in particular the HIV/AIDS epidemic, have plagued many developing countries in the last few decades. This chapter reviews the evidence on the impact of such extreme events on the well-being of young children, focusing on health and education outcomes. Using data from Burundi and Rwanda, de Walque reports on an emerging body of literature documenting the negative health and educational shocks endured by children in the aftermath of violent conflicts. Other papers reviewed in this chapter address the impact of parental death on schooling, a growing problem in Sub-Saharan Africa. Although such stress may be relatively more common in low-income countries, an evolving body of research on toxic stress on cognitive development also comes from the United States. De Walque's chapter links the two streams of literature. Although a first best strategy would be to avoid such stress, that conclusion is obvious. Thus, the chapter also explores measures to offset the challenge of toxic stress.

Longitudinal data indicate that the consequences of this stress are likely to persist even into adulthood with an adverse effect on future adult wages and productivity. Thus, De Walque concludes that after a conflict or a disaster it is important to protect and restore as quickly as possible children's relationship with their caregivers. For children who have lost their parents, it is crucial to provide nurturing caregivers; in most settings, orphans fare better if placed with close family members. Children's traumas are also mitigated when routines and opportunities to learn and play are maintained and supported and school activities are restored.

Although these three chapters describe the range of risks that children from low-income families face, the goal of the endeavor is to use this understanding to design programs and policies that will either prevent these impediments from determining a child's destiny or, failing that, to offset the initial obstacles. Susan Walker reviews a wide range of interventions aimed at children younger than three years of age in chapter 4, "Promoting Equity through Early Child Development Interventions for Children from Birth through Three Years of age." Given the evidence for the economic gradient and its timing presented in chapter 1, a clear need exists for programs to prevent the early loss of cognitive potential. More specifically, an urgent need has been identified for cost-effective strategies that can be scaled up in low-capacity environments. Because positive results are seen from interventions that utilize regular home visits by community workers, the next step is to capture these benefits in a manner that is less resource intensive. This chapter addresses the preventive nature and the potential for cost savings of outreach and community approaches necessary for sustainable scaling up that cover both nutrition interventions and parental enrichment programs. These include both those that entail periodic home visits by paraprofessional staff and those that focus on providing training to parents but do not necessarily involve visits by staff to the child's home. Thus, the chapter illustrates programs that integrate the communication of information about health and proper nutrition with the communication of information about care and early stimulation.

Walker notes that early interventions through home visits to improve caregiver-child interactions and increase stimulation benefit child development and can be delivered by trained paraprofessionals. These have sustained benefits for cognitive and psychological functioning, as well as educational achievements that are likely to benefit adult earning, functioning in society, and parenting of the next generation and thus promote equity. However, to achieve these improvements opportunities for integrating stimulation with existing services for children need to be identified, and provision of stimulation needs to be included as part of the core set of services provided for children younger than three years of age.

What if the coverage of such programs for very young children is not adequate to prevent a loss of potential? Can programs aimed at children four and five years of age increase a child's chance to benefit from his or her education? These questions are addressed in chapter 5, "The Convergence of Equity and Efficiency in ECD Programs" by Harold Alderman and Emiliana Vegas. The chapter explores how preschools—already considered an element of education strategies in many countries—can also be viewed as a component of a poverty reduction strategy. The chapter lays out the overall interplay of early ability and both preschool and primary school investments, indicating that some investments may close cognitive gaps. The chapter points out that even if ability and school readiness are malleable in the preschool period, the available evidence—largely from developed countries—suggests that interventions before a child enters preschool may be more cost-effective in narrowing the cognitive development gaps observed between children from poor socioeconomic families relative to those of their peers born to more advantaged families. Nevertheless, it remains an open question of the cost-effectiveness of such approaches relative to even earlier investments.

Alderman and Vegas note that evidence is accumulating regarding the impact of preschool programs in enhancing the results of subsequent schooling; it is less clear what features of such programs increase their effectiveness in terms of educational achievement. Still, the evidence indicates that the preschool enrollment gap between children of different socioeconomic backgrounds is currently a barrier to reaching the full potential of preschool education in reducing inequality of opportunity.

To briefly summarize the overarching theme of these five essays, in recent years governments and donors have aimed at reaching the Millennium Development Goals, which, among other objectives, strive to reduce child mortality and to achieve universal primary education. As progress is made on the former goal, however, meaningful gains on the latter become harder because new students who grew up in a resource-constrained environment are often poorly prepared to get full value from primary schools (Myers 1995). These children, moreover, are at risk of suffering long-term consequences when a climatic shock affects their communities or if they grow up during a low point of an economic cycle. They face further pervasive obstacles if their community is buffeted by civil strife. These crises as well as chronic barriers make ECD programs relatively hard to put in place, and more valuable if they can be established.

Thus, although in many countries ECD is promoted as a rights-based service (with universal coverage as an objective), rather than as a program designed to compensate a subpopulation for gaps in the child's home environment or to offset consequences of early malnutrition, focused preschool programs can serve as a key investment in a strategy to reduce the transmission of poverty from poor parents to their children.

Notes

1. See, among others, Heckman, Stixrud, and Urzua (2005).
2. Many organizations define ECD as the period of a child's growth until eight years of age. This volume, as well as other World Bank publications, however, covers a more restrictive period because the focus is on programs targeted to children before their entry into basic education.

References

Engle, P. L., M. M. Black, J. R. Behrman, C. O'Gara, A. Yousafzai, M. Cabral de Mello, M. Hidrobo, N. Ulkuer, I. Ertem, and S. Iltus. 2007. "Strategies to Avoid the Loss of Developmental Potential in More than 200 Million Children in the Developing World." *Lancet* 369 (9557): 229–42.

Grantham-McGregor, S., Y. B. Cheung S. Cueto, P. Glewwe, L. Richter, B. Strupp, and the International Child Development Steering Group. 2007. "Child Development in Developing Countries: Developmental Potential in the First 5 Years for Children in Developing Countries." *Lancet* 369 (9555): 60–70.

Heckman, James, Jora Stixrud, and Sergio Urzua. 2005. "The Effects of Cognitive and Non-cognitive Abilities on Labor Market Outcomes and Social Behavior." *Journal of Labor Economics* 24 (3): 411–82.

Lomborg, Bjørn, ed. 2004. *Global Crises, Global Solutions*. Cambridge: Cambridge University Press.

———. 2009. *Global Crises, Global Solutions: Costs and Benefits*. Cambridge: Cambridge University Press.

Myers, Robert. 1995. *The Twelve Who Survive: Strengthening Programmes of Early Childhood Development in the Third World*. Ypsilanti, MI: High Scope Press.

Naudeau, Sophie, Naoko Kataoka, Alexandria Valerio, Michelle Neuman, and Leslie Elder. 2010. "Investing in Young Children: An ECD Guide for Policy Dialogue and Project Preparation." World Bank, Washington, DC.

Nores, M., and W. S. Barnett. 2010. "Benefits of Early Childhood Interventions across the World: (Under) Investing in the Very Young." *Economics of Education Review* 29 (2): 271–82.

Shonkoff, J. P., and D. A. Phillips. 2000. *From Neurons to Neighborhoods: The Science of Early Childhood Development*. Washington, DC: National Academy Press.

Walker, Susan P., Theodore D. Wachs, Julie Meeks Gardner, Betsy Lozoff, Gail A. Wasserman, Ernesto Pollitt, Julie A. Carter, and the International Child Development Steering Group. 2007. "Child Development: Risk Factors for Adverse Outcomes in Developing Countries." *Lancet* 369 (9556): 145–57.

1

Cognitive Development among Young Children in Low-Income Countries

Sophie Naudeau, Sebastian Martinez, Patrick Premand, and Deon Filmer

Early childhood development encompasses children's cognitive development as well as their physical growth and well-being and socioemotional development. While endorsing the broad view of early childhood development highlighted in the introduction to this book, this chapter focuses on the cognitive domain, reflecting recent advances in the measurement of cognitive development in low-income countries. The objective of this chapter is to review the evidence that cognitive delays in early childhood can quickly accumulate among the poorest children and that indicators of cognitive development in early childhood strongly correlate with socioeconomic status.

The first part of the chapter takes stock of existing evidence on cognitive development in early childhood. A large share of evidence originates from developed countries, with more recent evidence coming from lower-middle-income countries in Latin America (in particular Ecuador and Nicaragua) as well as Madagascar. The second part of the chapter presents new evidence on patterns in cognitive development in Cambodia and Mozambique, two low-income countries. The chapter documents that young children in Cambodia and Mozambique are exposed to large cognitive delays that increase with age. It shows that cognitive development is associated with socioeconomic status as proxied by wealth and caregiver education, and that these gradients remain even when accounting for mediating factors such as nutrition and parenting. Overall, the patterns observed in Cambodia and Mozambique are remarkably consistent with those in the existing literature, suggesting that the prevalence of cognitive delays and socioeconomic gradients in early childhood development are likely to affect many children across low-income countries. The important policy implications of these findings are outlined in the conclusion.

A Review of the Literature

Long-Term Consequences of Cognitive Delays in Early Childhood

Low levels of cognitive and overall development in early childhood influence performance in school and throughout an individual's life. A substantial body of research suggests that delays in cognitive development during the early years of a child's life lead to negative consequences both in the short term, particularly regarding school readiness and performance, and in the long term through reduced employability, productivity, and overall well-being. Indeed, children who experience low levels of cognitive development in early childhood are more likely to repeat grades and to drop out of school early than those whose cognitive skills and overall school readiness were higher upon primary school entry (Feinstein 2003; Currie and Thomas 1999; Pianta and McCoy 1997). They are also more likely to have worse health and to engage in risky behavior such as smoking, risky sexual behavior, substance use and addiction, and criminal and violent activity as they become older (for a review on these topics, see Naudeau and others 2010).

These negative effects seriously undermine the social and economic benefits expected from the investment that parents and governments (in the case of publicly funded education and health policies) make in children. Moreover, these effects raise a fundamental question with regard to the quality of human resources available in the labor market and their capacity to make an effective contribution to facing the challenges of competitiveness and overall development of their country (Heckman and Masterov 2007).

Determinants of Cognitive Development

A range of environmental factors are likely to impact children's cognitive development in the early years. Research demonstrates that cognitive abilities are as strongly affected by the quality of the environment as they are by genetics, with genetic influences accounting for about half of the variance in cognitive abilities (for a review, see Fernald and others 2009; Plomin 1994).[1] In the United States, several studies show that low socio-economic status (SES), as measured by low income, wealth, or parental education, is associated with poor child development outcomes, including cognitive development (Aughinbaugh and Gittleman 2003; Baum 2003; Berger, Paxson, and Waldfogel 2005; Blau 1999; Guo and Harris 2000; Rhum 2004; Smith, Brooks-Gun, and Klebanov 1997; Taylor, Dearing, and McCartney 2004; Waldfogel, Han, and Brooks-Gun 2002). A large body of research also shows that a wide range of variables or "risk factors"[2] associated with poverty may act as "pathways" or "mediating variables" from low SES to poor cognitive development (Bradley and others 2001; Brooks-Gunn and Duncan 2007; Conger and Donnellan 2007; Evans and Miguel 2004). These risk factors include less responsive parenting, less stimulating learning environments, higher incidence of maternal depression and stress, lack of access to adequate nutrition, higher incidence of intrahousehold violence, poor housing, dangerous neighborhood, and pollution, among others.

SES and Cognitive Development in High- and Middle-Income Countries

There is evidence for a positive association between SES and cognitive development in high- and middle-income countries. Differences between children coming from households with low and high SES have been documented consistently in developed countries, especially in the areas of linguistic development and executive function.[3] See, for example, Bradley and Corwyn (2002), in the United States; Hackman and Farah (2009), also in the United States; and Siddiqi and others (2007), across 22 Organisation for Economic Co-operation and Development (OECD) countries.

In Turkey, a recent World Bank report (2009b) documents that both quality of the home environment for learning purposes and cognitive development among 36- to 47-month-old children significantly vary by SES. Figure 1.1 shows that children from various SES backgrounds receive starkly different inputs in support of their cognitive and overall development, including availability of learning materials in the home and parenting quality (as measured by the mother's responsiveness and language stimulation).

In turn, figure 1.2 shows that children from a wealthier background score much higher than those from lower SES in the areas of short-term memory and language comprehension (as measured by the Corsi and Tifaldi tests, respectively).[4]

Several studies from developed countries also reveal that early delays get worse as poor children get older. Findings also show that income gradients

Figure 1.1 Cognitive Development Inputs at Household Level for 36- to 47-Month-Old Children in Turkey

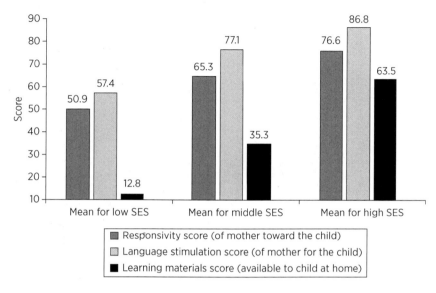

Source: World Bank 2009b. Data from the Study of Early Childhood Development Ecologies in Turkey, Koç University, 2008.

Note: SES = socioeconomic status.

widen as children get older, at least in terms of children's health, and it is now understood that these trends are at least partly due to the timing of development of various regions of the brain (see Fernald and others [forthcoming] for a review).

Prevalence of Early Childhood Delays in Low-Income Countries

Given general socioeconomic conditions, the prevalence of cognitive delays is likely to be high among young children in low-income countries. A recent study (Grantham-McGregor and others 2007) estimates that 219 million children under the age of five are disadvantaged.[5] Although this number represents 39 percent of all children under five in the developing world, the prevalence reaches a staggering 61 percent in the predominantly low-income region of Sub-Saharan Africa.

These children often experience a multiplicity of risk factors at the same time, including lack of access to basic water and sanitation infrastructure, lack of access to quality health services, inadequate nutritional inputs,

Figure 1.2 Cognitive Development Scores of 36- to 47-Month-Old Children in Turkey

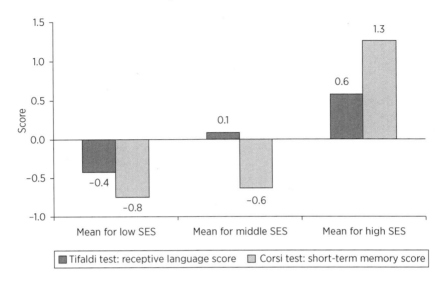

Source: World Bank 2009b. Data from the Study of Early Childhood Development Ecologies in Turkey, Koç University, 2008.

Note: SES = socioeconomic status.

parents with low education levels, and lack of access to quality day care centers and preschools (Naudeau and others 2010).

As a result, poor and otherwise disadvantaged children are likely to experience deficits in several areas of development, including in the cognitive domain. They are less likely than their peers to enroll in school at the right age, and they are also more likely to attain lower achievement levels or grades for their age (Vegas and Santibanez 2010).

Importance of Documenting Cognitive Delays in Low-Income Countries

Documenting the prevalence and magnitude of cognitive delays among young children in low-income countries is critical to design well-targeted, effective, and timely interventions. Early delays in cognitive and overall development can be costly to both individuals and societies. As mentioned above, children with early delays are likely to experience poor school performance and high morbidity rates, all of which contribute to costly inefficiencies in the public education and health sectors. As they get older, these children are also more likely to have low productivity and income, to provide poor care for their children, and to contribute to the intergenerational transmission of poverty. They are also less likely to contribute to the growth of their country's economy (see Naudeau and others 2010 for a review).

Developmental delays before age six are difficult to compensate for later in life because early childhood is a particularly sensitive period for brain formation. Indeed, neurological studies have shown that synapses (connections or pathways between neurons) develop rapidly during this period to form the basis of cognitive and emotional functioning for the rest of the child's life (Shonkoff and Phillips 2000). Both proper nutrition, especially from conception to age two, and early childhood stimulation in the first five years of life play a critical role in the process of brain formation and development (Nelson, de Hahn, and Thomas 2006; World Bank 2006). Some early stimulation inputs are particularly critical during specific subperiods (or windows of opportunity). For example, the capacity of a child to absorb language and to differentiate between sounds peaks at around nine months of age, well before the child can actually talk, thus indicating that it is critical for parents and other caregivers to verbally interact with children from birth onward (for a review, see Naudeau and others 2010). In turn, lack of proper nutrition and stimulation in the early years can lead to dramatic abnormalities in brain development (Shonkoff and Phillips 2000).

If wealth gradients can be documented among young children in low-income countries, then intervention strategies can be designed early to target beneficiaries accordingly. In addition, data can also be gathered on the relationship between cognitive development and other variables such as health and parenting quality that are likely to play a mediating role toward cognitive development. When such data are available, specific aspects of the child's environment can also be addressed in the design of early childhood development (ECD) interventions.

Recent Evidence from Ecuador, Nicaragua, and Madagascar

Although comparatively little is known about the link between SES and cognitive development in developing countries and about age-specific trends in this link, several recent studies are making important progress in these areas. Until recently, research on developing countries had placed greater emphasis on documenting the relationship between child health, particularly malnutrition, and cognitive development (for a review, see Paxson and Schady 2007), and little was known about whether socioeconomic gradients in cognitive development also existed among young children in developing countries (Schady 2006). In the last few years, however, several new studies taking place in developing countries, including

---

BOX 1.1

TVIP

The TVIP (Test de Vocabulario en Imagenes Peabody) is a version of the Peabody Picture Vocabulary Test (PPVT) that was adapted and normalized for Spanish-speaking populations in low-income settings. The test is administered by showing a child a series of plates containing four pictures. For each plate, an enumerator says a stimulus word and asks the child to identify the corresponding picture. The items are increasingly difficult, and the test stops when the child makes six errors out of eight consecutive items. The TVIP has been used in a range of studies in developing countries (Fernald and others 2009). While the TVIP is a measure of receptive language (a subdomain of language development), it is often used as a proxy for cognitive development because the two domains are closely interrelated in early childhood.

---

in Ecuador, Madagascar, and Nicaragua,[6] made great and consistent strides in this important area of research. As further documented below, all three studies demonstrate that (1) socioeconomic gradients also exist in low-income countries when it comes to cognitive development and (2) delays in cognitive and other areas of development increase quickly with age, to a point at which many poor children display signs of considerable delays well before primary school entry.

Ecuador. A study of cognitive development among young children in Ecuador shows that household wealth and parental education are associated with higher scores on a test of receptive language, and that development gaps are larger among older children. The study (Paxson and Schady 2007) uses a sample of more than 3,000 Ecuadoran children coming from predominantly young, poor families (98 percent had no school-age siblings, 82 percent were in the bottom two quintiles of the wealth distribution, and none had received social transfers in the six months preceding the survey, which took place in 2003–04). The main outcome measure for the analysis is a child's score on the Test de Vocabulario en Imagenes Peabody (TVIP: Peabody Picture Vocabulary Test), a test of receptive language further described in box 1.1. An important finding of the study, as shown in figure 1.3, is that steep socioeconomic gradients exist in this sample between children's cognitive development and their households' wealth. Similar associations are found with other measures of SES, including maternal and paternal education.

Figure 1.3 TVIP Vocabulary Scores of 36- to 72-Month-Old Ecuadoran Children by Wealth Quartiles

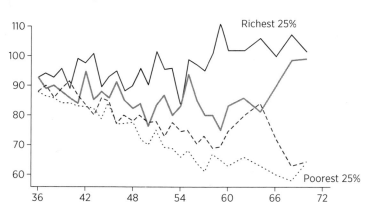

Source: Paxson and Schady 2007.

Note: The numbers on the y axis represent externally standardized TVIP scores. The mean of the reference population is 100, and the standard deviation is 15. Accordingly, children who score below 70 fall below the fifth percentile of the normative distribution. See box 1.2 for a discussion of external standardization and issues related to the reference population. TVIP = Test de Vocabulario en Imagenes Peabody.

Moreover, the damaging effect of poverty appears to increase with the age of the child. Indeed, although differences in the age-adjusted scores of three-year-old children in this sample are generally small, by age six children in the poorest 25 percent households have fallen far behind their counterparts in wealthier ones (richest 25 percent).[7] This pattern is likely to be causal because poor children tend to receive less speech directed toward them and because the speech they do hear tends to have reduced lexical richness and sentence complexity (Fernald and others 2009).

The Ecuador study also shows that child health and parenting quality are associated with test performance, although they account for only a small fraction of the association between SES and cognitive development. The results suggest that although four measures of health (height-for-age, weight-for-age, hemoglobin level, and number of months of breast feeding after birth) are jointly significant in their association with TVIP scores, only the measures of height-for-age and hemoglobin levels are individually significant. The results also indicate that all three variables included to measure parenting quality (that is, number of children living in the household, scores on the HOME scale,[8] and whether children are read to) are associated with children's performance on the TVIP. However, large associations between SES and cognitive development remain even after controlling for child health and parenting quality (together, these two constructs reduce the coefficient on wealth by only 13 percent).

Nicaragua. Another study documents low levels of cognitive development among poor children in Nicaragua. The study (Macours, Schady, and Vakis 2008; Macours and Vakis 2010) uses a longitudinal dataset built from a sample of 4,000 households with 2,086 young children between 36 and 72 months old. The data were collected in 106 rural communities in six Nicaraguan municipalities that were eligible to receive cash and productive transfers from a pilot program. The six municipalities were particularly disadvantaged in that they met the two criteria: (1) they had been affected by a drought the previous year and (2) they had a high prevalence of extreme rural poverty based on the national poverty map. Data collected in 2005 (before any intervention) and in 2006 (in a control group of households that did not receive any transfers) indicate that children in this sample exhibit serious signs of developmental delays, particularly in the areas of language development and short-term memory. On average, 97 percent of children in the sample scored in the lowest quartile of the normed distribution of the TVIP, and 85 percent scored in the lowest decile. Children in this sample also scored poorly (85 percent in the lowest quartile of the normed distribution and 61 percent in the lowest decile) on the McCarthy test of short-term memory, a test in which the enumerator reads increasingly long sequences of numbers to the child and asks him or her to repeat them.

The Nicaragua study also shows that age-adjusted cognitive scores get worse as children near primary school entry. In the case of language, the fraction of children who scored in the lowest decile of the TVIP normed distribution increased from 70 percent for children aged 36–59 months to 97 percent for children aged 60–83 months. Similar patterns can be observed for the McCarthy memory test.

Madagascar. A third study shows similar trends, this time among poor children in madagascar. The study (Fernald and others forthcoming) uses a nationally representative sample of 1,332 young children across 150 communities in Madagascar, a low-income country with a gross national income per capita of US$340 (World Bank 2007). Data collected in 2007 indicate that socioeconomic gradients exist in this sample, especially in the areas of receptive language, working memory, and memory of phrases (as measured by adapted versions of the PPVT, a subtest of the Stanford Binet Intelligence Scales for Early Childhood [5th edition],[9] and a subscale from the Woodcock-Munoz assessment,[10] respectively), all of which can be mapped to the broader area of cognitive and linguistic development. Indeed, children in the poorest socioeconomic quintile of the sample scored significantly lower than children in the richest quintile across these three areas of development.

Further, as in the Ecuador study, the difference between children in the highest and lowest SES categories (as measured by household wealth and maternal education) increased as children got older. The largest gaps by age six were in the areas of receptive language and sustained attention (as measured by the nonverbal Leiter International Performance Scales). Indeed, the difference in children's age-adjusted score in receptive language between children of mothers with high education and those with low education was nearly three times higher among six-year-olds than among three-year-olds. For sustained attention, the difference in age-adjusted scores between the richest and poorest children was 2.4 times greater among six-year-olds than it was in the three-year-olds.

Taking Stock. The above results show strikingly similar patterns across three countries, but the extent to which these trends can be documented in a broader range of low-income countries remains to be seen. In the second part of this chapter, we present new data from two additional studies in low-income countries, one in East Asia (Cambodia) and the other in Sub-Saharan Africa (Mozambique). Both studies validate the trends previously established in Ecuador, Madagascar, and Nicaragua. These two new studies also offer important insights regarding the cognitive development of poor young children in these countries and about the associations that exist between cognitive development, SES, nutrition, and parenting quality.

New Evidence from Cambodia and Mozambique

As we have reviewed above, a large share of existing evidence on cognitive development in early childhood originates from high- and upper-middle-income countries, with new evidence coming from samples of predominantly poor children in lower-middle-income countries, mainly in Latin America and, more recently, from Madagascar.

In this section, we present new evidence on patterns in cognitive development in low-income countries by analyzing large-scale datasets collected in Cambodia and Mozambique. We measure cognitive development by using the TVIP test of receptive language for children aged 36 to 59 months. First, we assess the extent to which young children in the Cambodian and Mozambican samples show signs of cognitive delays and if these delays increase with age. Second, we consider whether there are socioeconomic gradients by analyzing whether cognitive development is associated with SES as proxied by household characteristics such as wealth and caregiver education. Finally, we study whether other inputs into cognitive development such as nutrition and parenting are also correlated with SES, and to what extent they account for the association between SES and cognitive development. In other words, we test whether SES influences cognitive development through channels other than nutrition and parenting. We also consider whether socioeconomic gradients are larger for older children.

Overall, by providing a snapshot of cognitive development in Cambodia and Mozambique, the contribution of this second part of the chapter is to document the degree to which patterns previously discussed in the review of the literature also hold in these two low-income countries in East Asia and Sub-Saharan Africa, respectively.

The Cambodian and Mozambican Datasets

The Cambodian and Mozambican datasets illustrate patterns in young children's cognitive development before ECD interventions are implemented. They constitute large-scale baseline surveys from ongoing impact evaluations of ECD interventions. Both datasets were collected in 2008 and allow measuring of cognitive development for children aged 36 to 59 months based on the TVIP receptive language test. The surveys also include a broad range of covariates such as individual, household, and caregiver characteristics.

The Cambodian and the Mozambican datasets contain samples of predominantly poor children. The Mozambican sample contains information on 2,000 children aged 36 to 59 months. The data were collected in 76 communities eligible to participate in a center-based ECD program in three districts of Gaza Province (Bruns and others 2010).[11] Poverty is estimated at 59.7 percent in Gaza Province, which is above the Mozambican average of 54.1 percent, according to the latest national figures (Fox, Bardasi, and Van den Broeck 2005).

The Cambodia survey was collected in the most disadvantaged areas of the country (Filmer and Naudeau 2010). The sample contains data for 4,072 children aged 36 to 59 months in 141 communities across seven provinces.[12,13] Those communities were surveyed because they were eligible to receive either a formal preschool intervention or informal ECD services.[14] Eligibility criteria to receive these new services included incomplete primary schools, a poverty rate exceeding 30 percent, and the presence of high numbers of children between birth and age five.[15] Because the national poverty rate was estimated at 30.1 percent in 2007 (World Bank 2009a), the Cambodian dataset is best seen as containing a sample of children poorer than the national average.

Overall, both samples contain predominantly poor children that have no access to ECD interventions. The top panel of table 1.1 provides descriptive statistics on basic characteristics of the Cambodian and Mozambican datasets: 82.1 percent of children live in rural areas in the Cambodian

Table 1.1 Descriptive Statistics for Cambodian and Mozambican Samples

	Cambodia			Mozambique		
	N	Mean	SD	*N*	Mean	SD
Basic characteristics						
Age (months)	4,072	47.0	6.8	2,000	46.6	7.2
Male	4,070	51.5%		2,000	50.6%	
Urban	4,072	17.9%		2,000	13.9%	
Caregiver education (years)	4,039	2.9	2.7	1,981	3.3	2.7
Caregiver without education	4,039	28.5%		1,981	30.3%	
Number of adults in household	4,072	2.8	1.3	2,000	2.8	1.66
Number of children in household	4,072	3.0	1.4	2,000	3.8	1.84
Caregiver age	4,061	34.3	10.4	1,950	34.5	12.20
Mother in household	4,072	95.8%		2,000	86.7%	
Father in household	4,072	91.5%		2,000	70.4%	
Nutritional status						
Height-for-age z-score	4,011	−1.96	1.0	1,944	−1.78	1.59
Stunted	4,011	47.6%		1,944	43.1%	
Cognitive development						
Raw TVIP score	4,015	8.6	6.4	2,000	5.7	5.99
Standardized TVIP score	4,015	82.7	10.9	1,996	78.7	11.3
Parenting indicators						
Household has paper or pen	4,070	84.1%		1,990	74.9%	
Household has book	4,071	14.7%		1,735	75.4%	
Child plays with purchased toy	4,070	73.9%		1,980	28.4%	
Child plays with homemade toy	4,068	67.2%		1,996	55.1%	
Linguistic Stimulation Index (0–3)	4,071	1.40	1.0	2,000	1.50	1.1
Caregiver thinks punishment is necessary	4,032	48.2%		1,990	24.7%	

Source: Authors' calculations based on data from Bruns and others 2010 (Mozambique) and Filmer and Naudeau 2010 (Cambodia).

Note: N= number of observations; SD = standard deviation; TVIP = Test de Vocabulario en Imagenes Peabody.

dataset, 86.1 percent in the Mozambican dataset; 47.6 percent of children are stunted in the Cambodian data, 43.1 percent in Mozambique. The gender composition of both samples is balanced. A noteworthy feature of the Mozambican dataset is that a large share of parents do not live in the same household as their children (13.3 percent of mothers, 29.6 percent of fathers), reflecting a high prevalence of HIV/AIDS as well as frequent migration. The indicators of cognitive development and parenting presented in table 1.1 will be discussed in the next sections.

Cognitive Development in Cambodia and Mozambique

The TVIP test was used to measure the cognitive development[16] of young children in both the Cambodian and Mozambican datasets (see box 1.1 for more details).[17] In Mozambique, the TVIP test was translated and administered in Changaña (the local spoken language).[18] In Cambodia, the TVIP test was translated and administered in Khmer. Raw TVIP test scores are obtained by adding the number of words correctly recognized by a child until the test is suspended.

TVIP scores are best not compared across countries. Indeed, although the same version of the test was translated and applied in both Cambodia and Mozambique, the mere fact of translating the test and using it in different cultural settings can introduce variations in the relative difficulty level of each item. Accordingly, we focus on highlighting common patterns that hold across datasets, without comparing the specific scores of children in Cambodia and Mozambique.

By the same token, in this chapter we prefer presenting raw TVIP scores (interpreted as the number of words correctly recognized by a child until the test is suspended) instead of externally standardized TVIP scores. Externally standardized TVIP scores would explicitly benchmark the scores of children in the samples to the scores obtained by children in the reference sample used to norm the test.[19] In box 1.2 we highlight issues with the standardization and the reference sample that explain why we chose to use the raw TVIP score in this chapter.[20] In graphical representations, we present raw TVIP scores for children in the Cambodian and Mozambican samples while displaying in parallel the average raw score for the normed population. This allows documenting the likely exposure to cognitive delays without making explicit cross-country comparisons.

Figure 1.4 presents average raw TVIP scores in Cambodian (top panel) and Mozambique (bottom panel).[21] The mean raw score of children in the reference sample used to norm the test is presented in each graph. The upward dashed line in figure 1.5 describes the trajectory of cognitive development for an "average" child in the reference sample, showing the indicative rate at which children are expected to increase their language comprehension over time.

BOX 1.2

Issues with Externally Standardized TVIP Scores

Externally standardized TVIP scores are obtained by comparing raw TVIP scores in the study samples with the score distribution in a reference sample used to norm the test. However, the reference sample consists of Mexican and Puerto Rican children for whom a Spanish version of the TVIP was conducted. Because the cross-cultural relevance of the test is not guaranteed and the characteristics of the populations may differ, the normed sample may not be the appropriate comparison group to benchmark cognitive development among very disadvantaged children in Cambodia or Mozambique. Fernald and others (2009) or Cueto and others (2009) discuss the many unresolved issues related to measurement of cognitive development across countries.

Figure 1.4 illustrates patterns in standardized TVIP scores for children in the Cambodian and Mozambican samples. The normed distribution has a mean of 100 and a standard deviation of 15 for each age group. By contrast, figure 1.4 shows that standardized scores in the Cambodian and Mozambican samples are well below the norm at age 36 months, and that there is a significant downward trend in standardized scores.

Figure 1.4 also illustrates structural issues with the standardized scores. First, the downward-sloping dashed line represents the lower bound in the reference distribution, that is, the lowest possible standardized score a child can be assigned. The structure of the test implies that the lowest possible standardized score a child can achieve decreases with age: as children grow older, the scope for delays increases. Second, as another sign that the structure of the TVIP test may not fully translate to developing country datasets, the standard deviation of the test remains consistently below the norm of 15 across studies and varies by age instead of remaining constant. Third, some children in the Cambodian or Mozambican samples cannot make any progress with the test and have a raw score of 0, which is below the minimum raw score that can be normed. If these children are assigned the lower bound of the reference distribution, their standardized score is censored and overestimates their level of cognitive development. Censoring may imply that the standardized scores of low-performing children are artificially inflated, which can create biases when trying to estimate differences in test scores due to covariates such as socioeconomic status.

Sources: Cueto and others (2009); Fernald and others (2009); Paxson and Schady 2007; Schady 2010.

Figure 1.4 Standardized TVIP Score by Age

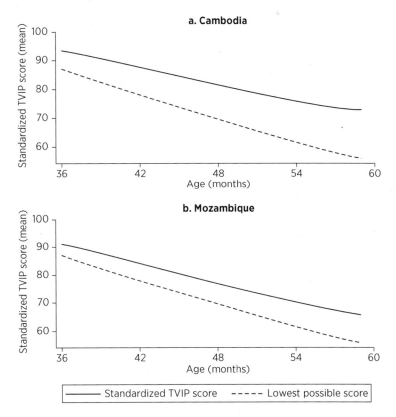

a. Cambodia

b. Mozambique

—— Standardized TVIP score - - - - - Lowest possible score

Source: Authors' calculations based on data from Bruns and others 2010 (Mozambique) and Filmer and Naudeau 2010 (Cambodia).

Note: The standardized scores are standardized based on the performance of children in the reference population used to norm the test. The lowest possible score is the lowest possible score that can be achieved for each age. The test is built such that the lowest possible score decreases with age. This external standardization may not be fully appropriate because it was established based on a Spanish version of the TVIP in a sample of Mexican and Puerto Rican children whose characteristics may differ (see box 1.2). TVIP = Test de Vocabulario en Imagenes Peabody.

The distance between the raw TVIP score in the Cambodian or Mozambican data and the mean score in the reference sample indicates the extent to which children in these two countries lag behind the reference sample. Figure 1.5 shows that there are strong signs of cognitive delays for children in both countries. Signs of delays are already apparent at age 36 months, when TVIP scores from the Khmer and Changaña tests appear significantly below the mean score in the reference sample. The exposure to delays

Figure 1.5 Raw TVIP Scores by Age

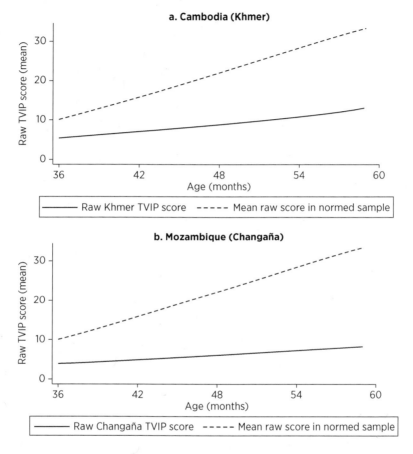

a. Cambodia (Khmer)

Raw Khmer TVIP score ———— Mean raw score in normed sample - - - - -

b. Mozambique (Changaña)

Raw Changaña TVIP score ———— Mean raw score in normed sample - - - - -

Source: Authors' calculations based on data from Bruns and others 2010 (Mozambique) and Filmer and Naudeau 2010 (Cambodia).

Note: The "mean raw score in the normed sample" is the mean raw TVIP score achieved by children in the reference population used to norm the test (see box 1.2). Comparisons between raw TVIP scores in Cambodia and Mozambique and the norm should be undertaken carefully. The norm may not be fully appropriate because it was established based on a Spanish version of the TVIP in a sample of Mexican and Puerto Rican children whose characteristics may differ. TVIP = Test de Vocabulario en Imagenes Peabody.

increases with age in the Cambodian and Mozambican samples, as shown by the widening gap between average raw scores in the samples and the mean score in the reference sample. In other words, although children are universally expected to demonstrate an increased understanding of language between ages three and five (as evidenced in the TVIP by the increasing number of words that a child can understand), five-year-old children in our Cambodian and Mozambican samples show only limited increased language understanding compared with their three-year-old peers.

Figure 1.5 displays average TVIP scores measured for different cohorts of children from a cross-sectional survey, not for a panel following the same cohort of children over time. As such, figure 1.5 illustrates cohort effects, not age effects. Conceptually, cohort effects may be driven by other factors that change over time and may explain differences in cognitive development between cohorts. However, the patterns in figure 1.5 are strikingly similar to those from the published literature documented earlier in this chapter, such as Paxson and Schady (2007) in Ecuador; Macours, Schady, and Vakis (2008) or Macours and Vakis (2010) in Nicaragua; or Fernald and others (forthcoming) in Madagascar. Taken together, these studies provide strong evidence that young children in developing countries show signs of large cognitive delays. In addition, that similar trends emerge across countries strongly suggests that observed cohort effects are not simply driven by other time-varying factors. Cognitive delays, indeed, appear to accumulate over time.

The Cambodian and Mozambican data also show that there are very large variations in cognitive development between children of the same age in each sample. Even children in the high end of the distribution in the Cambodian and Mozambican samples are showing substantial signs of delays.[22] At the same time, some children perform much better than their peers within each sample. The next section discusses a series of covariates that explains part of the large observed variation in raw TVIP scores, hence suggesting which factors contribute to improved cognitive development.

Socioeconomic Status and Cognitive Development

As we have discussed above, a variety of inputs and risk factors affect children's cognitive development (Fernald and others 2009; Naudeau and others 2010). SES, taken as including a set of household characteristics such as wealth and caregiver education, constitutes one of these inputs or risk factors. A pathway from SES to cognitive development raises important policy questions because it suggests that cognitive delays contribute to the intergenerational transmission of poverty from parents to their children. This section illustrates how correlates that proxy for SES are associated with cognitive development in early childhood. This association may capture the effect of other inputs that are also correlated with SES but not explicitly accounted for. Still, this section documents the overall association between SES and cognitive development. The next section will

Figure 1.6 Raw TVIP Score by Age and Wealth Quartile

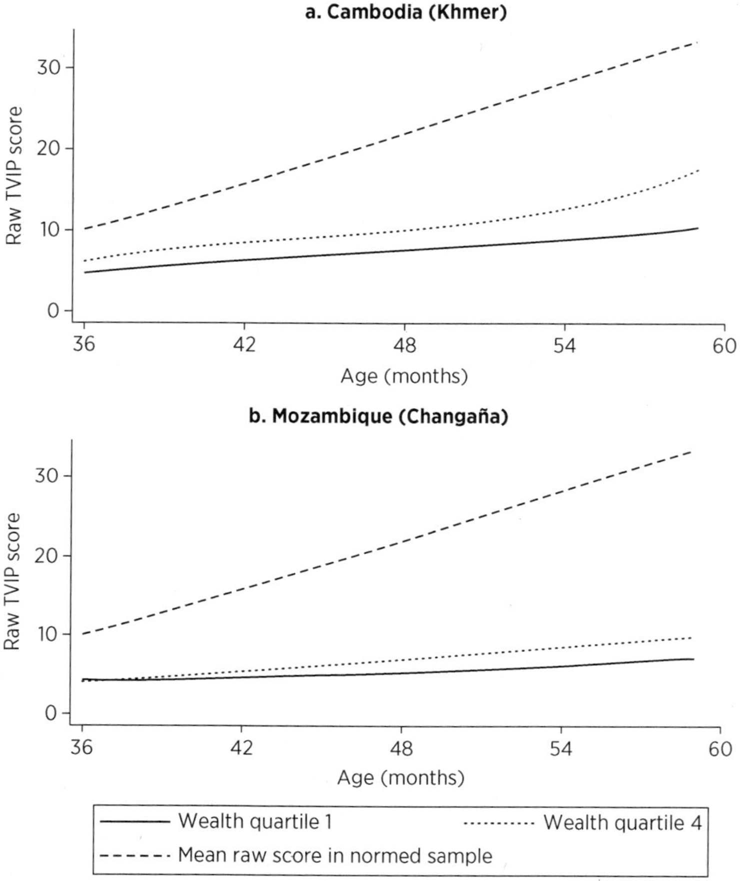

a. Cambodia (Khmer)

b. Mozambique (Changaña)

Wealth quartile 1 .... Wealth quartile 4
Mean raw score in normed sample

Source: Authors' calculations based on data from Bruns and others 2010 (Mozambique) and Filmer and Naudeau 2010 (Cambodia).

Note: The "mean raw score in the normed sample" is the mean raw TVIP score achieved by children in the reference population used to norm the test (see box 1.2). Comparisons between raw TVIP scores in Cambodia and Mozambique and the norm should be undertaken carefully. The norm may not be fully appropriate because it was established based on a Spanish version of the TVIP in a sample of Mexican and Puerto Rican children whose characteristics may differ. TVIP = Test de Vocabulario en Imagenes Peabody.

explicitly analyze the role of parenting and nutrition, two potential mediating factors that could account for part of the overall correlation between SES and cognitive development.

We use two proxies for SES: a wealth index and caregiver education. In the absence of comprehensive data on per capita household expenditures in the Cambodian and Mozambican datasets, we use a wealth index to proxy for per capita household expenditures.[23] The asset indices are derived from principal component analysis on ownership of household assets and durables.[24] Filmer and Scott (2008) show that asset indices constitute a good proxy for per capita household expenditures. Caregiver education is defined as the number of completed years of education from primary school onward. The measure of caregiver education essentially captures parental education for the broad majority of children who live with their parents. However, we prefer using a measure of caregiver education instead of parental education, given that many parents are absent, particularly in the Mozambican sample.[25]

Figure 1.6 plots raw TVIP scores for the bottom and the top quartiles of the asset distribution in the Cambodian and Mozambican samples.[26] Raw TVIP scores are, on average, higher for the top quartile of the asset index compared with the bottom quartile. In other words, differences in SES account for part of the large variation in test scores within each sample.[27] As we have discussed, similar socioeconomic gradients have been found in Ecuador, Madagascar, and Nicaragua. Still, it is quite remarkable to observe socioeconomic gradients in cognitive development in the Cambodian and Mozambican data, particularly because they contain rather homogeneous samples of mostly poor children in low-income countries. These results show that socioeconomic gradients in cognitive development appear even at very low levels of economic development.

Figure 1.7 displays raw TVIP scores by caregiver education, contrasting children whose caregiver has no primary education or only partial primary school education (one to four years of education) or has completed five or more years of primary school. The evidence on the role of caregiver education in cognitive development is more mixed. Patterns suggest some association between cognitive development and caregiver education in Cambodia, but not in Mozambique.

Table 1.2 presents a simple multivariate regression of the raw TVIP scores on SES, including wealth and caregiver education. The regression is estimated with the raw TVIP scores as an explanatory variable. Age fixed effects are included, so that results show how socioeconomic characteristics determine average TVIP scores across age groups. We impute the mean average education or age for caregiver when the variable is missing. We also include a dummy if the education or age variable is missing, which mostly occurs if parents do not reside in the household. All regressions include district fixed effects to account for constant differences between districts. Finally, standard errors are clustered at the village level.[28]

Although these regression coefficients cannot be interpreted causally, they confirm the significance of descriptive patterns in figures 1.6 and 1.7.[29] In Cambodia, children in the second, third, and fourth wealth quartiles

Figure 1.7 Raw TVIP Score by Age and Caregiver Education

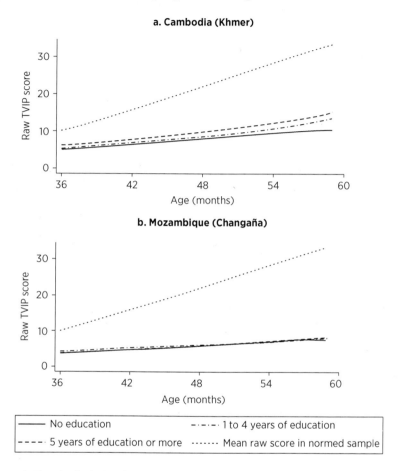

a. Cambodia (Khmer)

b. Mozambique (Changaña)

Source: Authors' calculations based on data from Bruns and others 2010 (Mozambique) and Filmer and Naudeau 2010 (Cambodia).

Note: The "mean raw score in the normed sample" is the mean raw TVIP score achieved by children in the reference population used to norm the test (see box 1.2). Comparisons between raw TVIP scores in Cambodia and Mozambique and the norm should be undertaken carefully. The norm may not be fully appropriate because it was established based on a Spanish version of the TVIP in a sample of Mexican and Puerto Rican children whose characteristics may differ. TVIP = Test de Vocabulario en Imagenes Peabody.

have significantly higher average TVIP scores than children in the bottom quartile. In Mozambique, children in the fourth quartile have significantly higher average TVIP scores than children in the bottom quartile. In short, significant socioeconomic gradients in cognitive development are present in both samples.

Table 1.2 Cognitive Development and Socioeconomic Status

	Raw TVIP score (Cambodia)	Raw TVIP score (Mozambique)
Socioeconomic status		
Second wealth quartile	0.67***	0.10
	(0.25)	(0.36)
Third wealth quartile	0.98***	0.78
	(0.24)	(0.68)
Fourth wealth quartile	2.42***	1.29**
	(0.34)	(0.51)
Caregiver education (years)	0.17***	−0.03
	(0.05)	(0.06)
Control characteristics		
Male child	0.19	0.09
	(0.18)	(0.31)
Urban household	−0.49	−0.02
	(0.41)	(0.21)
Number of adults in household	−0.19**	0.04
	(0.08)	(0.08)
Number of children in household	−0.19***	0.06
	(0.07)	(0.04)
Caregiver age (years)	0.01	0.02
	(0.01)	(0.02)
Missing mother	0.30	−0.89**
	(0.53)	(0.31)
Missing father	−0.39	−0.13
	(0.39)	(0.27)
Age fixed effects	Yes	Yes
District fixed effects	Yes	Yes
Constant	5.20***	3.25***
	(0.61)	(0.62)
Number of observations	4,013	2,000
Adjusted R^2	0.165	0.066

Source: Authors' calculations based on data from Bruns and others 2010 (Mozambique) and Filmer and Naudeau 2010 (Cambodia).

Note: Numbers in italics = coefficient/SE. Estimates and standard errors clustered at the community level in parentheses. * Significant at 10%; ** significant at 5%; *** significant at 1%. Regression also includes a series of dummies to account for some variables that were missing and had to be imputed (mother/caregiver's education, mother/caregiver's age, has paper and pen, has book, has bought toy, believes in punishment, and so on). SE = standard error; TVIP = Test de Vocabulario en Imagenes Peabody.

Results regarding the association between caregiver education and cognitive development are not robust across samples and confirm the mixed evidence presented in figure 1.7. In Cambodia, caregiver education is positively and significantly associated with TVIP scores. Caregiver education is not associated with TVIP scores in the Mozambican sample. However, the absence of the mother is statistically and negatively correlated with cognitive development. This result is particularly noteworthy because it suggests that the protective effect of nurturing caregivers may outweigh the role of caregiver education in settings with high prevalence of conflicts or epidemics. Chapter 3 will discuss in more details the impact of extreme events such as conflicts, epidemics, and orphanhood on outcomes in early childhood.

Socioeconomic Status, Nutrition, Parenting, and Cognitive Development

Despite the robust association between SES (particularly wealth) and cognitive development documented in the last section, substantial unexplained variation in raw TVIP scores remains. In addition, the association between SES and cognitive development may capture the effects of mediating variables that can be explicitly accounted for. For instance, nutrition and parenting are two of the channels through which SES can indirectly affect cognitive development. In this section, we consider whether nutrition and parenting are also determined by SES and whether socioeconomic gradients in cognitive development remain once differences in nutrition and parenting between households are controlled for.

Nutrition and parenting are proxied as follows. We use height-for-age to measure a child's nutritional status.[30] As displayed in table 1.1, 47.6 percent of children are stunted in the Cambodian sample, and 43.1 percent of children in the Mozambican sample.[31] We use a series of indicators that aim to measure parenting quality. First, four indicators measure if households have (1) paper or a pen or (2) a book and whether children play with (3) a homemade toy or (4) a purchased toy. Second, we build an index to measure the intensity of language stimulation a child receives in the household. The index ranges from zero to three and aggregates three variables that indicate whether anyone in the household sometimes (1) reads or looks at pictures with the child, (2) tells stories to the child, and (3) sings songs to the child. Finally, we also include a variable that captures whether the caregiver thinks that physical punishment is necessary to raise a child properly. All these proxies for parenting quality are measured consistently in the Cambodian and Mozambican surveys. Table 1.1 reveals some differences between samples in the parenting indicators. For instance, Mozambican households are much more likely to have a book in the household, and

Cambodian households are much more likely to have a purchased toy in the household.

SES is a significant determinant of both nutritional status and parenting quality.[32] For instance, the language stimulation index is significantly associated with the wealth index and caregiver education in both the Cambodian and Mozambican samples.[33] Nutritional status (as measured by height-for-age or stunting status) is significantly associated with the wealth index in Cambodia and Mozambique. In contrast, the correlation between nutritional status and caregiver education is statistically significant only in the Cambodian sample.[34] In general, the fact that SES codetermines nutritional status and parenting suggests that these two mediating variables may explain part of the association between SES and cognitive development observed in the previous section.[35]

Figure 1.8 shows the degree of correlation between cognitive development and stunting, and figure 1.9 plots cognitive development by level of language stimulation. Although nutrition, parenting, and cognitive development are codetermined by SES, figures 1.8 and 1.9 show that the correlation between those variables remains limited. There is substantial unexplained variation in TVIP scores even if nutritional status and parenting are accounted for.

Table 1.3 presents a multivariate regression with a full specification, including proxies for SES, nutrition, parenting, as well as a set of control characteristics, age, and district fixed effects. Results show that height-for-age is significantly associated with TVIP scores in both samples. In Cambodia, parenting variables such as the stimulation index and ownership of a book or a purchased toy are also significantly associated with cognitive development. In contrast, ownership of a purchased toy is significant and positive in the Mozambican sample, although a positive attitude toward punishment is negatively associated with cognitive development. Overall, the results show that parenting and nutrition account for part of the socioeconomic gradients observed in table 1.2.

Still, socioeconomic gradients in cognitive development remain, even accounting for the mediating effects of nutrition and parenting. The estimated coefficients for asset quartiles and parental education are of smaller magnitudes in table 1.2 than in table 1.3, however. In Cambodia, the coefficient for the second quartile in table 1.3 decreases by 30 percent, the coefficient of the third quartile by 39 percent, and the coefficient of the fourth quartile by 25 percent compared with table 1.2. In parallel, the coefficient of caregiver education decreases by 18 percent. In Mozambique, the coefficient of the fourth asset quartile variable decreases by 20 percent.[36] In the end, although nutrition and parenting account for a significant share of the association between SES and cognitive development, SES also affects cognitive development through other pathways. These results are remarkably

Figure 1.8 Raw TVIP Score by Age and Stunting Status

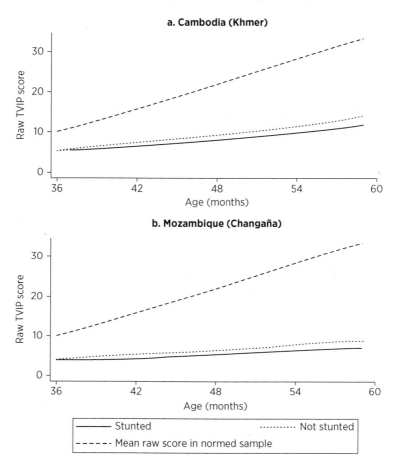

Source: Authors' calculations based on data from Bruns and others 2010 (Mozambique) and Filmer and Naudeau 2010 (Cambodia).

Note: The "mean raw score in the normed sample" is the mean raw TVIP score achieved by children in the reference population used to norm the test (see box 1.2). Comparisons between raw TVIP scores in Cambodia and Mozambique and the norm should be undertaken carefully. The norm may not be fully appropriate because it was established based on a Spanish version of the TVIP in a sample of Mexican and Puerto Rican children whose characteristics may differ. TVIP = Test de Vocabulario en Imagenes Peabody.

consistent with the findings of Paxson and Schady (2007) in Ecuador and suggest that the patterns found in lower-middle-income countries are robust in low-income countries as well.

Finally, additional results suggest that socioeconomic gradients as proxied by wealth quartiles increase with age. For example, in Cambodia, children

Figure 1.9 Raw TVIP Score by Age and Level of Language Stimulation

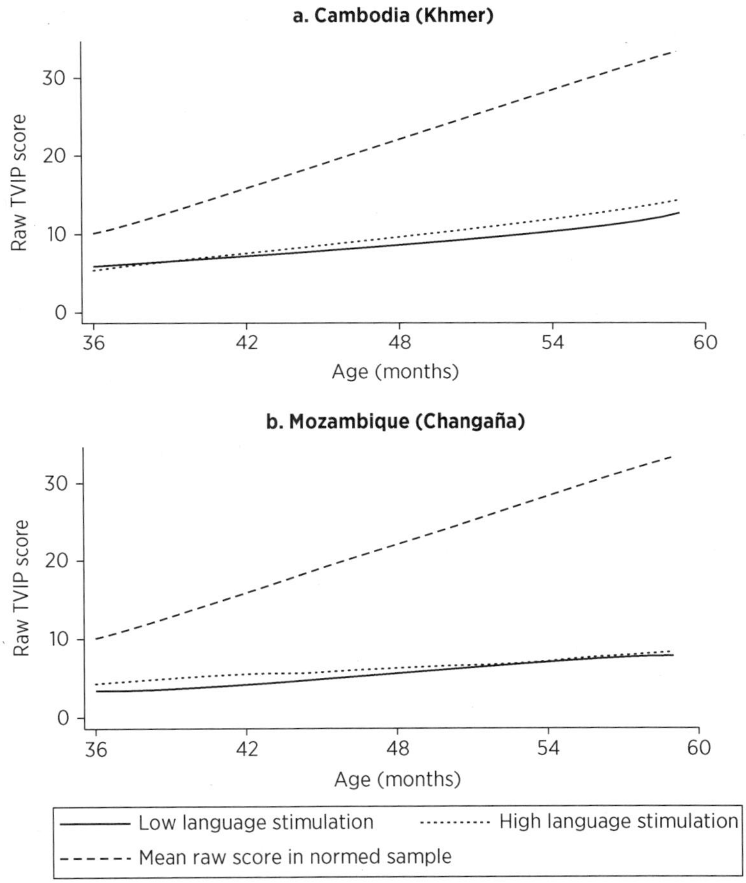

a. Cambodia (Khmer)

b. Mozambique (Changaña)

Low language stimulation .... High language stimulation
----- Mean raw score in normed sample

Source: Authors' calculations based on data from Bruns and others 2010 (Mozambique) and Filmer and Naudeau 2010 (Cambodia).

Note: The "mean raw score in the normed sample" is the mean raw TVIP score achieved by children in the reference population used to norm the test (see box 1.2). Comparisons between raw TVIP scores in Cambodia and Mozambique and the norm should be undertaken carefully. The norm may not be fully appropriate because it was established based on a Spanish version of the TVIP in a sample of Mexican and Puerto Rican children whose characteristics may differ. TVIP = Test de Vocabulario en Imagenes Peabody.

aged 48 to 59 months from the second and third quartiles have higher TVIP scores than children from the bottom quartile, but no significant differences in TVIP scores appear for children aged 36 to 47 months in the bottom three quartiles. In Mozambique, only in the older age group do children in the top asset quartile have higher TVIP scores than children in the bottom

Table 1.3 Cognitive Development, Socioeconomic Status, Nutrition, and Parenting

	Raw TVIP score (Cambodia)	Raw TVIP score (Mozambique)
Socioeconomic status		
Second wealth quartile	0.47* (0.24)	0.04 (0.36)
Third wealth quartile	0.60** (0.25)	0.59 (0.70)
Fourth wealth quartile	1.81*** (0.33)	1.03* (0.51)
Caregiver's education (years)	0.14*** (0.05)	−0.06 (0.07)
Nutrition and parenting		
Height-for-age z-score	0.61*** (0.11)	0.32* (0.14)
Stimulation index (0–3; reading, storytelling, singing)	0.30*** (0.11)	0.20 (0.13)
Has paper and pen	0.25 (0.20)	0.10 (0.22)
Has book	0.64** (0.30)	−0.46 (0.32)
Plays with purchased toy	0.68*** (0.21)	0.80** (0.26)
Plays with homemade toy	−0.20 (0.22)	−0.47 (0.26)
Believes in punishment	−0.25 (0.22)	−0.60** (0.19)
Control characteristics		
Male child	0.19 (0.19)	0.18 (0.35)
Urban household	−0.40 (0.40)	−0.17 (0.22)
Number of adults in household	−0.21*** (0.08)	0.03 (0.09)
Number of children in household	−0.15** (0.07)	0.07** (0.03)
Caregiver's age (years)	0.00 (0.01)	0.02 (0.02)

(continued next page)

Table 1.3 *(continued)*

	Raw TVIP score (Cambodia)	Raw TVIP score (Mozambique)
Missing mother	0.39	−0.90**
	(0.52)	(0.28)
Missing father	−0.33	−0.17
	(0.39)	(0.28)
Age fixed effects	Yes	Yes
District fixed effects	Yes	Yes
Constant	5.83***	4.01***
	(0.69)	(0.50)
Number of observations	3,915	1,942
Adjusted R^2	0.169	0.080

Source: Authors' calculations based on data from Bruns and others 2010 (Mozambique) and Filmer and Naudeau 2010 (Cambodia).

Note: Numbers in italics = coefficient/SE. Estimates and standard errors clustered at the community level in parentheses. * Significant at 10%; ** significant at 5%; *** significant at 1%. Regression also includes a series of dummies to account for some variables that were missing and had to be imputed (mother/caregiver's education, mother/caregiver's age, has paper and pen, has book, has bought toy, believes in punishment, and so on). SE = standard error; TVIP = Test de Vocabulario en Imagenes Peabody.

quartile.[37] The evidence on age patterns in socio-economic gradients in Cambodia and Mozambique is not as strong as the evidence provided by Paxson and Schady (2007) or Fernald and others (forthcoming) based on a sample representative of a larger share of the national population in Ecuador and Madagascar. Still, the Cambodian and Mozambican samples contain a rather homogeneous subset of the national population and as such the evidence remains noteworthy in suggesting that socioeconomic gradients are likely to increase with age, even at a very low level of economic development.

Conclusion and Policy Implications

The patterns observed in the Cambodian and Mozambican samples are remarkably consistent with those previously discussed in the literature,[38] particularly in Ecuador, Madagascar, and Nicaragua. In all five countries, significant socioeconomic gradients appear at an early age, and the poorest children exhibit serious signs of developmental delays by the time they reach age five. In the Cambodian and Mozambican samples, as in those from Ecuador, nutrition and parenting are also determined by SES and play a mediating role between SES and cognitive development, though only to a small extent.

Although we cannot extrapolate universal patterns from only five country-specific datasets, the fact that the findings described above are so consistent across low-income populations in five countries located in three different regions of the world (East Asia, Latin America, and Sub-Saharan Africa) suggests that similar patterns also exist in a wide range of low-income countries, or among low-income populations within wealthier countries. In other words, the external validity of these findings is likely to be high.

The chapter highlights pathways through which shocks and ECD interventions may affect cognitive development, as subsequent chapters will further discuss. To the extent that the associations between SES, nutrition, parenting, and cognitive development documented in this chapter are causal, any negative shock further affecting SES, nutrition, or parenting is likely to negatively affect cognitive outcomes as well (see chapters 2 and 3 for a review). In turn, policies and interventions that improve the welfare of young children in these areas (including center-based ECD programs, home-based programs designed to promote behavior changes among parents/caregivers, and cash transfers for families with young children) are likely to improve children's cognitive and overall development outcomes (see chapters 4 and 5 for a discussion). As chapter 4 further documents, interventions for very young children (below age three) are particularly critical.

As mentioned at the beginning of this chapter, early delays in children's cognitive and overall development lead to costly inefficiencies in the public health and education sectors because these children are more likely to be ill, to repeat grades, to drop out of school, and to engage in risky behaviors as they become older (see Naudeau and others 2010 for a review).

The questions of whether high-quality primary schools can counteract earlier delays and, if so, to what extent remain largely empirical in the developing world, and more research is needed in this area. Remedial interventions at older ages, such as education equivalency programs for school dropouts or therapeutic interventions for violent youth, can also compensate for some early delays. However, the longer a society waits to intervene in the life cycle of a disadvantaged child, the more costly it is to remediate the disadvantage (Heckman 2008a).

As the broader literature has shown, ECD interventions have not only a high cost-benefit ratio, but also a higher rate of return for each dollar invested than interventions directed at older children and adults (Heckman 2008b; Heckman, Stixrud, and Urzua 2006). Evidence suggests a potential rate of 7–16 percent annually from high-quality ECD programs targeting vulnerable groups (Heckman and others 2009; Rolnick and Grunewald 2007; see Naudeau and others 2010 for a review of the literature on the effectiveness of various types of ECD investments for different types of beneficiaries; see also chapter 5). Another economic advantage of ECD intervention is that it enhances both efficiency and equity: It offers a cost-efficient way to produce a well-trained and capable workforce, and leads to better outcomes for those at a greater disadvantage (see chapter 4 for a review on this topic).

Accordingly, some countries have begun to invest public resources in ECD, with a focus on the poorest children. For instance, in Cambodia, the government is using part of a Fast Track Initiative Catalytic Fund awarded for the period 2008–12 to scale up three different types of ECD programs among 1,500 of the poorest communities, including (1) formal preschools, (2) community-based preschools, and (3) home-based parenting programs. In Mozambique, the government is currently preparing a new ECD project that will aim to provide services to the most vulnerable communities.

In many other low-income countries, however, governments continue to underinvest in children's early years.[39] Although little data exist on the magnitude of the cognitive and overall delays that young children are likely to face in each of these countries, we can confidently hypothesize that the trends documented in this chapter for five countries across three continents are likely to hold there as well. In the absence of ECD interventions, poor children in these countries are likely to show serious signs of developmental delays by the time they enter primary school and to "play catch-up" for the rest of their lives.

Annex

Figure A.1 Quintiles 1, 3, and 5 of Raw TVIP Score Distribution by Age

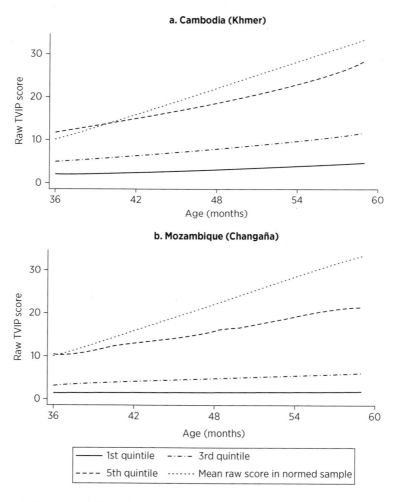

Source: Authors' calculations based on data from Bruns and others 2010 (Mozambique) and Filmer and Naudeau 2010 (Cambodia).

Note: The "mean raw score in the normed sample" is the mean raw TVIP score achieved by children in the reference population used to norm the test (see box 1.2). Comparisons between raw TVIP scores in Cambodia and Mozambique and the norm should be undertaken carefully. The norm may not be fully appropriate because it was established based on a Spanish version of the TVIP in a sample of Mexican and Puerto Rican children whose characteristics may differ. TVIP = Test de Vocabulario en Imagenes Peabody.

Figure A.2 Height-for-Age by Age and Wealth Quartile

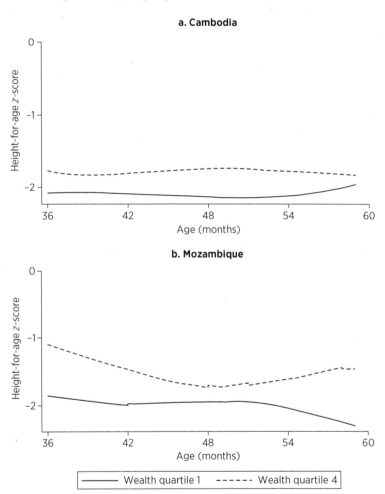

a. Cambodia

b. Mozambique

Wealth quartile 1   - - - - - Wealth quartile 4

Source: Authors' calculations based on data from Bruns and others 2010 (Mozambique) and Filmer and Naudeau 2010 (Cambodia).

Figure A.3 Height-for-Age by Age and Caregiver Education

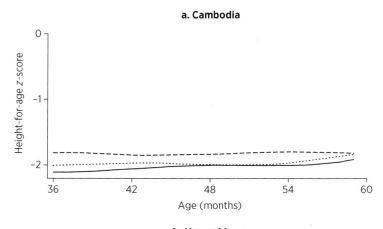

a. Cambodia

b. Mozambique

—— No education		······ 1 to 4 years of education
--- 5 years of education or more		

Source: Authors' calculations based on data from Bruns and others 2010 (Mozambique) and Filmer and Naudeau 2010 (Cambodia).

Figure A.4 Language Stimulation by Age and Wealth Quartile

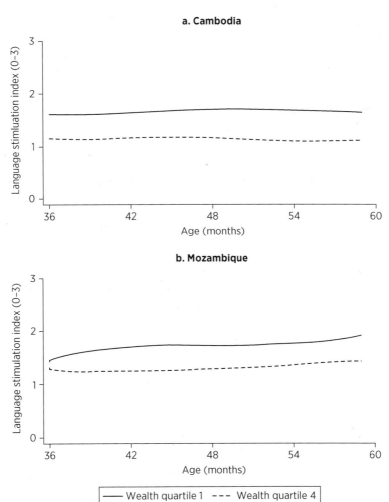

a. Cambodia

b. Mozambique

Wealth quartile 1 --- Wealth quartile 4

Source: Authors' calculations based on data from Bruns and others 2010 (Mozambique) and Filmer and Naudeau 2010 (Cambodia).

Figure A.5 Language Stimulation by Age and Caregiver Education

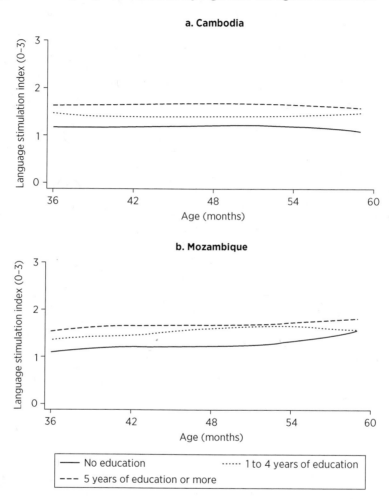

Source: Authors' calculations based on data from Bruns and others 2010 (Mozambique) and Filmer and Naudeau 2010 (Cambodia).

Table A.1 Correlates of Nutrition and Parenting in Cambodia and Mozambique

	Cambodia		Mozambique	
	Height-for-age z-Score	Parenting (stimulation index)	Height-for-age z-Score	Parenting (stimulation index)
Socioeconomic status				
Second wealth quartile	0.07	0.12**	0.23*	0.13*
	(0.05)	(0.05)	(0.11)	(0.05)
Third wealth quartile	0.13***	0.23***	0.27**	0.19**
	(0.04)	(0.05)	(0.11)	(0.05)
Fourth wealth quartile	0.24***	0.37***	0.46**	0.24**
	(0.05)	(0.05)	(0.16)	(0.07)
Caregiver's education (years)	0.01*	0.07***	0.02	0.06***
	(0.01)	(0.01)	(0.02)	(0.01)
Control characteristics				
Male child	0.03	-0.02	-0.17*	0.02
	(0.03)	(0.03)	(0.08)	(0.04)
Urban household	-0.10	-0.14*	0.17**	0.13***
	(0.08)	(0.08)	(0.07)	(0.02)
Number of adults in household	0.00	0.03**	-0.01	0.02
	(0.01)	(0.01)	(0.02)	(0.02)
Number of children in household	-0.05***	0.09***	0.02	0.02
	(0.01)	(0.01)	(0.02)	(0.02)

(continued next page)

43

Table A.1 Correlates of Nutrition and Parenting in Cambodia and Mozambique (continued)

	Cambodia		Mozambique	
	Height-for-age z-Score	Parenting (stimulation index)	Height-for-age z-Score	Parenting (stimulation index)
Caregiver's age (years)	0.00**	0.00	0.00	0.01**
	(0.00)	(0.00)	(0.00)	(0.00)
Missing mother	0.11	-0.08	-0.03	0.02
	(0.11)	(0.09)	(0.07)	(0.07)
Missing father	-0.12	-0.07	0.24**	-0.06
	(0.08)	(0.07)	(0.07)	(0.05)
Age fixed effects	Yes	Yes	Yes	Yes
District fixed effects	Yes	Yes	Yes	Yes
Constant	-1.92***	0.71***	-1.64***	0.66***
	(0.10)	(0.11)	(0.19)	(0.12)
Number of observations	4,010	4,069	1,944	1,997
Adjusted R^2	0.033	0.084	0.037	0.045

Source: Authors' calculations based on data from Bruns and others 2010 (Mozambique) and Filmer and Naudeau 2010 (Cambodia).

Note: Numbers in italics = coefficient/SE. Estimates and standard errors clustered at the community level in parentheses. * Significant at 10%; ** significant at 5%; *** significant at 1%. Regression also includes a series of dummies to account for some variables that were missing and had to be imputed (mother/caregiver's education, mother/caregiver's age, has paper and pen, has book, has bought toy, believes in punishment, and so on). SE = standard error.

Notes

1. Evidence distinguishing between genetic and environmental factors comes primarily from developed countries.
2. Risk factors are defined as "Personal characteristics or environmental circumstances that increase the probability of negative outcomes for children" (Cole and Cole 2000).
3. Executive function processes include impulse control, the ability to initiate action, the ability to sustain attention, and persistence, all of which are likely to significantly influence an individual's capacity to succeed in life. Executive function is often included in cognitive development, although both cognitive and socioemotional processes are typically involved. For more information, see Fernald and others (2009).
4. The Corsi test is an internationally standardized short-term memory test. The Tifaldi language test is designed specifically for Turkish language comprehension.
5. In this study, children are considered disadvantaged if they are stunted, living in poverty, or both.
6. Ecuador and Nicaragua are currently classified as lower-middle-income countries by the World Bank, whereas Madagascar is classified as a low-income country.
7. The broader literature summarized in this volume, and particularly in chapter 4, highlights the fact that delays in cognitive and overall development can accumulate quickly among poor children well before they reach the age of three. A limitation of the TVIP is that it can be used only for children aged 30 months and older, hence precluding the authors from presenting data for younger age groups.
8. The Home Observation for Measurement of the Environment (HOME) scale has been used in several countries to assess the quality of the home environment and parent-child interactions.
9. In this subtest, the child is scored based on his or her ability to find hidden objects or to reproduce a sequence according to a given model.
10. In this subscale, the child is scored based on his or her ability to repeat words and sentences spoken by the enumerator and that are increasingly long and difficult.
11. The three districts are Manjacaze, Xai Xai, and Bilene. The 76 communities were chosen from a total of 252 villages in the provinces, of which 167 villages were deemed eligible to receive the intervention. Bruns and others (2010) discuss the site selection procedure in detail.
12. The Cambodian datasets also include children aged 24 to 35 months old, but this chapter focuses on children aged 36 to 59 months for analysis for Cambodia and Mozambique to be consistent.
13. The following provinces are included: Battambang, Bantey Manchey, Kampong Cham, Kampong Thom, Kampot, Prey Veng, and Takeo.
14. In this context, informal ECD services include community preschools and home-based programs.
15. See Filmer and Naudeau (2010) for a detailed discussion of site selection.

16. As previously mentioned, scores on the TVIP are often used as a proxy for cognitive development (rather than linguistic development only).
17. The research teams decided to use the TVIP rather than the PPVT in both Cambodia and Mozambique because the TVIP was considered to be more appropriate for children in low-income settings. In both countries, steps were taken to translate and pilot the test. This was done in collaboration with a local child psychologist in Mozambique and with key informants (experts from the survey firm and teachers) in Cambodia.
18. In Mozambique, the TVIP test was also conducted in Portuguese after it was conducted in Changaña. However, Mozambican children in our sample were not exposed to the Portuguese language at baseline (they typically learn Portuguese upon primary school entry or in the context of ECD interventions). Therefore, we present only Changaña results in the following analyses.
19. One of the appealing features of externally standardized scores is that they can be used to compute the number of months children in the Cambodian and Mozambican data lag in comparison with an "average" child in the reference sample used to norm the test (see box 1.2). Such age equivalencies provide striking results. For instance, 59-month-old Cambodian children perform at the level that would be expected of 41-month-old children in the reference sample. This suggests that by the time Cambodian children are 59 months old, their cognitive development exhibits an average delay of a year and a half (18 months). Mozambican children who are 59 months old display signs of an average cognitive delay of two years (24 months), meaning that 59-month-old children perform at the level that would be expected of 35-month-old children in the reference sample. Those figures are staggering. However, they should be interpreted very carefully, given serious issues with the standardized score discussed in box 1.2 and the implicit cross-country comparisons it relies on.
20. Patterns in standardized TVIP scores are fully consistent with the patterns in raw TVIP scores discussed below.
21. The figures presented are smoothed by locally weighted regressions.
22. Figure A.1 shows the distribution of raw TVIP scores for each age group by displaying average scores for the bottom quintile, middle quintile, and top quintile of the score distribution. Figure A.1 shows that there are large variations in TVIP scores within the Cambodian and Mozambican samples.
23. Filmer and Scott (2008) discuss the degree of congruence in rankings between per capita expenditures and an asset index. Importantly, we do not use the asset indexes to compare socioeconomic gradients between countries. Rather, we use those indices to compare cognitive development between the most wealthy and the least wealthy in each sample.
24. The construction of asset indices, following the methodology proposed in Filmer and Pritchett (2001), is detailed in Bruns and others (2010) and Filmer and Naudeau (2010).
25. Fathers are the primary caregiver for 212 children in the Cambodian sample and 290 children in the Mozambican sample.
26. All results in the rest of this chapter are presented for raw TVIP scores. Results are robust if internally standardized TVIP scores are used instead.

27. See figure A.1.
28. The Cambodian dataset pools two different samples drawn using different methodologies (see Filmer and Naudeau 2010), and we also include a dummy for the formal sample to control for any constant differences between the two samples.
29. To repeat, the magnitude of coefficients should not be compared between countries, given potential cultural sensitivity of the TVIP test as well as the fact that the asset index varies between countries.
30. We use height-for-age because our measure of cognitive development is cumulative, so that short-term measures such as weight-for-height would not be appropriate. In addition, weight data are not available for the Cambodian sample.
31. A child with a height-for-age z-score below −2 is considered stunted.
32. Evidence on the association between SES, nutritional status, and parenting is presented in annex figures A.2 to A.5, as well as table A.1.
33. See figures A.4 and A.5, as well as table A.1.
34. See figures A.2 and A.3, as well as table A.1.
35. No significant negative trend is seen in language stimulation or height-for-age over time, in contrast with the patterns observed for cognitive delays, which accumulate over time.
36. Accounting for parenting only (without nutrition) leads to the following changes in the SES coefficient: In Cambodia, the coefficient for the second quartile in table 1.3 decreases by 14.9 percent, the coefficient of the third quartile by 23.5 percent, and the coefficient of the fourth quartile by 16.5 percent compared with table 1.2. The coefficient of caregiver education decreases by 17.6 percent. In Mozambique, the coefficient of the fourth asset quartile variable decreases by 13.2 percent. The coefficients of the first and second quartiles, as well as caregiver education, are not significant in table 1.2.
37. In both countries, similar patterns are found if the internally standardized TVIP score is used instead of the raw TVIP score. In both samples, coefficients for the 2nd asset quartile are also statistically higher for the older age group than for the younger age group.
38. It is also consistent with results from the literature in developed countries.
39. The OECD research study Starting Strong II (OECD 2006) suggests that 1.0 percent of GDP is the minimum public investment required to ensure provision of quality ECD services.

References

Aughinbaugh, A., and M. Gittleman. 2003. "Does Money Matter: A Comparison of the Effect of Income on Child Development in the United States and Great Britain." *Journal of Human Resources* 38 (2): 416–40.

Baum, C. L. 2003. "Does Early Maternal Employment Harm Child Development? An Analysis of the Potential Benefits of Leave Taking." *Journal of Labor Economics* 21 (2): 409–48.

Berger, L. M., C. Paxson, and J. Waldfogel. 2005. "Income and Child Development." Unpublished manuscript, Princeton University.

Blau, D. M. 1999. "The Effect of Income on Child Development." *Review of Economics and Statistics* 81 (2): 261–76.

Bradley, R. H., and R. F. Corwyn. 2002. "Socioeconomic Status and Child Development." *Annual Review of Psychology* 53: 371–99.

Bradley, R. H., R. F. Corwyn, H. P. McAdoo, and C. G. Coll. 2001. "The Home Environments of Children in the United States. Part I: Variations by Age, Ethnicity, and Poverty Status." *Child Development* 72 (6): 1844–67.

Brooks-Gunn, J., and G. J. Duncan. 1997. "The Effects of Poverty on Children." *Future of Children* 7: 55–71.

Bruns, B., S. Martinez, S. Naudeau, and V. Pereira. 2010. "Impact Evaluation of Save the Children Early Childhood Development Program in Mozambique. Baseline Results." World Bank, Washington, DC.

Conger, R. D., and M. B. Donnellan. 2007. "An Interactionist Perspective on the Socioeconomic Context of Human Development." *Annual Review of Psychology* 58: 175–99.

Cole, M., and S. R. Cole. 2000. *The Development of Children*. 4th ed. New York: Worth. Coots, J. J.

Cueto, S., J. Leon, G. Guerrero, and I. Munoz. 2009. "Psychometric Characteristics of Cognitive Development and Achievement Instruments in Round 2 of Young Lives." Young Lives Technical Note No. 15, University of Oxford, Oxford.

Currie, J., and D. Thomas. 1999. "Early Test Scores, Socioeconomic Status and Future Outcomes." NBER Working Paper 6943, National Bureau of Economic Research, Cambridge, MA.

Evans, D., and E. Miguel. 2004. "Orphans and Schooling in Africa: A Longitudinal Analysis." Unpublished manuscript. Harvard University and University of California, Berkeley.

Feinstein, L. 2003. "Inequality in the Early Cognitive Development of Children in the 1970 Cohort." *Economica* 70: 73–97.

Fernald, L. C. H., P. Kariger, P. Engle, and A. Raikes. 2009. "Examining Early Child Development in Low-Income Countries: A Toolkit for the Assessment of Children in the First Five Years of Life." World Bank, Washington, DC.

Fernald, L., A. Weber, E. Galasso, and L. Ratsifandrihamanana. Forthcoming. "Socio-Economic Gradients and Child Development in a Very Low Income Population." *Developmental Science*.

Filmer, D., and S. Naudeau. 2010. "Impact Evaluation on Early Childhood Care and Development (ECCD Programs in Cambodia, Baseline Report)." World Bank, Washington, DC.

Filmer, D., and L. Pritchett. 2001. "Estimating Wealth Effects without Expenditure Data—or Tears: An Application to Educational Enrollments in India." *Demography* 38 (1):115–32.

Filmer, D., and K. Scott. 2008. "Assessing Asset Indices." World Bank Policy Research Working Paper No. 4605, World Bank, Washington, DC.

Fox, L., E. Bardasi, and K. Van den Broeck. 2005. "Poverty in Mozambique. Unraveling Challenges and Determinants." Africa Region Working Paper Series No. 87. World Bank, Washington, DC.

Grantham-McGregor, S., Y. B. Cheung, S. Cueto, P. Glewwe, L. Richer, B. Trupp, and the International Child Development Steering Group. 2007. "Child Development in Developing Countries: Developmental Potential in the First Five Years for Children in Developing Countries." *Lancet* 369 (9555): 60–70.

Guo, G., and K. M. Harris. 2000. "The Mechanisms Mediating the Effects of Poverty on Children's Intellectual Development." *Demography* 37 (4): 431–47.

Hackman, D. A., and M. J. Farah. 2009. "Socioeconomic Status and the Developing Brain." *Trends in Cognitive Science* 13 (2): 65–73.

Heckman, J. J. 2008a. "The Case for Investing in Disadvantaged Young Children." In *Big Ideas for Children: Investing in Our Nation's Future,* ed. First Focus, 49–58. Washington, DC: First Focus.

———. 2008b. "Schools, Skills, and Synapses." *Economic Inquiry* 46 (3): 289–324.

Heckman, J. J., and D. V. Masterov. 2007. "The Productivity Argument for Investing in Young Children." *Review of Agricultural Economics* 29 (3): 446–93.

Heckman, J. J., S. H. Moon, R. Pinto, P. A. Savalyev, and A.Yavitz. 2009. "The Rate of Return to the High/Scope Perry Preschool Program." Working Paper 200936, Geary Institute, University College Dublin, Dublin. http://www.ucd.ie/geary/static/publications/workingpapers/gearywp200936.pdf.

Heckman, J. J., J. Stixrud, and S. Urzua. 2006. "The Effects of Cognitive and Noncognitive Abilities on Labor Market Outcomes and Social Behavior." *Journal of Labor Economics* 24 (3): 411–82.

Macours, K., N. Schady, and R. Vakis. 2008. "Cash Transfers, Behavioral Changes, and Cognitive Development in Early Childhood: Evidence from a Randomized Experiment." World Bank Policy Research Working Paper No. 4759, World Bank, Washington, DC.

Macours, K., and R. Vakis. 2010. "Seasonal Migration and Early Childhood Development." *World Development* 38 (6): 857–69.

Naudeau, S., N. Kataoka, A. Valerio, M. J. Neuman, and L. K. Elder. 2010. *Investing in Young Children: An Early Childhood Development Guide for Policy Dialogue and Project Preparation.* Washington, DC: World Bank.

Nelson, C. A., M. de Haan, and K. M. Thomas. 2006. *Neuroscience and Cognitive Development: The Role of Experience and the Developing Brain.* New York: John Wiley.

OECD (Organisation for Economic Co-operation and Development). 2006. *Starting Strong II: Early Childhood Education and Care.* Paris: Education Directorate, OECD.

Paxson, C., and N. Schady. 2007. "Cognitive Development among Young Children in Ecuador: The Roles of Wealth, Health, and Parenting." *Journal of Human Resources* 42 (1): 49–84.

Pianta, R. C., and S. J. McCoy. 1997. "The First Day of School: The Predictive Validity of Early School Screening." *Journal of Applied Developmental Psychology* 18: 1–22.

Plomin, R. 1994. *Genetics and Experience: The Interplay between Nature and Nurture.* Thousand Oaks, CA: Sage Publications.

Rolnick, A. J., and R. Grunewald. 2007. "The Economics of Early Childhood Development as Seen by Two Fed Economists." *Community Investments* 19 (2): 13–14, 30.

Ruhm, C. J. 2004. "Parental Employment and Child Cognitive Development." *Journal of Human Resources* 39 (1): 155–92.

Schady, N. 2006. "Early Childhood Development in Latin America and the Caribbean." *Economia* 6 (2): 185–225.

———. 2010. "Parental Education, Vocabulary, and Cognitive Development in Early Childhood: Longitudinal Evidence from Ecuador." Paper presented at the Annual Meeting of the Latin American Economic Association, Medellin, Colombia, November 11–13.

Shonkoff, J. P., and D. A. Phillips. 2000. *From Neurons to Neighborhoods: The Science of Early Childhood Development.* Washington, DC: National Academy Press.

Siddiqi, A., I. Kawachi, L. Berkman, S. V. Subramanian, and C. Hertzman. 2007. "Variation of Socioeconomic Gradients in Children's Developmental Health across Advanced Capitalist Societies: Analysis of 22 OECD Nations." *International Journal of Health Services* 37 (1): 63–87.

Smith, J. R., J. Brooks-Gunn, and P. K. Klebanov. 1997. "Consequences of Living in Poverty for Young Children's Cognitive and Verbal Ability and Early School Achievement." In *Consequences of Growing Up Poor,* ed. J. Duncan and J. Brooks-Gunn, 132–89. New York: Russell Sage Foundation.

Taylor, B., E. Dearing, and K. McCartney. 2004. "Incomes and Outcomes in Early Childhood." *Journal of Human Resources* 39 (4): 980–1007.

Vegas, E., and L. Santibanez. 2010. *The Promise of Early Childhood Development in Latin America and the Caribbean.* Washington, DC: World Bank.

Waldfogel, J., W. Han, and J. Brooks-Gunn. 2002. "The Effects of Early Maternal Employment on Child Cognitive Development." *Demography* 30 (2): 369–92.

World Bank. 2006. *Repositioning Nutrition as Central to Development: A Strategy for Large-Scale Action.* Washington, DC: World Bank.

———. 2007. *World Development Indicators.* Washington, DC: World Bank.

———. 2009a. "Poverty Profile and Trend in Cambodia. Findings from the 2007 Cambodia Socio-Economic Survey (CSES)." Report No. 48618-KH, World Bank, Washington, DC.

———. 2009b. "Turkey: Expanding Opportunities for the Next Generation. A Report on Life Chances." Report No. 48627-TR, World Bank, Washington, DC.

2

The Influence of Economic Crisis on Early Childhood Development: A Review of Pathways and Measured Impact

Jed Friedman and Jennifer Sturdy

Human capital, understood broadly in terms of skills, both cognitive and noncognitive, as well as capabilities, such as health or social functioning, is one of the foremost determinants of welfare. Increased attention has focused on the disproportionate influence of early life conditions in the production of adult human capital, and various investments in early life have been shown to be highly cost-effective (Bärnighausen and others 2008; Horton, Alderman, and Rivera 2008). These investments also have far-reaching potential for reducing the intergenerational transmission of poverty. Not only do children who develop cognitive and noncognitive skills grow up to be more productive, but increasing evidence shows that improved parental education and skill are subsequently related to improved child survival, health, nutrition, cognition, and education (Helmers and Patnam 2010; Lam and Duryea 1999; Psacharopoulos 1989; Rosenzweig and Wolpin 1994).

One of the major risks to skill formation in children is poverty. Conditions associated with poverty are in turn associated with worse physical health, psychosocial health, and cognitive outcomes observed in children

(Bradley and Corwyn 2002), and the greater cumulative exposure to these conditions or risk factors is associated with significantly lower cognitive development (Sameroff and others 1993). Much recent scholarship has delineated and explored the various interlinkages between poverty and low early childhood development (ECD) outcomes, summarized in chapter 1. This chapter instead focuses on the possible ECD consequences of one important category of impoverishing event: the economic crisis.

As the 2008 global financial crisis has again demonstrated, economic crises are an unfortunate recurring event in the world and can have severe consequences for household livelihoods. Economic crises, defined as sharp, negative fluctuations in aggregate income, are especially common in developing countries (Loayza and others 2007), and the frequency with which they occur has been increasing in recent history (Montiel and Serven 2005). Declines in household and community resources are not the only risks that arise from an economic crisis because of its aggregate nature. At the same time as households cope with the possibility of reduced income from aggregate economic contractions, vital public services may also experience a decline in quality or availability, which in turn may have an additional impact on skill development among children. For example, the economic crisis that hit Latin America in 1982 led to a decrease in public health spending and had a disproportionate effect on the poorest groups (Musgrove 1987).

This chapter reviews the existing rigorous empirical evidence that links economic crisis to adverse ECD-related outcomes. The studies reviewed all involve ex post analysis that contrasts outcomes assessed with population-representative data with equivalent data measured before the crisis period (more speculative studies that infer crisis impacts from previously estimated parameters, perhaps extrapolated from different populations, are not included here). The pre- and post-data bracket an arguably exogenous event, the economic crisis, and so differences in observed outcomes can be ascribed to the influence of crisis as long as the gap between pre- and post-observations is of suitably short duration. Only results estimated to be statistically significant at conventional levels are discussed. Very few of these reviewed studies have directly investigated the influence of aggregate economic shocks on the cognitive and noncognitive skills of young children. However, numerous studies have explored the relationship between economic crisis and intermediate outcomes, such as nutritional status, that play a key role in ECD. This broad literature is summarized herein.

The next section begins with a discussion that delineates the in utero and early life pathways that determine ECD to establish a framework to assess the possible effects of economic crisis on these pathways and ultimately, perhaps, on ECD. The following sections then review the existing evidence concerning the impacts of recent economic crises on these nutritional and environmental pathways. The chapter concludes with a discussion of policy responses that may serve to mitigate the detrimental effects from aggregate economic shocks.

Early Childhood Development Pathways

To understand how aggregate shocks can affect ECD, we first review the determinative mechanisms for ECD. Conservative estimates from Grantham-McGregor and others (2007) suggest that over 200 million children under five years of age living in developing countries fail to reach their cognitive development potential because of a range of factors, including poverty, poor health and nutrition, and lack of stimulation in home environments. It is possible that this burden increases during times of crisis as poverty increases and food security is threatened. However, to investigate this claim more carefully it is necessary to understand the pathways through which poverty influences skill acquisition in children.

Walker and others (2007) list three functional domains in early childhood that affect readiness for school and subsequent school performance: cognitive ability, social-emotional competence, and sensory-motor development. The authors then extensively review the existing evidence to identify risk factors that may inhibit these functional domains. Based on the consistency of evidence, as well as the magnitude of the risk factor in terms of both prevalence and influence on development outcomes, the authors identify four key risk factors that each affect at least 20 percent of children in developing countries: stunting (31 percent of children under age five), iron deficiency (23–33 percent of children under age four), iodine deficiency (35 percent of the population worldwide), and inadequate cognitive stimulation. In addition, the authors argue there is enough evidence to suggest additional risk factors, including intrauterine growth restriction (11 percent of births) and maternal depression (17 percent prevalence).

These nutritional and environmental pathways are summarized in table 2.1, which lists the operational measure of each risk factor and sources of evidence for the inclusion of each risk factor, as well as the measured impacts on ECD. The majority of these measures are nutritional, concerning either the nutrition of the child or the in utero environment, and an existing literature documents the impacts of economic crisis on nutrition; this is reviewed in a later section. Two other risk factors, maternal depression and inadequate cognitive stimulation in the home and community, have been studied far less in regard to potential impacts from economic crisis; the case of maternal depression is also explored in a later section. The next section, however, first discusses the possible

Table 2.1 Main Pathways for Early Childhood Development Outcomes

Risk factor/Indicator	Summary of evidence	Source (country)	Impact on ECD
Nutritional			
Intrauterine growth restriction/ *Infants at term with low birth weight (<2,500 g; ≥37 weeks' gestation)*	Cohort studies indicate develop-mental deficits up to age 3 years.	Grantham-McGregor et al. 1998 (Brazil)	Lower developmental levels
		Gorman and Pollitt 1992 (Guatemala)	Lower cognitive scores at age 2 years
		Gardner et al. 2003 (Jamaica)	Poor problem-solving ability at 7 months
		Walker et al. 2004 (Jamaica)	Lower developmental levels at 15 and 24 months
Childhood undernutrition/ *Stunting (height-for-age below − 2 SD of reference values)*	Prospective cohort studies show stunted children have poorer cognitive outcomes. Supplementary feeding trials all show concurrent benefits, although long-term benefits are less consistent.	Berkman et al. 2002 (Peru)	Children with severe stunting in second year of life scored 10 points lower on WISC-R test at 9 years old
		Mendez and Adair 1999 (Philippines)	Children with stunting at age 2 were associated with significant deficits (−0.14 SD) in cognitive test z-scores at age 8 years old
Iodine deficiency	Iodine-deficient groups are consistently shown to have lower development.	Bleichrodt et al. 1987 (Meta-analysis)	Meta-analysis of 18 studies showed IQ scores 13.5 points lower with iodine deficiency
	Maternal supplementation trials are sufficiently robust to establish that iodine deficiency in utero causes congenital hyperthyroidism and poor development in childhood.	Qian et al. 2005 (China)	Meta-analysis of 37 studies in China for children under 16 years found IQ scores 12.5 points lower

Iron deficiency/*Iron deficiency anemia*	Iron deficiency anemia in infancy is associated with short- and long-term development deficits. Supplementation trials show benefits to motor and social-emotional development, with cognitive benefits reported in preschool children.	Grantham-McGregor and Ani 2001 (Meta-analysis)	Longitudinal studies indicate consistently that anemic children (<2 years) continue to have poor cognitive and motor development and school achievement into middle childhood

Environmental

Cognitive stimulation or learning opportunities	Consistent evidence from intervention studies shows that providing cognitive stimulation or learning opportunities to young children significantly increases both cognitive and social-emotional competence.	Gardner et al. 2003 (Jamaica)	Significantly higher cognitive functioning in young children given cognitive stimulation or learning opportunities
Maternal depression	Consistent evidence from associational studies shows significantly lower cognitive and social-emotional competence in infants of depressed mothers.	Galler et al. 2000 (Barbados)	Reduced levels of cognitive function and higher levels of behavior problems reported in young children of depressed mothers

Source: Adapted from Walker and others 2007.

Note: ECD = early childhood development; SD = standard deviation.

influence of economic crisis on decidedly the most adverse ECD outcome: infant mortality.

Aggregate Shocks and Infant Mortality

The most severe condition affecting ECD is infant and early child mortality. Country-level investigations that examine the influence of aggregate economic shocks on infant mortality reveal a mixed picture. Much of the initial evidence was derived from developed economies and concluded that the likelihood of infant survival, like many health indicators, actually improves during recessions. For example, Dehejia and Lleras-Muney (2004) find that infant mortality is generally pro-cyclical in the United States. A variety of transmission mechanisms have been proposed to explain why economic recessions lead to improved child health in developed countries, including reductions in air pollution (Chay and Greenstone 2003), reductions in health-damaging behaviors such as smoking and drinking, and increases in the probability that mothers engage in time-intensive activities such as exercise and prenatal care (Ruhm 2000; Ruhm and Black 2002).

Country-level studies from the developing world have shown a less definitive pattern. Sharp economic downturns were associated with increases in infant mortality in Mexico (Cutler and others 2002), Peru (Paxson and Schady 2005), and India (Bhalotra 2010). However, when looking at the 1997 financial crisis in Southeast Asia, little impact on mortality has been identified in Indonesia (Strauss and others 2004).

One recent comprehensive study of developing countries has identified a clear link between aggregate economic contractions of sufficient magnitude and increases in the likelihood of mortality in the first year of life. Baird, Friedman, and Schady (2010) pool all available Demographic and Health Surveys (DHS) from 59 developing countries around the world to construct a dataset of 1.7 million live births over series of varying lengths, depending on the timing and number of surveys taken, in each country. The authors identify a large negative association between infant mortality in a given year and their measure of crisis—deviations of per capita gross domestic product (GDP) from trend. A 1 percent decrease in per capita GDP results in an increase in infant mortality of between 0.24 and 0.40 deaths per 1,000 children born. On average, the country-specific year-on-year decrease in infant mortality in their data is 2.5 deaths per 1,000 live births; thus, a 1 percent shortfall in per capita GDP from expected trends results in an increase in infant mortality of between 10 and 15 percent of the average annual mortality decline (and a crisis on the order of 7–10 percentage points of GDP completely erases the expected secular gain).

Furthermore, Baird, Friedman, and Schady (2010) identify important heterogeneity within this average relationship between infant mortality and economic crisis. The mortality of children born to rural and less edu-cated women is more sensitive to economic shocks, which suggests that the poor are disproportionately affected during most economic crises, and per-haps the poor face important credit constraints that bind in tragic ways during large contractions.

The mortality of girls is also significantly more sensitive to aggregate economic shocks than that of boys. This gender differential exists even in regions such as Sub-Saharan Africa that are not particularly known for son preference and indicates a behavioral dimension where households conserve resources to better protect young sons at the expense of daugh-ters. Finally, the relation between economic shocks and infant mortality is decidedly nonlinear. Figure 2.1 reproduces a figure from the Baird, Friedman, and Schady (2007) working paper that nonparametrically relates

Figure 2.1 Relation between IMR (Detrended) and Log Per Capita GDP (Detrended)

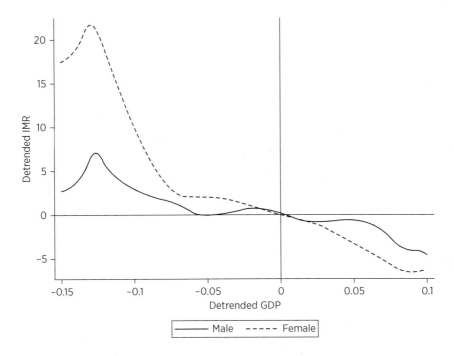

Source: Baird, Friedman, and Schady 2007.

Note: Estimated with locally weighted least squares. GDP is measured in year 2000 inter-national (purchasing power parity) dollars. GDP = gross domestic product; IMR = infant mortality rate.

deviations from trend for both the infant mortality rate (IMR) and GDP. For small departures from trend (noncrisis years), little relation is seen between IMR and GDP. However, as negative departures grow in magnitude, that is, as the magnitude of the economic shock increases, the influence on the mortality of female infants is particularly apparent.

Even though the gender difference in mortality response to crises observed in many regions suggests a behavioral dimension related to declines in household income, little evidence is available to illuminate the causal pathway by which economic shocks are translated into elevated mortality. Baird, Friedman, and Schady (2010) leverage birth timing to reveal that it is the economic conditions "around" the time of birth (a three-month window) that appear to be most determinative of survival in the first year of life. However, the pathways by which shocks in this vulnerable period translate into increased likelihood of death are still not clear.

Christian (2010) argues for the importance of maintaining adequate nutrition during crisis periods to avert increases in child mortality and morbidity but does not present evidence that this is a dominant causal channel for elevated mortality. A decline in the quality or quantity of public health services during periods of crisis is another potential mechanism, and Ferreira and Schady (2009) contrast the experiences of Indonesia and Peru to indicate the likely importance of maintaining critical health services. However, the evidence does not extend beyond these two case studies.

Emerging findings indicate that the negative relation between economic crisis and infant survival is attenuated in middle- and upper-middle-income developing countries, perhaps delineating a bridge where the counter-cyclicality of IMR and aggregate income in low-income countries switches to the pro-cyclicality observed in high-income countries. Miller and Urdinola (2010) observe that child mortality is positively related to the coffee price in coffee-growing regions of Colombia, whereas Schady and Smitz (2010) investigate recent economic crises in 17 middle-income countries and find that IMR rose during only two contractions—in Armenia and Peru—that also happened to experience some of the most severe shocks. Currently, however, in much of the developing world the risks to infant survival are still present. Friedman and Schady (2009) estimate that the 2008 global financial crisis led to 35,000–50,000 excess infant deaths in Sub-Saharan Africa the following year.

Aggregate Shocks and Nutritional Pathways

If economic crises affect the mortality of infants and young children, it is highly probable that crisis can also influence the health of surviving children to a substantial degree. One long-standing concern that has received much of the attention in the literature is the effect of crises on nutritional status. For example, in a speculative exercise that uses data available from the 1997 East Asian crisis, Bhutta and others (2009) model the plausible impacts of the 2008 economic crisis on various infant and child health indicators for the Asia region. While noting the insufficiency of some data, their results suggest maternal anemia rates may increase 10–20 percent, the prevalence of low birth weight by 5–10 percent, childhood stunting by 3–7 percent, wasting by 8–16 percent, and under-age-five mortality by 3–11 percent. The most notable potential pathway for these impacts is lower quantity and quality of nutritional intake resulting from increased food insecurity and lower household income.

If these adverse impacts have indeed occurred, the implications for ECD outcomes are clear, given that these affected domains are some of the critical developmental risk factors listed in table 2.1. Although the crisis impacts mentioned above are hypothetical based on a model calibrated with historical data, a substantial body of work has investigated the ex post impacts of aggregate shocks on various nutritional measures, including birth weight, child stunting, underweight and wasting, and child anemia. This section reviews this empirical evidence base, and the empirical findings are summarized in table 2.2.

Birth Weight

Low birth weight, defined as less than 2,500 grams at birth, is a significant determinant for infant mortality (McCormick 1985) and reduced developmental outcomes (Gardner and others 2003; Gorman and Pollitt 1992; Grantham-McGregor and others 1998; Walker and others 2004). The importance of such a risk factor in determining ultimate ECD is clear. However, empirical evidence is limited on the causal impacts of aggregate shocks on birth weight.

One piece of evidence comes from Argentina, where the 1999–2001 recession and consequent 2001–02 economic collapse resulted in a 17 percent drop in GDP from 2000 to 2002. Although the economic recovery was relatively quick, the crisis had a potentially lasting effect on human development levels. Cruces, Gluzmann, and Lopez Calva (2010) use data over the 1993–2006 period and leverage regional variation in GDP and health outcomes to estimate a low birth weight to GDP elasticity. For years in which there is contraction in regional GDP, the authors estimate an elasticity of 0.25 case of low birth weight per 1,000 births for every percentage point decline in GDP per capita. Applying this estimate to the growth shortfall from the 2007–09 crisis in Argentina, the authors project an increase in the rate of low-weight births from 68.1 to 70.1 per 1,000. Interestingly, the authors' estimates find no significant impact from an increase in GDP on

Table 2.2 Impacts of Aggregate Shocks on Main Pathways for Early Childhood Development Outcomes

Risk factor indicator	Summary of evidence	Source	Crisis type, year, and country	Impact on ECD
Pathway: Nutritional				
Intrauterine growth restriction/*Infants at term with low birth weight (<2,500 g; ≥37 weeks' gestation)*	There is limited empirical evidence on the effects of shocks on infant birth weight; however, the current available evidence suggests increases in the risk of low birth weight. Further empirical research is required.	Cruces et al. (2010)	Economic, 2001–02, Argentina	Low-weight births to GDP elasticity of –0.25 per 1,000 births during crisis period
		Burlando (2010)	Month-long blackout, 2008, Tanzania	Reduced birth weight between 50–100 grams
Childhood undernutrition/ *Stunting (height-for-age below –2 SD of reference values)*	There is evidence of increased stunting from extreme shocks and some more moderate shocks. Impacts are found among those aged under 24 months during the period of exposure, suggesting the youngest are the most vulnerable. However, there is little evidence on the lasting impacts of these increases in early childhood undernutrition, whether catch-up is possible and to what degree.	Strauss et al. (2004)	Economic, 1997–98, Indonesia	No negative consequences from 1997 crisis
		Paxson and Schady (2004)	Economic, 1988–92, Peru	Reduction of 0.25 z-score at age 4 observed for children born during the crisis
		Hoddinott and Kinsey (2001)	Drought, 1994–95, Zimbabwe	Reduction of 1.5–2 cm of growth for children 12–24 months, but not older cohort
		Alderman et al. (2006)	Civil war and drought, 1982–84, Zimbabwe	Reduction of z-score 0.58 SD
		Yamano et al. (2003)	Drought, insect attack, and crop disease, 1995–96, Ethiopia	Reduction of 0.12–0.17 cm for children 6–24 months
		Hidrobo (2010)	Economic, 1998–2000, Ecuador	Reduction of z-score by 0.1 SD

Indicator	Description	Source	Crisis	Impact
Iodine deficiency	To our knowledge, there is no evidence on the impacts of crises on iodine deficiency.	N/A	N/A	N/A
Iron deficiency/ *Iron deficiency anemia*	There is little direct evidence concerning the effects of economic crisis on child or mother micronutritional status, although it is possible that where macronutritional deficits arise due to aggregate income shortfalls, micro-nutritional deficits may also occur. Further empirical research is required.	Block et al. (2004)	Economic and drought, 1997–98, Indonesia	Decrease of 6.1% in child hemoglobin concentration
		Frankenberg et al. (1999)	Economic, 1997–98, Indonesia	No impact on child or mother hemoglobin levels
Child malnutrition/ *Wasting (weight-for-height z scores –2 SD or more below the mean)*	Although wasting is often used to assess the severity of emergencies because it is strongly related to mortality, we find little empirical evidence on the impacts of aggregate shocks on wasting. Further empirical research is required.	Block et al. (2004)	Economic and drought, 1997–98, Indonesia	Similar to Waters et al. (2003), no impact on weight-for-age. However, wasting increased from 6% to 12%.
Child malnutrition/ *Underweight (weight-for-age z scores –2 SD or more below the mean)*	To our knowledge, there is little empirical evidence to suggest that aggregate shocks impact childhood underweight status, as measured by weight-for-age. Further empirical research is required.	Waters et al. (2003)	Economic, 1997–98, Indonesia	No impact on weight-for-age, although women (potential mothers) with BMI less than 18 increased from 14.1% to 14.7%

(continued next page)

Table 2.2 Impacts of Aggregate Shocks on Main Pathways for Early Childhood Development Outcomes (continued)

Risk factor indicator	Summary of evidence	Source	Crisis type, year, and country	Impact on ECD
		Frankenberg et al. (1999)	Economic, 1997–98, Indonesia	No impact on weight-for-age
		Pongou et al. (2006)	Economic and subsequent structural adjustment reform, 1990s, Cameroon	Increase in malnutrition for children 0–3 years from 16% to 23%
Pathway: Environmental				
Cognitive stimulation	To our knowledge, there is no evidence on the impacts of crises on child cognitive stimulation.			N/A
Maternal depression	No study has yet linked a rise in economic crisis–induced adult psycho-social morbidity to adverse child outcomes. This is a clear gap in the literature that needs to be addressed before we can confidently point to maternal depression as another relevant channel for economic crisis influencing ECD outcomes.		Economic, Thailand	Increase in suicidal ideation among recently unemployed adults
			Economic, Indonesia	Increase in symptoms related to depression and anxiety among adults

Source: Authors' compilation.

Note: BMI = body mass index; ECD = early childhood development; GDP = gross domestic product; N/A = not available; SD = standard deviation.

low birth weight, suggesting an asymmetric relation between changes in low-birth-weight prevalence and changes in aggregate income similar to that observed for infant mortality referenced above.

Although not an economic crisis on a large scale, Burlando (2010) combines data from a 350-household survey, as well as 20,000 birth records covering a multiyear period, to demonstrate that income loss associated with a month-long power outage in Tanzania resulted in reductions in birth weights of infants born seven to nine months later. For women who were at most seven weeks pregnant when the power outage began to those who became pregnant two weeks after the end of the blackout, the author observes a reduction in birth weight of between 50 and 100 grams. These birth weights were recorded in the main maternity ward in the urban area of Zanzibar Town, which caters mostly to the urban population hardest hit during the power outage. Explanations such as a change in the composition of hospital-seeking women, prenatal care consultations, and food shortage are ruled out as significant determinants for the difference in birth weight. Although evidence was found of a change in fertility behavior due to the blackout, with a higher number of subsequent births in the affected cohort and an increase in the number of teenage mothers, higher fertility could not explain why low birth weights were observed for women already pregnant during the blackout. The author proposes reduced maternal nutritional intake resulting from the temporary income shock as the main transmission mechanism for reduced birth weights. When compared with other cohorts, data suggest that women who were visibly pregnant during the blackout received insurance from shocks, whereas women who may not have known they were yet pregnant or had conceived during the blackout did not receive the same protection.

Stunting

Childhood stunting is primarily an indicator of chronic malnutrition, especially in utero and in early childhood, and is calculated by comparing the height-for-age of a child with a reference population of well-nourished and healthy children. Stunting (height-for-age z scores 2 standard deviations or more below the mean) has a demonstrated increased risk for poorer cognitive outcomes, including performing poorly in school, decreased scores on cognitive function tests (Berkman and others 2002; Mendez and Adair 1999). Stunted children fail to acquire skills at normal rates compared with nonstunted children (Grantham-McGregor and others 1997), and for this reason the impacts of aggregate shocks on childhood stunting may have severe consequences for ECD. The evidence largely, although not exclusively, points to the presence of such impacts from crisis, especially for shocks of the very largest magnitudes.

Paxson and Schady (2004), who use DHS data from 1992, 1996, and 2000 to estimate the impact of the 1988–92 Peruvian crisis on child nutritional status, find that children born at the beginning of the crisis and observed at four years of age in 1992 had significantly lower height (approximately 0.25 z-scores lower) compared with the same aged peers in 1996 and 2000 who exhibited no differences from each other. The lack of data on stunting for the precrisis period makes this finding suggestive but not definitive. In contrast Strauss and others (2004) find no negative consequences from the 1997 Indonesian crisis on stunting when comparing a panel of children measured in 1997 and then 2000 (consistent with the null finding for infant mortality in Indonesia cited earlier).

Using panel data from households living in rural Zimbabwe, Hoddinott and Kinsey (2001) estimate the impact of an extreme crisis, the 1994–95 drought, on childhood stunting. The authors use data from households first interviewed in 1983 to 1984, interviewed again in 1987, then annually from 1992 to 1997. This enables a comparison of height-for-age between children in similar age cohorts in years of average rainfall (measured in 1993 and 1994) with those in drought years (measured in 1995 and 1996). The analysis finds that children aged 12–24 months lost 1.5–2.0 centimeters of growth, with no impact on older children. The evidence suggests that the drought had an impact only on children residing in poorer households (measured in terms of livestock holdings) who are arguably less able to buffer income shortfalls with asset sales. The nutritional effects of the drought for those affected also persisted to the end of the study period, indicating that growth was not able to catch up. In a similar analysis, using data on children's nutritional status as preschoolers, the nutritional status of their siblings at a comparable age and information on both civil war and drought shocks, the Zimbabwe civil war resulted in a reduction in the child height-for-age z-score of 0.5, and the 1982–84 drought shock resulted in a reduction of 0.6 (Alderman, Hoddinott, and Kinsey 2006).

Yamano, Alderman, and Christiaensen (2003) use data from three national surveys carried out in 1995–96 in Ethiopia to assess the impact of food aid programs on stunting in the presence of crop damage resulting from recent droughts, insect attacks, and crop disease. Through this analysis, the authors find that a 10 percent increase in crop damage corresponds to a 0.12-centimeter reduction in growth over a six-month period for children 6–24 months old. When food aid is controlled for in the analysis, the crop damage corresponds to a 0.17-centimeter reduction in child height, indicating the partially protective effects of such aid. Similar to other findings, no significant impact of crop damage is seen on child growth for children 25–50 months old, highlighting the vulnerability of this younger critical age group (under 24 months) to shocks.

In summary, evidence has been found of increased stunting from extreme shocks, such as drought and perhaps the very large economic contractions witnessed in Peru over the 1988–92 period, although impacts from more moderate crises are somewhat mixed. In addition, little is known about the lasting impacts of these increases in childhood stunting, if catch-up is possible, and if so to what degree.

Other Nutritional Outcomes

Pongou, Salomon, and Ezzati (2006) use pooled cross-sectional Cameroon DHS data from 1991 and 1998 to estimate the combined effect of economic crisis and subsequent government adjustment programs (which reduced public expenditures) on child malnutrition. Child malnutrition is defined in this analysis as underweight (weight-for-age z-scores 2 standard deviations or more below the mean) for children under age three. The data cover a period of increasing poverty at least in part due to economic crisis and related reductions in public expenditures, and so the authors are able to test how malnutrition may be affected by an aggregate shock, as well as how this impact may be mediated by economic status and accessibility to formal health care.

The authors find that underweight status for children under age three increased from 16 percent in 1991 to 23 percent in 1998. Declines in economic status and health care accessibility were both correlated with an increase in malnutrition in urban areas, with the children of educated mothers the most protected from adverse changes. In rural areas, reductions in health access, but not economic status, were correlated with an increase in malnutrition, and children born either to low-educated mothers or into poor households experienced the largest increases in underweight status. However, what is not clear from the analysis is whether this change in health access was due to a reduced ability to pay on the part of households or a reduced ability of the health system to provide care.

A handful of studies have documented the impact of the 1997 Indonesia crisis on other health outcomes that can be ultimately linked to child development, including micronutritional deficiencies and general access to health care. Waters, Saadah, and Pradhan (2003) examine the impact of the 1997–98 East Asian crisis on health utilization and outcomes in Indonesia. During the crisis, inflation was at an annual rate of 58 percent, food prices increased an estimated 80 percent, and the overall poverty level increased from 11 to 20 percent. Utilization of public facilities declined 8 percent, while private facility utilization declined 4 percent from 1997 to 1998. The authors found no impact of the crisis on child nutritional status, as measured by weight-for-age. However, evidence for the same period was found for slight decreases in women's body mass index (BMI)

(Frankenberg, Thomas, and Beegle 1999). This suggests that women and perhaps other adults served as a buffer for children during the shock period.

Using nutritional surveillance data from rural Central Java, Block and others (2004) also estimate the impact of Indonesia's 1997–98 drought and financial crisis on child health outcomes. The authors decompose data trends into time, age, and cohort effects using 14 rounds of data from December 1995 to January 2001. The authors argue that failure to control for age and cohort effects will substantially underestimate the impact of the crisis on nutritional outcomes. Similar to Waters, Saadah, and Pradhan (2003), the authors find no impact on child underweight status (weight-for-age). However, they find large and long-lasting impacts on other measures of nutritional status, including wasting (weight-for-height z-scores 2 standard deviations or more below the mean) and micronutrient status. The analysis shows that prevalence of wasting doubled from 6 to 12 percent, with limited recovery by 2001. The effects on mean hemoglobin concentration from December 1996 to July 1998 show a decrease of 6.1 percent. With larger impacts on hemoglobin concentration in children born or conceived during the crisis, it appears that maternal malnutrition was an additional pathway for increased risk of iron deficiency anemia in children. This conclusion is validated through observed decreases in egg, dark green leafy vegetable, and cooking oil consumption at the household level.

Micronutritional deficits such as iron or iodine deficiency are two of the six ECD risk factors in table 2.1; however, little further direct evidence has been identified concerning the effects of economic crisis on child or mother micronutritional status, although it is possible that where macronutritional deficits arise because of aggregate income shortfalls (see above), micronutritional deficits may also occur. The only other evidence on child anemia and crisis also derives from the 1997 crisis in Indonesia. Strauss and others (2004) and Frankenberg, Thomas, and Beegle (1999) find no change in hemoglobin levels of children or mothers, although the relatively limited frequency of data collection may not have been able to identify the impacts observed in Block and others (2004). This is an area for further inquiry.

Aggregate Shocks and Environmental Pathways

Psychosocial morbidity, especially maternal depression, is yet another risk factor for ECD (Sohr-Preston and Scaramella 2006). Factors associated with poverty such as unemployment and increased material risk are also associated with poorer adult psychosocial health, at least in developed countries, thus highlighting another causal channel linking poverty with potentially lower ECD measures. In the United States, low-income respondents have lower odds of having no psychosocial disorder relative to high-income respondents (odds ratio [OR] = 0.6), as do respondents with less than a high school education relative to college graduates (OR = 0.3) (Kessler and others 2005). In a series of studies sponsored by the International Consortium in Psychiatric Epidemiology, the odds of experiencing two or more (comorbid) disorders in the past 12 months increase with declining income and education in Canada, the Netherlands, and the United States, but not in Mexico (WHO International Consortium in Psychiatric Epidemiology 2000).

Researchers have taken an interest in investigating the causal mechanisms and direction of this observed association. Competing theories include the social causation hypothesis, whereby low socioeconomic status leads to mental disorders through pathways such as stress and relative deprivation, and the drift or selection hypothesis, in which mental ill-health leads to declines in socioeconomic status via reduced educational and occupational attainment. This distinction is relevant for understanding the possible impacts of economic crisis on ultimate ECD outcomes, because the selection hypothesis would preclude strong effects of crisis on parental psychosocial well-being whereas the social causation hypothesis would allow for it.

Several tests of these theories, all based on data from developed countries, suggest that both mechanisms are probably relevant. A New Zealand–based study (Miech and others 1999) finds that internalizing disorders (anxiety and depression) do not affect subsequent educational attainment, whereas externalizing disorders (conduct and attention deficit disorders) do. Social causation effects explain the relationship between anxiety disorders and educational attainment, whereas both causation and selection effects apply to conduct disorder. Johnson and others (1999), following a cohort of young children in New York State for almost 20 years, find support for the social causation hypothesis for anxiety, depressive, disruptive, and personality disorders, whereas disruptive and substance use disorders appeared to select respondents into lower educational attainment. The root cause behind social causation may very well be stressors related to perceptions of loss of autonomy rather than low income per se; for example, indebtedness is a greater predictor of depression and anxiety than low income levels in the United Kingdom (Jenkins and others 2008). This is a suggestive finding that may be salient for understanding the psychosocial impacts of economic crisis on adult caretakers of young children.

Turning to the relatively sparse evidence from developing countries, the linkages between poverty and poor psychosocial health in the developing world are less clear. Patel and Kleinman (2003) find significant associations between socioeconomic status (broadly interpreted) and common mental disorders in 10 out of 11 developing-country studies, and Das and others (2007) review population-representative samples from five developing countries and find no association between consumption-based poverty measures and psychosocial health. Nevertheless, the emerging evidence base suggests that negative (or positive) life shocks are linked to worse (or improved) psychosocial health among adults in developing countries (Das and Das 2006; Stillman, McKenzie, and Gibson 2009), which indicates that it may not be poverty per se that is linked to an increased likelihood of poor mental health, but rather transitions into poverty and the conditions associated with transition.

The handful of studies looking at the psychosocial impact of economic crises in developing countries find them to be severe. In Thailand after the 1997 financial crisis, rates of suicidal ideation rose dramatically among the recently unemployed (Tangcharoensathien and others 2000), and panel data from Indonesia find a dramatic rise in symptoms related to depression and anxiety, particularly among the groups most adversely affected, such as the less educated, urban, and landless populations (Friedman and Thomas 2009). Figure 2.2 reports the prevalence of anxiety and depressive symptoms in a population-representative panel of adult individuals taken at three points in time: 1993, before the crisis; 1998, immediately after the crisis; and 2000. The rise in psychosocial morbidity is apparent in all ages over the crisis period, and this increase appears to be sustained even as other measures of economic welfare such as household income and consumption have largely recovered by the year 2000.

The Friedman and Thomas (2009) study may be the most directly applicable to establishing some link between economic crisis and worsened parental depression and other psychosocial morbidity. However, no study has yet attempted to link a rise in economic crisis–induced adult psychosocial morbidity to adverse child outcomes of any sort. This is a clear gap in the literature that needs to be addressed before we can confidently point to maternal depression as another relevant channel for economic crisis influencing ECD outcomes. In one suggestive study, Costello and others (2003) exploit a natural experiment in the form of an income supplement to American Indian families from a new casino to test the social causation hypothesis. The casino opened in the middle of a longitudinal study on child and adolescent psychiatric morbidity in North Carolina, lifting a sizable proportion of American Indian families out of poverty during the study. Before the casino's opening, psychiatric morbidity was more common among children of persistently poor families and of families who would later exit poverty relative to children of families that were never poor. After the casino opened, symptoms in children of previously poor households fell to levels matching those of the never-poor, whereas symptoms of the persistently poor children remained high. The effect was specific to conduct and oppositional/defiant disorders; no effects were observed

Figure 2.2 Incidence of Sadness or Anxiety in Each of the Three Survey Years among Indonesian Adults, by Age of Respondent

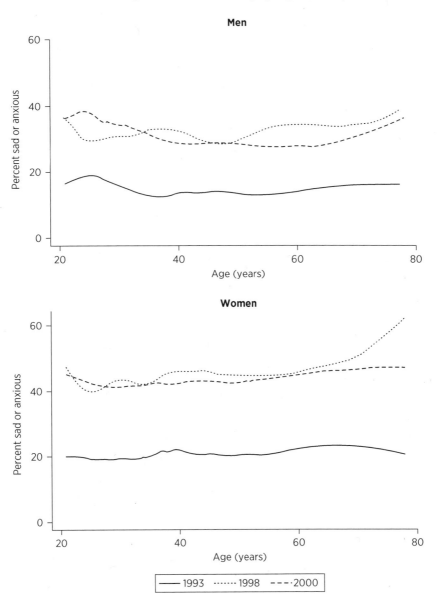

Source: Friedman and Thomas 2009.

for anxiety and depression. Unfortunately, measures of cognitive skills of the children were not included in the study.

A similar result was also identified in Mexico among beneficiaries of the conditional cash transfer program Oportunidades (Opportunities). Ozer and others (2009) investigate the effect of program participation on child behavior by exploiting the randomized rollout of the pilot program and find a 10 percent decrease in oppositional or defiant disorders among beneficiaries but no change in symptoms related to anxiety and depression. Aizer, Stroud, and Buka (2009) find a robust negative link between maternal stress during pregnancy, as measured through cortisol levels in the blood, and subsequent educational attainment of those infants exposed to elevated levels of cortisol. This last finding is particularly relevant because it suggests that even transitory crisis impacts on the psychosocial health of pregnant mothers can have long-lasting impacts on children. Further work is necessary in a variety of settings to definitively establish and quantify the ECD impacts of crisis that operate through the psychosocial health of the mother; however, the variety of work cited here suggests that this pathway may indeed be an important one by which economic crisis affects ECD.

Long-Term Consequences of Economic Crisis

An important question related to any possible ECD consequence of economic crisis is that of duration of impact. Duncan, Brooks-Gunn, and Klebanov (1994) and McLoyd (1998) argue that it is the conditions associated with persistent rather than transitory poverty that result in low levels of child development and subsequent adult functioning, at least for U.S. populations. Because crises are by definition transitory events (although severe ones can last several years), do any of the influences on risk factors discussed in previous sections have an impact on the individual that lasts into later childhood, adolescence, and, ultimately, on into adulthood?

That conditions in early life can have long-term consequences for health (Barker 1992; 1995), education, and socioeconomic outcomes for individuals is well established. Case and Paxson (2010), using a within-family estimator, find that children who are born heavier and longer score higher on cognitive tests later in life, attain more education, are more likely to be employed, and earn more, conditional on employment. Grantham-McGregor, and others (2007) look at the effect of stunting and poverty on both school attainment and learning and come to a similar conclusion: Stunted children have poorer performance in school, with an estimated reduction of 0.7–0.8 standard deviation on test scores (a reduction equivalent to two years of schooling). With the assumption that every year of schooling is equivalent to an increase of 9 percent in adult annual income, the authors estimate a loss in adult income from being stunted of between 22 and 30 percent. If an economic crisis leads to lower birth weight or stunting among children during the critical period of in utero development and the first two years of life, as suggested by the material reviewed previously, then crisis will likely lead to lower cognitive skills or earnings for that same cohort later in life.

Direct observations of long-term impacts of crisis, however, are rare. One recent study provides evidence on the medium-term impacts of economic crisis on child nutritional status, as measured by height-for-age, as well as one direct measure of early childhood cognitive development, a vocabulary test score—indeed, this is the first study to our knowledge that directly investigates impacts of economic crisis on cognitive measures. Hidrobo (2010) observes children who were three years old or younger during the 1998–2000 economic crisis in Ecuador first in 2003 (when they were three to five years old) and then again in 2005 (at between five and seven years of age). The author identifies the impact of the crisis by comparing sibling differences in outcomes across households exposed to the crisis with other sibling sets observed at similar ages but not exposed to the crisis, where crisis exposure is determined by birth month and province. The author proposes three major pathways through which the crisis can affect child health and cognitive development: (1) reductions in household real income, (2) reductions in the amount of time parents spent at home, and (3) decreases in the health environment. The author finds that one year of crisis exposure resulted in a significant decrease in height-for-age by 0.1 standard deviation, as well as a reduction in vocabulary test scores of 2.4 points (corresponding to a 3 percent reduction). The author also examines how exposure to the crisis may vary by age and finds that the largest negative impact on height is found for children 12–17 months old during the crisis period, whereas the impact on the cognitive development measure is largest for those 18–29 months old over the crisis period.

Hidrobo (2010) investigates possible heterogeneous impacts of the crisis and finds that rural farming households were able to better protect their children as measured by height-for-age, but not by the vocabulary score. This suggests that although farm households were somewhat insured from a reduction in food consumption experienced by other households, they may not have been as protected from the deterioration in the general health environment and may also have experienced reduced parental time at home. Similarly, households with access to health centers, and presumably free health services and food supplements for children, were significantly more protected from the impacts of the crisis on child height-for-age, but not for the vocabulary score. This finding emphasizes that multiple causal pathways are determinative of ECD (table 2.1), and economic crises can adversely affect several pathways simultaneously. Effective protection policies implemented in the wake of an economic crisis would need to consider all of these transmission channels to be most effective.

Although Hidrobo (2010) provides evidence that the negative impacts of a crisis may persist three to five years after recovery, do the consequences of crisis during early childhood extend far into adulthood? The relative lack of long-run longitudinal studies in developing countries has limited this area of inquiry. However, numerous studies identify important long-term impacts of climatic shocks and extreme disruptive events, such as famine, that link impacts measured in adulthood to event exposure on the basis of date and location of birth. These studies may shed light on the long-term impacts of at least the most severe crises that can result in dramatic nutritional declines. Maccini and Yang (2009) demonstrate that positive weather conditions around the time of birth for the 1953–74 birth cohorts in Indonesia decreased the likelihood of female self-reported poverty and poor health, increased female height, and completed years of schooling, as well as improved economic status. Negative shocks early in life can also have long-term negative consequences for adult outcomes. Alderman, Hoddinott, and Kinsey (2006) use aggregate shocks, such as civil war and drought, as an instrument for preschool nutritional status. The authors estimate that preschool malnutrition results in loss of stature, schooling, and potential work experience for a total estimated loss of lifetime earnings of around 14 percent.

Two studies of famine reveal particularly detailed findings. In Almond and others (2007), the authors explore the long-term economic, health, and marital outcomes for individuals affected by the 1959–62 Chinese famine. The authors use month and year of birth, as measured in the 2000 Chinese census, as the base measure of exposure to famine, which is then supplemented with a measure of famine intensity as identified by geographic variation in overall death rates. Focusing on cohorts born in 1956–64, the authors find that greater famine intensity is associated with a higher likelihood of being illiterate (8 percent more likely for women and 9 percent for men), not currently working (3 percent for women and 6 percent for men), and disability (13 percent for women) in 2000. Additionally, men exposed to the famine period as young children were 9 percent more likely to be financially dependent on other household members and experienced higher rates of mortality, as defined by survival to age 40.

One challenge for the Almond and others (2007) analysis is that the three-year duration of the Chinese famine makes it impossible to distinguish between the consequences of exposure to the famine in utero separated from exposure during the first years of life. However, Neelsen and Stratmann (2010) are able to use the eight-month Greek famine of late 1941 to early 1942 to distinguish the long-term effects of undernourishment at specific ages: in utero and first and second year of life. Using data from the Greek National Population Housing Census, the authors include 11 cohorts born between 1936 and 1946. For these cohorts, the authors observed them when 25–36 years old in 1971 and then again at 10-year intervals for the next three decades. Using a regression discontinuity analysis, the exposed groups are the 1940 birth cohort (exposed during the second year of life), 1941 birth cohort (first year of life), and 1942 birth cohort (in utero), with 1936–39 and 1943–46 cohorts included for comparison purposes.

The findings are similar to those from Almond and others (2007), as the authors estimate that being exposed to famine conditions at a young age lowers the likelihood of being literate, likelihood of completing upper secondary schooling, and total number of years of education. For those exposed in the second year of life, the authors find a reduction of 0.5 percentage point in literacy, as well as reductions in upper secondary and technical schooling of between 1.3 and 1.8 percentage points. For this cohort, a reduced total attainment in education between 1.2 to 1.4 months is also seen, as well as reduced occupational prestige.

The cohort most affected by the famine appears to be those in the first year of life when the famine struck. Reductions in literacy range from 0.4 to 1.1 percentage points and are significant for all rounds of census data. The negative impact on upper secondary and technical schooling completion is 1.8–2.4 percentage points, with years of education reduced 1.4–2.4 months. A significant reduction is also found in the occupational prestige of adults from this birth cohort. The cohort least affected by the famine was the exposed in utero 1942 cohort, which shows no significant reductions in literacy, although years of education are reduced 1.3–1.7 months, with similar reductions in occupational prestige. The authors suspect that positive selection through fertility as well as mortality may explain the mitigated negative impacts for this cohort; however, this requires further study.

In summary, clear long-lasting adult life consequences are found from extreme temporal events such as famine and drought, but as yet little evidence from more moderate (and arguably typical) economic crises exist. The results from the relatively milder Ecuador crisis find impacts lasting up to five years into late childhood, and future longitudinal studies may be able to trace out these impacts further into young adulthood. The clearest pathway through which these lifelong effects occur is again nutrition, especially nutrition during the critical period of very early childhood. The studies cited here have found evidence for stunting and low-birth-weight impacts, at least in the Latin American crises experienced by Argentina, Ecuador, and Peru, and these same nutritional deficits have been linked to lower subsequent cognitive outcomes in a variety of settings. It is thus probable that crises can have long-term ECD-related outcomes operating through these channels. The Ecuadoran study also suggests the importance of nonnutritional pathways that can also be affected by crisis. Future work is needed to robustly identify the impacts of crisis on these pathways and the subsequent shorter- and longer-run consequences for affected children.

Discussion and Policy Responses

This chapter has reviewed the pathways through which ECD outcomes can, in principle, be impacted by economic crisis. These pathways include elevated mortality, reduced nutritional intake, and degradations to the home, school, and health environment. The chapter then reviewed existing rigorous empirical evidence, where rigor is defined as contrasting population-representative outcomes taken from points measured both before and after the plausibly exogenous crisis event. These studies are summarized in table 2.2. Empirical evidence suggests that infant mortality and poor nutritional status, measured through low birth weight, stunting, underweight, and wasting, increase in times of economic crisis in a variety of settings. This suggests salient short-run risks for ECD in the face of aggregate shocks. When reviewing the evidence on longer-run outcomes, the picture is not as definitive, except in the case of the most extreme shocks such as famine. However, sufficient evidence is available on the importance of nutrition at critical ages to suggest that any crisis-induced malnutrition will also have long-run consequences.

Many questions remain unanswered. The findings on mortality suggest an important gender component, with female infants being more vulnerable. Infants born to rural and less-educated mothers are also more likely to die during crisis. Does this same heterogeneity arise when looking at the nutritional and other ECD-related influences of crisis? Evidence from Ecuador suggests that food-producing rural households may be able to buffer much of the nutritional consequences of a financial crisis, so heterogeneity may very well exist along a variety of dimensions that are important to the design of protective policies. This possible heterogeneity in crisis impacts needs to be carefully explored in multiple settings. Even less is known about how crisis affects nonnutritional pathways. Although nutritional deficits at critical ages appear to have long-lasting consequences, what about consequences from a transitory deterioration in the stimulative environment or the psychosocial health of caregivers? The evidence for these questions is in a very nascent stage. Understanding how, and in what context, crisis affects each individual risk factor is a research priority if countries wish to design effective policy responses to the apparently inevitable future macroeconomic shocks.

During crisis periods in developing countries one often finds calls for donors and governments to maintain public health expenditures to protect maternal and child health. Although in many countries civil service salaries in the health sector are protected, nonsalary expenditures, such as drugs and infrastructure investment, are the most likely to decline during a crisis. While richer countries tend to exhibit counter-cyclical government spending, low-income countries often curtail government spending in a crisis (Lewis and Verhoeven 2010). This has implications for the ability of facilities, particularly at the primary health level, to maintain quality service delivery. Maintaining the pre-crisis levels of government health expenditures is therefore desirable; however, health spending by itself does not guarantee that pro-poor services will be protected (World Bank 2009).

Evidence addressing the potential protective effect of maintaining or increasing supply-side activities during a crisis is severely limited. However, Indonesia is one example where the supply-side response to the 1997 crisis appears to have been a critical factor in the protection of child health. The Indonesian government instituted several health-related policies in the crisis aftermath, including a supplementary feeding program aimed at maintaining the nutritional status of children under five years old, with a particular emphasis on children under two. Giles and Satriawan (2010) find that this program had a significant protective effect on the height-for-age of children aged 12–24 months during the crisis period and that longer exposure to the program, because the program start date varied by region, resulted in ever greater protective effects. They find no impact for children of other ages.

Another protective effort by the Indonesian government was a health card program that served as both a supply- and demand-side policy aimed at mitigating the observed decrease in utilization of key health services. The health card was distributed to households identified as those most vulnerable to the disruptions from the financial crisis and provided household members free services at public health facilities, including outpatient and inpatient care, prenatal care, and assistance at birth. Those facilities that provided subsidized care received additional financing to compensate for the increase in demand. Pradhan, Saadah, and Sparrow (2007) find that utilization of outpatient facilities would have fallen further in 1999 if the program had not been introduced. The authors argue that a considerable portion of the program impacts are a result of the increased facility financing, rather than the demand-side aspects of the health cards. In addition, although the distribution of health cards was pro-poor, the actual benefits of the program (for example, increased utilization) were stronger for the wealthier quintiles, suggesting these households were more likely to benefit from the increased financing in the public health facilities.

In a similar vein, evidence from Thailand shows that the government was able to counteract decreased demand for health services during the 1997–98 crisis through an expansion of the social insurance program. During this time, health care utilization in Thailand actually increased (Waters, Saadah, and Pradhan 2003). Besides the two examples of Indonesia and Thailand, though, little additional evidence links maintenance of public sector spending to protected health and development outcomes. Future research on this issue will be especially beneficial to the global community's efforts to design effective supply-side-oriented protection policies.

By contrast, a more substantial body of evidence suggests that policy interventions directed at the demand side can be useful in mitigating the effects of economic crisis, especially if they are already in place at the outset of a crisis or can be rapidly established. Fafchamps and Minton (2007) use data from Madagascar to demonstrate how an unanticipated macroshock can result in an immediate decrease in health service utilization due primarily to reduced real incomes. The authors find that a removal of user fees resulted in a 22 percent increase in health service utilization. Although this is not an argument for universal removal of user fees, it suggests that removal of user fees for a limited period of time maintains utilization when household poverty is the main driver behind a decline in access to services.

For the purposes of mitigating adverse impacts of economic crisis on ECD outcomes, health care utilization is, of course, just one concern. As detailed in previous sections, nutritional status is a primary pathway for ECD outcomes. For this reason, policy makers need also look toward interventions that directly target household consumption, especially food consumption, during times of economic crisis. Food for Work (FFW) or Cash for Work programs may provide immediate relief to households during crisis periods. As discussed in Gentilini (2007), the transfer selection, whether cash or food, should be based on a thorough and comprehensive assessment of local capacities, including careful analysis of market conditions. However, little evidence is available on which mechanism, or whether a combination of the two, may be the best to mitigate adverse effects during crisis on child nutritional outcomes. Although evidence suggests that FFW programs in Ethiopia improved food security, improved targeting is required to maximize program benefits (Gedamu 2006; Gilligan and Hoddinott 2007).

In terms of ECD pathways, limited evidence is available concerning the impact of FFW programs on child nutritional status. The Ethiopian FFW program did have a positive impact on child weight-for-height (Quisumbing 2003). In Indonesia, a pilot FFW program introduced to mitigate the adverse effects of the 1997–98 crisis transferred rice, cooking oil, and legumes to participant households. However, a program evaluation found no impact on the principal outcome of interest, child and maternal anemia rates, suggesting that to affect micronutrient status the FFW program should have provided foods linked to iron intake (Moench-Pfanner and others 2005). This underscores the argument that food transfers not only need to be well targeted but also well constituted to address the wide range of ECD pathways.

Another widespread protective policy tool is the conditional cash transfer (CCT) program. A large body of evidence is at hand on the positive impacts of CCT programs on health and education in a variety of contexts (Fiszbein and Schady 2009; Gertler 2004; Schady and Araujo 2008). Although the evidence base is not as extensive, CCT programs have also demonstrated positive impacts on child height (Fernald, Gertler, and Neufeld 2008, 2009). Macours, Schady, and Vakis (2008) provide evidence on the potential for CCT programs to yield improvements in ECD outcomes through several diverse pathways. In Nicaragua, the conditional cash transfer program Atencion a Crisis (Attention to Crisis) provided payments conditional on school-aged child enrollment and attendance as well as preventive care visits for preschool-aged children. Parents were also exposed to informational campaigns concerning the importance of nutrition in household food choices. The CCT program resulted in significant gains for a variety of cognitive and noncognitive outcomes. Child recipients of the program experienced increases of 0.13 and 0.17 standard deviation in social-personal and language measures, as well as a gain of 0.22 standard deviation in receptive vocabulary. In terms of the causal pathways influenced that explain these gains, the program shifted household expenditures toward more diversified diets and more nutrient-rich food for young children, as well as stimulation materials such as books, paper, and pencils. In addition, beneficiary children were found to be more likely to have had a self-reported growth check-up and to have received vitamins, iron, and deworming medicine. Thus, the provision of additional directed resources can propel households to invest more in the early development of their children. Presumably if programs of this nature are already in place before the onset of crisis, they should serve to mitigate the most deleterious effects of crisis on child health, nutrition, and cognition. In addition, these programs can serve as a platform to deliver well-targeted enhanced services deemed necessary in a crisis aftermath.

References

Aizer, A., L. Stroud, and S. Buka. 2009. "Maternal Stress and Child Well-Being: Evidence from Siblings." Unpublished manuscript, Brown University, Providence, RI.

Alderman, H., J. Hoddinott, and B. H. Kinsey. 2006. "Long Term Consequences of Early Childhood Malnutrition." *Oxford Economic Papers* 58 (3): 450–74.

Almond, D., L. Edlund, H. Li, and J. Zhang. 2007. "Long-Term Effects of the 1959–1961 China Famine: Mainland China and Hong Kong." NBER Working Paper 13384, National Bureau of Economic Research, Cambridge, MA.

Baird, S., J. Friedman, and N. Schady. 2007. "Aggregate Income Shocks and Infant Mortality in the Developing World." World Bank Policy Research Working Paper No. 4346, World Bank, Washington, DC.

———. 2010. "Aggregate Income Shocks and Infant Mortality in the Developing World." *Review of Economics and Statistics*. Forthcoming.

Barker, D. J. P. 1992. *Fetal and Infant Origins of Adult Disease.* London: BMJ Books.

———. 1995. "Fetal Origins of Coronary Heart Disease." *BMJ* 311 (6998): 171–74.

Bärnighausen, T., D. E. Bloom, D. Canning, A. Friedman, O. Levine, J. O'Brien, L. Privor-Dumm, and D. Walker. 2008. "The Economic Case for Expanding Vaccination Coverage of Children." Best Practice Paper: New Advice from Copenhagen Consensus 08, Copenhagen Consensus Center, Copenhagen.

Berkman, D. S., A. G. Lescano, R. H. Gilman, S. L. Lopez, and M. M. Black. 2002. "Effects of Stunting, Diarrhoeal Disease, and Parasitic Infection during Infancy on Cognition in Late Childhood: A Follow-Up Study." *Lancet* 359 (9306): 564–71.

Bhalotra, S. 2010. "Fatal Fluctuations? Cyclicality in Infant Mortality in India." *Journal of Development Economics* 93 (1): 7–19.

Bhutta, Z. A., F. A. Bawany, A. Feroze, A. Rizvi, S. J. Thapa, and M. Patel. 2009. "Effects of the Crises on Child Nutrition and Health in East Asia and the Pacific." *Global Social Policy* 9: 119–43.

Bleichrodt, N., I. Garcia, C. Rubio, G. Morreale de Escobar, and F. Escobar del Rey. 1987. "Developmental Disorders Associated with Severe Iodine Deficiency." In *The Prevention and Control of Iodine Deficiency Disorders,* ed. B. Hetzel, J. Dunn, and J. Stanbury, 65–84. Amsterdam: Elsevier.

Block, S. A., L. Keiss, H. Keller, S. Kosen, R. Moench-Pfanner, M. W. Bloem, and C. P. Timmer. 2004. "Macro Shocks and Micro (Scopic) Outcomes: Child Nutrition during Indonesia's Crisis." *Economics and Human Biology* 2 (1): 21–44.

Bradley, R. H., and R. F. Corwyn. 2002. "Socioeconomic Status and Child Development." *Annual Review of Psychology* 53: 371–99.

Burlando, A. 2010. "When the Lights Go Out: Permanent Health Effects of Transitory Shocks." Unpublished paper, Boston University, Boston.

Case, A., and C. Paxson. 2010. "Causes and Consequences of Early-Life Health." *Demography* 47 (Supp.): S65–S85.

Chay, K. Y., and M. Greenstone. 2003. "The Impact of Air Pollution on Infant Mortality: Evidence from Geographic Variation in Pollution Shocks Induced by a Recession." *Quarterly Journal of Economics* 118 (3): 1121–67.

Christian, P. 2010. "Impact of the Economic Crisis and Increase in Food Prices on Child Mortality: Exploring Nutritional Pathways." *Journal of Nutrition* 140 (1): 177S–81S.

Costello, E. J., S. N. Compton, G. Keeler, and A. Angold. 2003. "Relationships between Poverty and Psychopathology: A Natural Experiment." *JAMA* 290 (15): 2023–29.

Cruces, G., P. Gluzmann, and L. F. Lopez Calva. 2010. "Permanent Effects of Economic Crisis on Household Welfare: Evidence and Projections from

Argentina's Downturn." Paper prepared for UNDP-RB-LAC project The Effects of the Economic Crisis on the Well-Being of Households in Latin America and the Caribbean.

Cutler, D. M., F. Knaul, R. Lozano, O. Mendez, and B. Zurita. 2002. "Financial Crisis, Health Outcomes, and Ageing: Mexico in the 1980s and 1990s." *Journal of Public Economics* 84 (2): 279–303.

Das, J., and V. Das. 2006. "Mental Health in Urban India: Patterns and Narratives." Manuscript, World Bank, Washington, DC.

Das, J., Q. T. Do, J. Friedman, D. McKenzie, and K. Scott. 2007. "Mental Health and Poverty in Developing Countries: Revisiting the Relationship." *Social Science and Medicine* 65 (3): 467–80.

Dehejia, R., and A. Lleras-Muney. 2004. "Booms, Busts, and Babies' Health." *Quarterly Journal of Economics* 119 (3): 1091–130.

Duncan, G. J., J. Brooks-Gunn, and P. K. Klebanov. 1994. "Economic Deprivation and Early Childhood Development." *Child Development* 65 (2): 296–318.

Fafchamps, M., and B. Minten. 2007. "Public Service Provision, User Fees and Political Turmoil." *Journal of African Economies* 16 (3): 485–518.

Fernald, L. C. H., P. J. Gertler, and L. M. Neufeld. 2008. "Role of Cash in Conditional Cash Transfer Programmes for Child Health, Growth, and Development: An Analysis of Mexico's Oportunidades." *Lancet* 371 (9615): 828–37.

———. 2009. "10-Year Effect of Oportunidades, Mexico's Conditional Cash Transfer Programme, on Child Growth, Cognition, Language, and Behaviour: A Longitudinal Follow-Up Study." *Lancet* 374 (9706): 1997–2005.

Ferreira, F. H. G., and N. Schady. 2009. "Aggregate Economic Shocks, Child Schooling, and Child Health." *World Bank Research Observer* 24 (2): 147–81.

Fiszbein, A., and N. Schady. 2009. *Conditional Cash Transfers: Reducing Present and Future Poverty.* Washington, DC: World Bank.

Frankenberg, E., D. Thomas, and K. Beegle. 1999. "The Real Costs of Indonesia's Economic Crisis: Preliminary Findings from the Indonesia Family Life Surveys." DRU-2064-NIA/NICHD. RAND Corporation, Santa Monica, CA.

Friedman, J., and N. Schady. 2009. "How Many More Infants Are Likely to Die in Africa as a Result of the Global Financial Crisis?" World Bank Policy Research Working Paper 5023, World Bank, Washington, DC.

Friedman, J., and D. Thomas. 2009. "Psychological Health before, during, and after an Economic Crisis: Results from Indonesia 1993–2000." *World Bank Economic Review* 23 (1): 57–76.

Galler, J. R., R. H. Harrison, F. Ramsey, V. Forde, and S. C. Butler. 2000. "Maternal Depressive Symptoms Affect Infant Cognitive Development in Barbados." *Journal of Child Psychology and Psychiatry* 41 (6): 747–57.

Gardner, J. M., S. P. Walker, C. A. Powell, and S. Grantham-McGregor. 2003. "A Randomized Controlled Trial of a Home-Visiting Intervention on Cognition and Behavior in Term Low Birth Weight Infants." *Journal of Pediatrics* 143 (5): 634–39.

Gedamu, A. 2006. "Food for Work Program and Its Implications on Food Security: A Critical Review with a Practical Example from the Amhara Region, Ethiopia." *Journal of Agriculture and Rural Development in the Tropics and Subtropics* 107 (2): 177–88.

Gentilini, U. 2007. "Cash and Food Transfers: A Primer." World Food Programme Occasional Paper 18, Rome, Italy.

Gertler, P. 2004. "Do Conditional Cash Transfers Improve Child Health? Evidence from PROGRESA's Controlled Randomised Experiment." *American Economic Review* 94 (2): 331–36.

Giles, J., and E. Satriawan. 2010. "Protecting Child Nutritional Status in the Aftermath of a Financial Crisis: Evidence from Indonesia." World Bank Policy Research Working Paper No. 5471, World Bank, Washington, DC.

Gilligan, D. O., and J. Hoddinott. 2007. "Is There Persistence in the Impact of Emergency Food Aid? Evidence on Consumption, Food Security, and Assets in Rural Ethiopia." *American Journal of Agricultural Economics* 89 (2): 225–42.

Gorman, K. S., and E. Pollitt. 1992. "Relationship between Weight and Body Proportionality at Birth, Growth during the First Year of Life, and Cognitive Development at 36, 48, and 60 Months." *Infant Behavior and Development* 15 (3): 279–96.

Grantham-McGregor, S., and C. Ani. 2001. "A Review of Studies on the Effect of Iron Deficiency on Cognitive Development in Children." *Journal of Nutrition* 131 (2): 649S–66S.

Grantham-McGregor, S., Y. B. Cheung, S. Cueto, P. Glewwe, L. Richter, and B. Strupp. 2007. "Child Development in Developing Countries: Developmental Potential in the First Five Years for Children in Developing Countries." *Lancet* 369 (9555): 60–70.

Grantham-McGregor, S. M., P. I. Lira, A. Ashworth, S. S. Morris, and A. M. Assuncao. 1998. "The Development of Low Birth Weight Term Infants and the Effects of the Environment in Northeast Brazil." *Journal of Pediatrics* 132 (4): 661–66.

Grantham-McGregor, S., C. Walker, S. Chang, and C. Powell. 1997. "Effects of Early Childhood Supplementation with and without Stimulation on Later Development in Stunted Jamaican Children." *American Journal of Clinical Nutrition* 66 (2): 247–53.

Helmers, C., and M. Patnam. 2010. "The Formation and Evolution of Childhood Skill Acquisition: Evidence from India." *Journal of Development Economics.* Forthcoming.

Hidrobo, M. 2010. "The Effects of Ecuador's 1998–2000 Economic Crisis on Child Health and Cognitive Development." November. Department of Agricultural and Resource Economics, University of California, Berkeley.

Hoddinott, J., and B. Kinsey. 2001. "Child Growth in the Time of Drought." *Oxford Bulletin of Economics and Statistics* 63 (4): 409–36.

Horton, S., H. Alderman, and J. A. Rivera. 2008. "The Challenge of Hunger and Malnutrition." Copenhagen Consensus 2008 Challenge Paper, Copenhagen Consensus Center, Copenhagen.

Jenkins, R., D. Bhugra, P. Bebbington, T. Brugha, M. Farrell, J. Coid, T. Fryers, S. Weich, N. Singleton, and H. Meltzer. 2008. "Debt, Income, and Mental Disorders in the General Population." *Psychological Medicine* 38 (10): 1485–93.

Johnson, J. G., P. Cohen, B. P. Dohrenwend, B. G. Link, and J. S. Brook. 1999. "A Longitudinal Investigation of Social Causation and Social Selection Processes Involved in the Association between Socioeconomic Status and Psychiatric Disorders." *Journal of Abnormal Psychology* 108 (3): 490–99.

Kessler, R. C., W. T. Chiu, O. Demler, and E. E. Walters. 2005. "Prevalence, Severity, and Comorbidity of 12-Month DSM-IV Disorders in the National Comorbidity Survey Replication." *Archives of General Psychiatry* 62 (6): 617–27.

Lam, D., and S. Duryea. 1999. "Effects of Schooling on Fertility, Labor Supply, and Investments in Children, with Evidence from Brazil." *Journal of Human Resources* 34 (1): 160–92.

Lewis, M., and M. Verhoeven. 2010. "Financial Crises and Social Spending: The Impact of the 2008–2009 Crisis." *World Economics* 11 (4): 79–110.

Loayza, N. V., R. Ranciere, L. Serven, and J. Ventura. 2007. "Macroeconomic Volatility and Welfare in Developing Countries: An Introduction." *World Bank Economic Review* 21 (3): 343–57.

Maccini, S., and D. Yang. 2009. "Under the Weather: Health, Schooling, and Economic Consequences of Early-Life Rainfall." *American Economic Review* 99 (3): 1006–26.

Macours, K., N. Schady, and R. Vakis. 2008. "Cash Transfers, Behavioral Changes and Cognitive Development in Early Childhood: Evidence from a Randomized Experiment." World Bank Policy Research Working Paper 4759, World Bank, Washington, DC.

McCormick, M.C. 1985. "The Contribution of Low Birth Weight to Infant Mortality and Childhood Morbidity." *New England Journal of Medicine* 312 (2): 82–90.

McLoyd, V. 1998. "Socioeconomic Disadvantage and Child Development." *American Psychologist* 53 (2): 185–204.

Mendez, M. A., and L. S. Adair. 1999. "Severity and Timing of Stunting in the First Two Years of Life Affect Performance on Cognitive Tests in Late Childhood." *Journal of Nutrition* 129 (8): 1555–62.

Miech, R. A., A. Caspi, T. E. Moffitt, B. R. E. Wright, and P. A. Silva. 1999. "Low Socioeconomic Status and Mental Disorders: A Longitudinal Study of Selection and Causation during Young Adulthood." *American Journal of Sociology* 104 (4): 1096–131.

Miller, G., and B. P. Urdinola. 2010. "Cyclicality, Mortality, and the Value of Time: The Case of Coffee Price Fluctuations and Child Survival in Colombia." *Journal of Political Economy* 118 (1): 113–55.

Moench-Pfanner, R., S. de Pee, M. W. Bloem, D. Foote, S. Kosen, and P. Webb. 2005. "Food-for-Work Programs in Indonesia Had a Limited Effect on Anemia." *Journal of Nutrition* 135 (6): 1423–29.

Montiel, P., and L. Serven. 2005. "Macroeconomic Stability: The More, the Better?" In *Economic Growth in the 1990s: Lessons from a Decade of Reform*, 95–120. Washington, DC: World Bank.

Musgrove, P. 1987. "The Economic Crisis and Its Impact on Health and Health Care in Latin America and the Caribbean." *International Journal of Health Services* 17 (3): 411–41.

Neelsen, S., and T. Stratmann. 2010. "Effects of Prenatal and Early Life Malnutrition: Evidence from the Greek Famine." CESIFO Working Paper No. 2994, Munich, Germany.

Ozer, E. J., L. C. H. Fernald, J. G. Manley, and P. J. Gertler. 2009. "Effects of a Conditional Cash Transfer Program on Children's Behavior Problems." *Pediatrics* 123 (4): 630–37.

Patel, V., and A. Kleinman. 2003. "Poverty and Common Mental Disorders in Developing Countries." *Bulletin of the World Health Organization* 81 (8): 609–15.

Paxson, C., and N. Schady. 2004. "Child Health and the 1988–92 Economic Crisis in Peru." World Bank Policy Research Working Paper No. 3260, World Bank, Washington, DC.

———. 2005. "Child Health and Economic Crisis in Peru." *World Bank Economic Review* 19 (2): 203–33.

Pongou, R., J. A. Salomon, and M. Ezzati. 2006. "Health Impacts of Macroeconomic Crises and Policies: Determinants of Variation in Childhood Malnutrition Trends in Cameroon." *International Journal of Epidemiology* 35 (3): 648–56.

Pradhan, M., F. Saadah, and R. Sparrow. 2007. "Did the Health Card Program Ensure Access to Medical Care for the Poor during Indonesia's Economic Crisis?" *World Bank Economic Review* 21 (1): 125–50.

Psacharopoulos, G. 1989. "The Determinants of Early Age Human Capital Formation: Evidence from Brazil." *Economic Development and Cultural Change* 37 (4): 683–708.

Qian, M., D. Wang, and W. E. Watkins. 2005. "The Effects of Iodine on Intelligence in Children: A Meta-Analysis of Studies Conducted in China." *Asia Pacific Journal of Clinical Nutrition* 14 (1): 32–42.

Quisumbing, A. R. 2003. "Food Aid and Child Nutrition in Rural Ethiopia." *World Development* 31 (7): 1309–24.

Rosenzweig, M. R., and K. I. Wolpin. 1994. "Are There Increasing Returns to the Intergenerational Production of Human Capital—Maternal Schooling and Child Intellectual Achievement." *Journal of Human Resources* 29 (2): 670–93.

Ruhm, C. 2000. "Are Recessions Good for Your Health?" *Quarterly Journal of Economics* 115 (2): 617–50.

Ruhm, C., and W. Black. 2002. "Does Drinking Really Decrease during Bad Times?" *Journal of Health Economics* 21 (4): 659–78.

Sameroff, A. J., R. Seifer, A. Baldwin, and C. Baldwin. 1993. "Stability of Intelligence from Preschool to Adolescence: The Influence of Social and Family Risk Factors." *Child Development* 64 (1): 80–97.

Schady, N., and C. Araujo. 2008. "Cash Transfers, Conditions, and School Enrollment in Ecuador." *Economía* 8 (2): 43–70.

Schady, N., and M. F. Smitz. 2010. "Aggregate Economic Shocks and Infant Mortality: New Evidence for Middle-Income Countries." *Economics Letters* 108 (2): 145–48.

Sohr-Preston, S. L., and L. V. Scaramella. 2006. "Implications of Timing of Maternal Depressive Symptoms for Early Cognitive and Language Development." *Clinical Child and Family Psychology Review* 9 (1): 65–83.

Stillman, S., D. McKenzie, and J. Gibson. 2009. "Migration and Mental Health: Evidence from a Natural Experiment." *Journal of Health Economics* 28 (3): 677–87.

Strauss, J., K. Beegle, A. Dwiyanto, Y. Herawati, D. Pattinasarany, E. Satriawan, B. Sikoki, Sukamdi, and F. Witoelar. 2004. "Indonesian Living Standards before and after the Financial Crisis." RAND Labor and Population, ISBN 0-8330-3558-4. RAND Corporation, Santa Monica, CA.

Tangcharoensathien, V., H. Piya, P. Siriwan, and K. Vijj. 2000. "Health Impacts of Rapid Economic Changes in Thailand." *Social Science and Medicine* 51 (6): 789–807.

Walker, S. P., S. M. Chang, C. A. Powell, and S. M. Grantham-McGregor. 2004. "Psychosocial Intervention Improves the Development of Term Low Birth-Weight Infants." *Journal of Nutrition* 134 (6): 1417–23.

Walker, S. P., T. D. Wachs, J. M. Gardner, B. Lozoff, G. A. Wasserman, E. Pollitt, and J. A. Carter. 2007. "Child Development: Risk Factors for Adverse Outcomes in Developing Countries." *Lancet* 369 (9556): 145–57.

Waters, H., F. Saadah, and M. Pradhan. 2003. "The Impact of the 1997–98 East Asian Economic Crisis on Health and Health Care in Indonesia." *Health Policy and Planning* 18 (2): 172–81.

WHO International Consortium in Psychiatric Epidemiology. 2000. "Cross-National Comparisons of the Prevalences and Correlates of Mental Disorders." *Bulletin of the World Health Organization* 78 (4): 413–26.

World Bank. 2009. "Averting a Human Crisis during the Global Downturn." Conference Edition. http://siteresources.worldbank.org/NEWS/Resources/AvertingTheHumanCrisis.pdf.

Yamano, T., H. Alderman, and L. Christiaensen. 2003. "Child Growth, Shocks and Food Aid in Rural Ethiopia." World Bank Policy Research Working Paper 3128, World Bank, Washington, DC.

3

Conflicts, Epidemics, and Orphanhood: The Impact of Extreme Events on the Health and Educational Achievements of Children

Damien de Walque

Conflicts and epidemics, in particular the HIV/AIDS epidemic, have plagued many developing countries in the last few decades. This situation is especially true in Africa. This chapter will review the existing evidence for the impact of such extreme events on the well-being of young children; it will focus on mental and physical health as well as education outcomes. The impact of conflict and epidemics on children could be direct when their health is directly impacted or if access to school is denied. It might also be indirect as a consequence of the death or morbidity of their parents, depriving them of the presence of one or more caregivers.

The literature on the mental health of children has documented how childhood trauma has a profound impact on the emotional, behavioral, cognitive, social, and physical functioning of children (Perry and others 1995). Developmental experiences determine the organizational and functional status of the mature brain. Various adaptive mental and physical responses are found to trauma, including physiological hyper-arousal and dissociation. Because the developing brain organizes and internalizes new information in a use-dependent fashion, the more a child is in a state of hyper-arousal or dissociation, the more likely he or she is to have neuro-psychiatric symptoms following trauma. The acute adaptive states, when they persist, can become maladaptive traits and have long-term implications for brain development. The intensity and duration of a response to trauma in children are dependent on a wide variety of factors.

The National Scientific Council on the Developing Child defines the concept of toxic stress (National Scientific Council on the Developing Child 2005), which provides an overview of biological reactions to stressful environments and how these reactions can have a lasting effect on child development. By "toxic stress" they mean experiences of severe, uncontrollable, and chronic adversity.

Stress responses include activation of a variety of hormone and neuro-chemical systems throughout the body, and sustained or frequent activation of the hormonal systems that respond to stress can have serious developmental consequences, some of which may last well past the time of stress exposure. Increases in the level of cortisol interfere with gene expression: High, sustained levels of cortisol or corticotropin-releasing hormone result in damage to the hippocampus. Stressful events can be harmful, tolerable, or beneficial, depending on how much of a bodily stress response they provoke and how long the response lasts. These responses, in turn, depend on whether the stressful experience is controllable, the frequency and duration of the periods that the body's stress system has been activated in the past, and the support systems available to the child. Consensus is emerging that the origins of adult disease are often found among developmental and biological disruptions occurring during the early years of life. These early disruptions can affect adult health in two ways—either by cumulative damage over time or because the adversities occurred during sensitive developmental periods. With both channels, a lag of many years, even decades, may be seen before early adverse experiences are expressed in the form of disease (Shonkoff and others 2009). The extent to which stressful events have lasting adverse effects is determined more by the individual's response to the stress, based in part on past experiences and the availability of support systems, rather than by the nature of the stressor itself.

The physiology of toxic stress should be universal, even if triggers and responses are more cultural. For example, a set of studies investigated the effect of severe deprivation in Romanian institutions on child development and cognitive function by comparing the outcomes of Romanian adoptees subsequently adopted in the United Kingdom with other children adopted in the United Kingdom but who had not experienced deprivation in institutions (Kreppner and others 2007; Stevens and others 2008). They found persistent impairment following early institutional deprivation of six months or more, which suggests a possible pathway to impairment through some form of neuro-developmental programming during critical periods of early development.

Research on conflicts, epidemics, and disasters, given their unpredictability and disruptive nature, and their impact on child development is a challenging field: Very often data are available only post-disaster, obtaining a representative sample is difficult, and longitudinal studies are hard to conduct (Masten and Osofsky 2010; Norris and others 2002a). Generally, it is also rare to have data immediately after the events. Most researchers use datasets collected several years after the shocks and try to measure their consequences based on the status and the welfare of the child at the time of data collection. This makes it difficult to obtain direct evidence about the traumas experienced by young children. The review of the literature conducted found only a very limited number of studies that collected outcome data from children under age six. This is an important limitation of the current literature that needs to be acknowledged upfront. This chapter will highlight the studies that included such measures taken during early childhood (Akresh and others 2007; Baillieu and Potterton 2008; Ferguson and Jelsma 2009; Kithakye and others 2010; Potterton and others 2010; Van Rie and others 2008). It will also rely, however, on many studies measuring outcomes for older children who have been affected by conflicts or epidemics earlier in life. Even if in those analyses it is more difficult to ascertain the timing of the trauma or to pinpoint its causes, such studies have the benefit of documenting the long-term impacts of those events.

In addition to the direct impact of conflicts and disasters on children, the trauma might also indirectly affect the inputs that parents or caregivers can contribute to early child development (ECD). A very important factor in how children respond to stress is the presence of a caregiver, because a caregiver can mitigate the alarm and dissociative response to trauma (Perry and others 1995; Shonkoff and Phillips 2000). Analyses using data from Indonesia and Mexico show that controlling for changes in household economic status (consumption) does not reduce the negative effect of parental death on children's health and educational status (Gertler and others 2003). This suggests that the loss of a parent has consequences that go well beyond the economic shock associated with the death of the breadwinner.

An important question is: What are the policy implications of documenting the negative consequences of violence and epidemics on ECD? A consensus is found that every effort should be made to prevent conflicts, disasters, and epidemics. Nevertheless, it is important to point out that lasting consequences are seen even after the school buildings have been restored and reopened. It is also crucial to realize that these lasting impacts have implications in terms of equity and in the intergenerational transmission of human capital. Further, documenting the long-term impact of trauma does highlight the importance of trying to understand which steps in the classroom or in psychological services could help traumatized children progress normally through school, which strategies can help stimulate HIV-infected children, and which programs could give a second chance to youth who have dropped out of school because of traumas experienced early in their childhood.

The next section reviews the evidence for the impact of violence on ECD, looks at mediating and mitigating factors, and investigates resilience to trauma. The next sections focus on the impact of violence on children's nutrition and education, respectively. This chapter then reviews studies documenting how the HIV/AIDS epidemic directly affects children. The following section looks into the consequences of orphanhood, independent of the cause of the parental death. After reviewing the evidence for the impact of orphanhood on early childhood, the section contrasts the results obtained by cross-sectional and longitudinal studies on measuring how orphan status affects educational outcomes, and it ends by investigating how living arrangements for orphans affect their schooling. The final section concludes.

Violence and Early Childhood Development

An overview focused on the prevalence of psychological morbidities in children who have been exposed to war-related traumas or terrorism outlines the psychological responses to war-related stressors in three categories: (1) little or no reaction, (2) acute emotional and behavioral effects, and (3) long-term effects (Shaw 2003). This synthesis documents that children exposed to war-related stressors experience a spectrum of psychological morbidities, including posttraumatic stress symptoms, mood disorders, externalizing and disruptive behaviors, and somatic symptoms determined by exposure dose effect.

Several studies of individual conflicts or disasters document the consequences of such events on a child's psychosocial development. Very few studies include young children under the age of five. One study in Kenya (Kithakye and others 2010) examined pre- and post-conflict data from 84 children, between three and seven years of age, living in Kibera, Kenya, during the December 2007 political conflict. The results indicate that children's experiences during the conflict (destruction of their home, death of a parent, harm to parent and child) are associated with adjustment difficulties. Specifically, the severity of the traumatic experience was associated with increased aggression and decreased pro-social behavior.

More studies interview older children and adolescents, but in many cases the traumatic events took place, at least for part of the sample, during early childhood. The interval between the traumatic event and the interview generally has an impact on the magnitude of the measured trauma. For example, a study interviewed a group of 94 children in Iraq who had been exposed to the bombing of a shelter where more than 750 people were killed in the 1991 Gulf war (Dyregrov and others 2002). The interviews took place six months, one year, and two years after the war. Measurement scales summarized the impact of trauma on two dimensions: intrusion and avoidance. Intrusion is characterized by distressing thoughts, feelings, and nightmares, whereas avoidant thinking and behavior as well as psychic numbing characterize avoidance. Findings show no significant decline in intrusive and avoidance reactions as measured six months to one year following the war. Reactions were reduced two years after the war, although the scores were still high, indicating that symptoms persist, with somewhat diminished intensity over time.

In a follow-up study of Cambodian refugee adolescents who had endured as children the horrors of the Khmer Rouge regime in Cambodia from 1975 to 1979, the diagnosis of posttraumatic stress disorder (PTSD) was found to persist, but the symptoms appeared less intense over time (Sack and others 1993). The prevalence of depression dropped markedly between a 1987 survey and a similar survey in 1990. The follow-up sample appeared to be functioning well despite their PTSD profiles. In two comparative groups of nondisplaced ($N = 64$) and displaced children ($N = 70$) from Croatia (Kuterovac, Dyregrove, and Stuvland 1994), a majority of the children had been exposed to armed combat, with displaced children significantly more exposed to destruction of home and school as well as to acts of violence, and loss of family members, than the nondisplaced children. Results from the Impact of Event Scale (IES) indicated that displaced children had been more exposed (higher total score) and experienced higher scores for the intrusion and avoidance subscales. For girls, the total score and intrusion score were significantly higher than for boys.

In Rwanda, a total of 3,030 children 8 to 19 years of age were interviewed about their war experiences and reactions approximately 13 months after the genocide that started in April 1994 (Dyregrov and others 2000). The results from the interviews demonstrate that Rwandan children had been exposed to extreme levels of violence in the form of witnessing the death of close family members and others in massacres, as well as other violent acts. A majority of these children (90 percent) believed that they would die; most had to hide to survive, and 15 percent had to hide under dead bodies to survive. A shortened form of the IES used for a group of

1,830 of these children documented high levels of intrusion and avoidance. In another study focusing on Lebanon (Macksoud and Aber 1996), a sample of 224, 10- to 16-year-old children were interviewed using measures of war exposure, mental health symptoms, adaptational outcomes, and PTSD. The number and type of the children's war traumas varied meaningfully by their age, gender, father's occupational status, and mother's educational level. As predicted, the number of war traumas experienced by a child was positively related to PTSD symptoms, and various types of war traumas were differentially related to PTSD, mental health symptoms, and adaptational outcomes. For example, children who were exposed to multiple war traumas, were bereaved, became victims of violent acts, witnessed violent acts, and/or were exposed to shelling or combat exhibited more PTSD symptoms.

A prospective study to investigate psychosocial adjustment in male and female former child soldiers (ages 10–18; N = 156, 12 percent female; Betancourt and others 2010) that began in Sierra Leone in 2002 found that over the two-year period of follow-up, youth who had wounded or killed others during the war demonstrated increases in hostility. Youth who survived rape had higher levels of anxiety and hostility.

Several studies also analyzed the consequence of natural disasters on the psychosocial development of young children. For example, Kronenberg and others (2010) assessed trauma symptoms, recovery patterns, and life stressors of children between the ages of 9 and 18 (n = 387) following Hurricane Katrina. Based on assessments two and three years after the hurricane, most children showed a decrease in posttraumatic stress and symptoms of depression over time. In a study of the consequences of earthquakes in Turkey (Celebi Oncu and Metindogan Wise 2010), the authors compared two groups of children. The first group (n = 53; 26 females, 27 males) experienced two major earthquakes at age seven, three months apart, in Turkey, whereas a similarly matched control group (n = 50; 25 females, 25 males) did not. The results indicated that the traumatized group evinced a range of trauma-related symptoms two years after experiencing the earthquakes.

Similarly, a study from Sri Lanka after the 2004 tsunami (Catani and others 2010) examines the impact of children's exposure to a natural disaster against the backdrop of exposure to other traumatic events and psychosocial risks. Here 1,398 Sri Lankan children 9–15 years old were interviewed in four cross-sectional studies about exposure to traumatic life events related to the war, the tsunami experience, and family violence. Symptoms of PTSD, somatic complaints, psychosocial functioning, and teacher reports of school grades served as outcome measures. The results showed extensive exposure to adversity and traumatic events among children in Sri Lanka. Findings of regression analyses indicated that all three event types—tsunami and disaster, war, and family violence—significantly contributed to poorer child adaptation.

Mediating or Mitigating Factors

Many studies attempt to identify factors that mitigate or that, on the contrary, might exacerbate the reaction to the violence. For example, still in the context of Sri Lanka after the tsunami and during the war, one study documents that daily stressors may mediate the relation between exposure to disaster-related stressors and psychological and psychosocial distress among youth in disaster-affected countries (Fernando and others 2010). A sample of 427 Sri Lankan youth (mean age 14.5) completed a survey with measures of exposure to disaster-related stressors and daily stressors, psychological distress (posttraumatic stress, depression, and anxiety), and psychosocial distress. The results indicated that daily stressors significantly mediated relations between war- and tsunami-related stressors and psychological and psychosocial distress. These results point to the need for policies and interventions that focus on reducing proximal daily stressors that are salient to Sri Lankan youth exposed to disasters. In their study of the aftermath of Hurricane Katrina, Kronenberg and others (2010) found that age, gender, and life stressors were related to the recovery patterns. Their findings highlight the importance of building and maintaining supportive relationships following disasters.

A general finding is indeed that children who are not protected at the time of a disaster by effective caregivers are more vulnerable (Masten and Osofsky 2010). For example, in Lebanon, children who were separated from parents reported more depressive symptoms. However, some of these same traumas—namely, separation from parents and loss of someone close to the child—in addition to witnessing violent acts and remaining in one's own community during shelling and combat also seem to impose adaptive adjustments on children in the form of pro-social and intentional behavior (Macksoud and Aber 1996). In their studies of soldier children in Sierra Leone, Betancourt and others (2010) found that of the potential protective resources examined, improved community acceptance was associated with reduced depression at follow-up and improved confidence and pro-social attitudes regardless of levels of violence exposure. Retention in school was also associated with greater pro-social attitudes.

However, a study from Rwanda found that although children living in shelters were exposed to more trauma, they demonstrated less posttraumatic reactions (Dyregrov and others 2000). Children living in the community evidenced higher intrusion and arousal scores than those living at centers. The authors argued that this initially surprising finding could be explained by the unique circumstances in Rwandan society in the aftermath of the genocide. Indeed, the UNICEF Trauma Recovery Program initially targeted the centers for training caregivers who worked with children on basic methods of trauma healing, whereas very few schools and family members received this training in the first 6–10 months after the genocide. The higher distress level in the community is even more compelling, as children living at centers initially experienced more losses and greater violence exposures than children in the community, although community children did report more threats to their life. In general, one of the primary goals of emergency programming for children involves initial support for the speedy return of children to the community, preferably with their families. Often, as in Rwandan society, a tradition is found of caring for parentless children where no blood ties exist. This study suggests that we should not adopt such strategies indiscriminately. Some situations, such as the Rwanda genocide, may render communities less able to care for children in the immediate aftermath of a widespread disaster such as this. Nevertheless, in the same context of Rwanda after the 1994 genocide, other results suggest that over the longer term orphans obtained better schooling outcomes when placed with relatives (de Walque 2009).

Resilience

Several studies also document cases of resilience among children exposed to traumatic stress and the factors associated with it. Youth who survived rape had higher levels of anxiety and hostility. Nevertheless, they also demonstrated greater confidence and pro-social attitudes at follow-up. Based on interviews with 330 former Ugandan child soldiers (age = 11–17, female = 48.5 percent), one study examines posttraumatic resilience in children and adolescents who have been extensively exposed to violence (Klasen and others 2010). Despite severe trauma exposure, 27.6 percent showed posttraumatic resilience, as indicated by the absence of PTSD, depression, and clinically significant behavioral and emotional problems. Among these former child soldiers, posttraumatic resilience was associated with lower exposure to domestic violence, lower guilt cognitions, less motivation to seek revenge, a better socioeconomic situation in the family, and more perceived spiritual support. In a similar study population, former combatants in Uganda, both children and adults, the analysis (Blattman and Annan 2010) also provides a nuanced view of the impact of violence on psychosocial outcomes, emphasizing resilience more than permanent social exclusion. Most of the former combatants showed moderate signs of emotional distress, with serious and debilitating distress concentrated in a minority of them who experienced extreme violence. The majority of them recover over time without psychological interventions, depending on the environment (families and communities) to which they return.

In the study of young children in Kenya, results indicated that emotion regulation was associated with less aggression and more pro-social behavior post-conflict (Kithakye and others 2010). Emotion regulation involves components of temperament (such as affect, activity, and attention) typically defined in terms of the effortful processes that afford young children the ability to inhibit dominant responses and activate subdominant responses in times of stress (Eisenberg, Hofer, and Vaughan 2007; Rothbart and Bates 2006).

Such cases of resilience highlight the importance of having policy recommendations tailored to the different groups of victims, those who have been deeply impacted by the violence experienced, and those who have, for multiple reasons, demonstrated more resilience. Understanding the factors and interventions that favor the emergence of resilience is also key from a policy perspective.

More generally and from a policy perspective (Ager and others 2010; Masten and Osofsky 2010), the research suggests that after a conflict or a disaster, it is important to protect and restore as quickly as possible the children's relationship with their caregivers. For children who have lost their parents, it is crucial to provide nurturing caregivers. Children's traumas are also mitigated when routines and opportunities to learn and play are maintained and supported and school activities are restored.

Violence and Nutrition

Few studies directly look at the impact of conflicts on the physical health of children. One important and relatively easy-to-measure indicator of health is the nutritional status of children. One study (Akresh and others 2007) focuses on stunting and examines the effect of civil conflicts and crop failures on the health of Rwandan children born between 1987 and 1991. They use an integrated household survey, combining health and agricultural data with event data from reports by nongovernmental organizations, and exploit the local nature of the crop failure (confined to provinces in southern Rwanda) and the civil war (confined to provinces in northern Rwanda) to identify the causal effect of these exogenous shocks on child health by calculating height-for-age z-scores for a birth cohort of children under age five who experienced the shock, and then they compare measurements several years later. Their results demonstrate that boys and girls born after the shock in regions experiencing civil conflict are both negatively impacted with lower height-for-age z-scores. Conversely, only girls are negatively impacted by crop failure, and this is amplified for girls in poor households. Those results are robust to using sibling difference estimators, household-level production, and rainfall shocks as alternative measures of crop failure.

These results potentially go beyond physical health and suggest a long-term effect on education, given the general finding that stunted children are less likely to be enrolled in school, more likely to enroll late, and more likely to attain lower achievement levels of grades for their age (Beasley and others 2000; Daniels and Adair 2004; Hall 2001; Hutchinson and Powell 1997; Jamison 1986; Moock and Leslie 1986; Sharrif and others 2009; Sigman and others 1989). Analyses of panel data (Glewwe and others 2001; Yamauchi 2008) indicate that the effect of stunting in decreasing schooling outcomes is at least partially causal. A study in Zimbabwe used civil wars and drought shocks as instrumental variables to identify differences in the nutritional status of children before entering school and confirm that the effect of poor nutrition on schooling is causal (Alderman, Hoddinott, and Kinsey 2006). The authors found that improvements in height-for-age in preschoolers are associated with increased height as a young adult and the number of grades of schooling completed.

Violence and Educational Outcomes

Using data from Cambodia, Rwanda, and Tadjikistan, a body of literature is emerging that documents the negative educational shocks endured by children in the aftermath of violent conflicts (Akresh and de Walque 2008; de Walque 2006; Shemyakina forthcoming) .

In his study of the long-term consequences of the Khmer Rouge period in Cambodia, de Walque (2006) documents that individuals, especially men, who were of secondary school age at the end of the 1970s had less secondary education than the preceding and subsequent birth cohorts. The analysis suggests, however, that the educational deficit is more due to a collapse of the school system under the Khmer Rouge than to long-lasting effects of childhood traumas because the birth cohorts who were young children in the 1975–79 period enjoyed substantially higher schooling outcomes.

Shemyakina (forthcoming) examines the effect of conflict on schooling outcome enrollment and the probability of completion of mandatory schooling through grade 9 by adults in Tajikistan. Her results demonstrate that exposure to the conflict, as measured by past damage to household dwellings, had a large significant negative effect on the enrollment of girls and little, or no, effect on the enrollment of boys. Furthermore, girls who were of school age during the conflict and lived in conflict-affected regions were 12.3 percent less likely to complete mandatory schooling as compared with girls who had the opportunity to complete their schooling before the conflict started, and 7 percent less likely to complete school than girls of the same age who lived in regions relatively unaffected by conflict. Interestingly, these negative impacts were not completely explained by the unavailability or the destruction of schools and other education-related infrastructure in the regions affected by conflict.

Akresh and de Walque (2008) combine two nationally representative cross-sectional household surveys, one collected in 2000 (six years after the genocide ended) and one collected in 1992 (two years before the genocide), to examine the impact of Rwanda's 1994 genocide on primary school enrollment and the probability of completing a particular grade for those exposed children. The identification strategy uses prewar data to control for an age group's baseline schooling and exploits variation across provinces in the intensity of killings and which children's cohorts were school-aged when exposed to the war. The findings show a strong negative impact of the genocide on schooling, with exposed children completing half a year less education, representing an 18.3 percent decline.

Understanding the specific mechanisms by which the genocide impacted children's schooling is critical for developing adequate policy responses to protect children from the negative conflict effects. Although the data do not allow definitive conclusions, the results do offer indications as to the likely mechanism. One possible mechanism is orphanhood. The large proportion of orphans in post-1994 Rwanda suggests that the absence of one or both parents could be the principal driving factor. However, the results of Akresh and de Walque (2008) do not confirm this intuition. It is true that orphans do slightly worse than non-orphans in terms of schooling outcomes in 2000, but it is striking that non-orphans in 2000 are doing worse than orphans in 1992.

Another possible mechanism is that households were made poorer because of the conflict (loss of crops and assets and disruption of business activities) and, given the more difficult economic circumstances, might further discriminate against the schooling of girls. However, the results indicate that the negative impact on education was actually larger for boys and for children from nonpoor families, which suggests that the genocide had a leveling-off effect that brought boys and the nonpoor to the same lower level of schooling as girls and poor children. Finally, another potential explanation is the destruction of schools or lack of teachers because of the genocide and the subsequent impact on children's schooling. However, the authors do not find evidence that infrastructure problems are driving the decline in educational attainment because they find almost no impact for grade 1 completion rates, and the largest impact is not seen until grades 3 and 4. This seems to indicate that the most likely mechanism linking the genocide to reduced educational attainment is through grade progression, as opposed to not entering the school system. Such a mechanism is consistent with early childhood traumas that would impair the children's ability to progress normally through the school system.

Another study (Blattman and Annan 2010) investigates the long-term consequences of being a child soldier. They used a survey of former child soldiers who had been forcefully enrolled by a rebel group in Uganda to avoid the problem of self-selection. They conclude that the economic and educational effects are widespread and persistent: Schooling falls by nearly a year, skilled employment is cut in half, and earnings drop by a third.

Documenting the long-term impact of trauma on schooling outcomes and education highlights the importance of trying to understand which steps in the classroom or in psychological services—for example, remediation services for children with learning difficulties—could help traumatized children progress normally through school and which programs could give a second chance to youth who have dropped out of school because of traumas experienced early in their childhood.

So far, most of the studies reviewed document the consequences of covariate shocks, wars, violence, and disasters that affect the entire communities in which the children live. Being enrolled as a child soldier is more of an idiosyncratic shock that affects the child individually (Betancourt and others 2010; Blattman and Annan 2010; Klasen and others 2010). Similarly, HIV/AIDS infection and orphanhood, covered below, are idiosyncratic shocks, except when they overwhelm communities so that traditional fostering breaks down. Although the distinction between covariate and idiosyncratic shocks is useful from a methodological point of view, in practice great variation is also seen in individual exposure to covariate shocks so that it might be more helpful to consider the shocks as multilevel phenomena rather than maintain a strict dichotomy.

HIV/AIDS and Early Childhood Development

The HIV/AIDS epidemic affects directly and indirectly a very large number of children. UNAIDS estimates that in 2008, worldwide, 2.1 million children under age 15 were living with HIV, 430,000 became newly infected, and 280,000 died from AIDS (UNAIDS 2009). It was estimated that only 28 percent of children in resource-poor countries who need pediatric antiretroviral treatments are receiving them (WHO/UNAIDS/UNICEF 2010). In 2008, more than 14.1 million children in Sub-Saharan Africa were estimated to have lost one or both parents to AIDS (UNAIDS 2009).

Reviews conclude that HIV infection is associated with cognitive impairments in children, a result of direct and indirect effects of the virus on the developing brain, and that, in addition to damage to the central nervous system, HIV-infected children face developmental delays secondary to associated illnesses, poor nutritional status, and adverse living conditions, such as due to caretaker illness and death, abandonment, and poverty (Sherr and others 2009; Van Rie and others 2007). A study from Johannesburg, South Africa, determines the extent of delay in acquisition of language, cognitive, and motor skills of children infected with HIV (Baillieu and Potterton 2008). Forty HIV-positive, anti-retrovirus-naive children aged 18 to 30 months were assessed using the Bayley Scales of Infant Development II (BSID II). The facet-scoring section was used to descriptively analyze cognitive, language, and motor development. The Mental and Psychomotor Developmental Indices of the BSID II were used to determine the extent of mental and motor delays. The results indicate that mean cognitive development was 7.63 months delayed and mean motor development was 9.65 months delayed, with 97.5 percent of the sample functioning below expected motor and cognitive age. Eighty-five percent of the sample demonstrated gross motor delay, which was the most adversely affected skill. They report global language delay in 82.5 percent of the children. The authors suggest that gross motor delay may be attributed to decreased strength or to HIV encephalopathy (global brain dysfunction). Additionally, cognitive delay may be because of disease progression and structural damage to the brain, and language delay may be attributed to neurological impairment, cognitive delay, or environmental deprivation.

Comparing HIV-positive children with other children allows a better measure of the impact caused by the disease. A study in Cape Town, South Africa, assesses the effect of pediatric HIV/AIDS on cognitive development and motor performance in a group of HIV-infected children (Ferguson and Jelsma 2009). The BSID II was administered to 51 HIV-infected children, of whom 34 were receiving antiretroviral therapy. Their performance was compared with an age-matched reference sample ($N = 35$), whose HIV status was unknown. The HIV-infected sample and the age-matched sample were comparable with regard to the caregiver's level of education, employment status, and income. However, the HIV-infected sample had significantly more hospital admissions, and their caregivers were mostly single. The prevalence of significant motor delay was 66.7 percent in the HIV-infected sample compared with 5.7 percent in the age-matched sample. The performance of the HIV-infected sample was significantly poorer than the age-matched sample, even if a significant number of healthy children also displayed delayed performance.

It is also interesting to extend the comparison to children who are not directly infected by HIV but are affected because their parents either died from AIDS or are suffering from it. Recent literature reviews have come to different conclusions about the situation of HIV-exposed, uninfected children. One concludes that little evidence is available for a difference in the early growth of HIV-exposed but uninfected children compared with healthy controls (Isanaka and others 2009), whereas the other assesses that those children are at increased risk of mortality, morbidity, and slowed growth. A study in Kinshasa, Democratic Republic of Congo, compared the neurodevelopment of preschool-aged HIV-infected, HIV-affected (HIV-uninfected AIDS orphans and HIV-uninfected children whose mother had symptomatic AIDS), and healthy control children (Van Rie and others 2008). Thirty-five HIV-infected, 35 HIV-affected, and 90 control children aged 18 to 72 months were assessed using the BSID II, Peabody Developmental Motor Scales, Snijders-Oomen Nonverbal Intelligence Test, and Rossetti Infant-Toddler Language Scale, as appropriate for age. Sixty percent of HIV-infected children had severe delays in cognitive function, 29 percent had severe delays in motor skills, 85 percent had delays in language expression, and 77 percent had delays in language comprehension, all significantly higher rates as compared with control children. Young HIV-infected children (aged 18–29 months) performed worse, with 91 and 82 percent demonstrating severe mental and motor delay, respectively, compared with 46 and 4 percent in older HIV-infected children (aged 30–72 months). HIV-affected children had significantly more motor and language expression delays than control children. The impact of the HIV pandemic on children's neurodevelopment extends beyond the direct effect of the HIV virus on the central nervous system. AIDS orphans and HIV-negative children whose mothers had AIDS demonstrated significant delays in their neurodevelopment, although to a lesser degree and in fewer developmental domains than HIV-infected children. Young HIV-infected children were the most severely afflicted group, indicating the need for early interventions. Older children performed better as a result of a "survival effect," with only those children with less aggressive disease surviving.

A recent review assessed the different strategies used to support young children and families affected by HIV/AIDS, including home visits, cash transfers, ECD programs, and legal protection (Engle and others 2010). The review singled out a home stimulation program taught to caregivers in South Africa that was rigorously evaluated and significantly improved cognitive and motor development in young children infected with HIV (Potterton and others 2010). Otherwise, the review concludes that research and evidence are insufficient on which strategies have an impact.

Orphanhood

For many children one of the most immediate consequences of conflicts, disasters, and epidemics is the loss of their parents. However, not all orphans lost their parents in the wake of such events, and it is often difficult, in standard datasets, to identify the cause of orphanhood. This section will first review the evidence for the impact of orphanhood on ECD and health outcomes. Then the longer-term impact of losing one or two parents on educational achievement will be investigated. Finally, the evidence for which living arrangements present the best options for the welfare of orphans will be summarized.

Orphanhood and Early Childhood Development

In a study investigating the effect of severe deprivation on child development and cognitive function by comparing the cognitive outcomes of 131 Romanian adoptees from institutions to 50 children adopted in the United Kingdom (Beckett and others 2006), the authors examine the links between duration and timing of deprivation and IQ scores as measured on the WISC III test when the children were 6 and 11 years old. The findings indicate persistent effects of deprivation on cognitive development at age 11, but significant improvement over time for the children with the lowest IQ scores at age 6. A dose-response relationship was observed between age at entry (length of deprivation) and IQ at age 6, but this did not extend to age 11.

One study uses data comparing 41 orphans whose fathers or mothers, or both, had died from AIDS with 41 matched non-orphans from the same poor urban areas in Tanzania to assess the psychological well-being of orphans (Makame and Grantham-McGregor 2002). Participants were given an arithmetic test and a semistructured questionnaire concerning any internalizing problems, their attendance at school, and their experiences of punishment, reward, and hunger. They found that most orphans were significantly less likely to be in school, but those who did attend school attended regularly and had similar arithmetic scores. The orphans not currently attending school had markedly poorer arithmetic scores. Significantly more orphans went to bed hungry in the previous week compared with non-orphans. Comparing them on an "internalizing problem scale" designed to capture problems related to mood, pessimism, somatic symptoms, sense of failure, anxiety, positive affect, and emotional ties, orphans had markedly more problems compared with non-orphans, and 34 percent reported they had contemplated suicide in the past year.

Another study assessed the psychological effects of maternal death on 1,000 children who had lost their mothers due to AIDS and from other causes using the data from a survey in Ethiopia (Bhargava 2005). The analysis measured scores from the Minnesota Multiphasic Personality Inventory-2 (MMPI) and school participation. The scores on MMPI items reflect emotional and social adjustment. The main findings were that although AIDS orphans scored lower on MMPI items, variables such as presence of the father, household income, feeding, clothing conditions, and attitude of the fostering family were also significant predictors of scores. Girls scored lower in terms of the scores on MMPI items.

One study using data from Tanzania examines the impact of adult mortality on three measures of health among children under five (Ainsworth and Semali 2000): morbidity, height-for-age, and weight-for-height. Stunting is significantly higher among orphans than other children, even if other factors are controlled for. Although nonpoor families are reported to be able to cope with this risk, loss of a parent raises the incidence of stunting to levels found among the poor; the impact is particularly severe for poor households. Ainsworth and Semali (2000) also show how much three important health interventions—immunization against measles, oral rehydration salts, and access to health care—can mitigate the impact of adult mortality. These programs disproportionately improve health outcomes among the poorest children and, within that group, among children affected by adult mortality. Another analysis, using data from Burundi, documents that a higher percentage of double and maternal orphans are malnourished compared with children who have both parents living (Subbarao, Mattimore, and Plangemann 2001).

Orphanhood and Educational Achievement: Cross-Sectional Studies

Cross-sectional studies of the educational outcomes of orphans have the advantage of highlighting the diversity of circumstances and heterogeneity in the link between orphanhood and schooling across countries and their interaction with poverty. However, typically, cross-sectional data have the ability only to identify who is an orphan and not the timing of parental death, making it difficult to know whether the measured outcomes are transitory or permanent. The cross-sectional data can examine the enrollment outcomes only after a parental death; they cannot assess the dynamic impacts of morbidity and mortality on children's school attendance both before and after death of an adult, the impact on the hours at school, or the ultimate impact on learning outcomes. For example, if orphans are placed in relatively better-off households that have a higher demand for schooling, the cross-sectional estimates may underestimate the true impact of school enrollment.

One study estimated multivariate models that relate enrollment to the survival status of each parent, as well as socioeconomic household characteristics in seven Sub-Saharan African countries using cross-sectional Demographic and Health Survey (DHS) data from the early 1990s (Lloyd and Blanc 1996). These authors conclude that the death of a parent appears to make relatively little difference to children's educational chances, which implies that strong family support networks continue to cushion the impact of orphanhood on children. Furthermore, the survival of parents seems to be even less important to children's likelihood of advancing at an appropriate pace through school than to their current enrollment status. In most cases, enrollment rates are only slightly higher for children with living parents, and these effects are rarely sizable (five percentage points or greater), statistically significant, or both.

Pooling DHS data from several countries to create an East African sample (Kenya, Tanzania, and Zimbabwe) and a West African sample (Ghana and Nigeria), one analysis estimated multivariate models explaining whether or not a child is at or above his or her appropriate grade level and adjusted for residence, child's age, household economic status, and head of household's characteristics (Bicego and others 2003). The findings indicate that orphans are less likely than non-orphans to be at the appropriate educational level, with the effect stronger at younger ages (ages 6–10) than older ages (11–14). Loss of both parents places a child at a particular disadvantage, and loss of a mother appears more detrimental than loss of a father with regard to educational attainment. Using school and student surveys to analyze the effects of orphanhood on education outcomes in Botswana, Malawi, and Uganda, one study finds that absenteeism rates were not consistently higher among orphans than non-orphans, and repetition rates were sometimes higher, but often lower, than among non-orphans (Bennell 2005). In almost all cases, student orphans were more likely to have stopped attending school at some point than non-orphans.

To explore the extent to which orphans are under-enrolled, and to assess the magnitude of this potential under-enrollment relative to other selected factors, another study examines the relation between parental survival, poverty, gender, and school enrollment using 102 large and nationally representative datasets from 51 developing countries and four regions (Africa, Asia, the Caribbean, and Latin America) (Ainsworth and Filmer 2006). The authors find considerable diversity in the orphan/non-orphan differential across countries and conclude that it is difficult to draw generalizations about the extent to which orphans are disadvantaged. Although examples are found of large differentials in enrollment by orphan status, in the majority of cases the orphan enrollment gap is dwarfed by the gap between children from richer and poorer households. In some cases, even children from the top of the wealth distribution have low enrollments, a result that points to fundamental issues in the supply or demand for schooling that are a constraint to higher enrollments of all children. The gap in enrollment between female and male orphans is not much different from the gap between girls and boys with living parents, which suggests that female orphans are not disproportionately affected in terms of their enrollment in most countries. These diverse findings demonstrate that the extent to which orphans are under-enrolled relative to other children is country specific, at least in part because the correlation between orphan status and poverty is not consistent across countries. The authors further acknowledge that the enrollment rate captures only one dimension of schooling and does not provide information about attendance, repetition rates, completion rates, dropout rates, or the ultimate variables of interest: learning and achievement (Ainsworth and Filmer 2006; Yamano and Jayne 2005).

Using data from 10 Sub-Saharan African countries between 1992 and 2000 to estimate the impact of parental death on school enrollment, a different study analyzes 19 DHS datasets from Sub-Saharan Africa from the 1990s (Case and others 2004). As opposed to the other cross-sectional studies, the authors used a household fixed-effects estimation strategy, which compares orphans and non-orphans in the households that take in orphans. Using household fixed effects, they find that orphans are disadvantaged relative to other children within the same household. In eight of the 19 surveys they find that children who have lost their father have statistically significantly lower enrollment; in eight of the 19 surveys they find that children who have lost their mother have statistically significantly lower enrollment, and in 13 of the 19 surveys they find that two-parent orphans have statistically significantly lower enrollment. The household fixed-effects approach is useful for comparing orphans with non-orphans in the same household, controlling for household characteristics. However, if orphans are strategically placed in better-off households within the extended family, by assuming that before orphanhood those children had the same characteristics as the non-orphans in the fostering household, the household fixed-effects approach might overestimate the differences between them.

Another study isolates the impact of the death of a parent on schooling by comparing single-parent children whose other parent died within the 12 months before the survey with a matched sample of non-orphans in a pooled dataset from three years of Indonesia's National Sample Survey (Gertler and others 2004). They find that the enrollment of orphans is statistically significantly lower than non-orphans and that the difference increases with the expected grade level, ranging from two to five percentage points at the primary level (grades 1–6) and five to seven percentage points at the lower secondary level (grades 7–9). Overall primary school enrollment (ages 7–12) was 95 percent, and overall lower secondary school enrollment (ages 13–15) was 79 percent.

Orphanhood and Educational Achievement: Longitudinal Studies

Longitudinal studies allow assessing the dynamic impacts of morbidity and mortality on children's school attendance both before and after death of an adult and therefore allow a richer assessment of the impact of orphanhood on schooling outcomes.

Using panel data from the Kagera region of northwestern Tanzania, one study measures the impact of adult deaths and orphan status on a household's decision to send children to primary school and, conditioned on that decision, on the number of hours that children spend at school (Ainsworth and others 2005). Their analysis is done using a three-year panel dataset (1991–94) that allows relating the timing of adult deaths to school attendance. The overall attendance rate in their sample of children ages 7–14 was only 59 percent. They find no evidence that children dropped out of school because of orphan status or a recent adult death in the household, although they do find that attendance was delayed for maternal orphans or poor children who experienced an adult death. Among children already attending school, school hours were significantly lower in the months before an adult death in the household and recovered following the death. Girls sharply reduced their school hours immediately after the death of a parent.

Using a difference-in-differences identification strategy with a three-year panel dataset of rural Kenyan households implemented in 1997, 2000, and 2002, another analysis found that children's school attendance is adversely affected by the death of working-age adults among the bottom half of households ranked by initial asset levels in 1997, but no significant effects are detected among households in the top half of the asset distribution (Yamano and Jayne 2005). Working-age adult mortality negatively affects school attendance even before the death in poor households. The negative impact is greater among girls than boys. These results suggest that children, particularly girls, are sharing the burden of caring for sick working-age adults, that school fees tend to be among the first expenditures curtailed in relatively poor households after one of their adult members becomes chronically ill, or both. By contrast, school attendance among boys, but not girls, in relatively poor households drops sharply after the adult member dies. These results indicate the importance of differentiating among gender, impacts before as well as after the occurrence of mortality, and initial wealth conditions of the household in empirical assessments of the effects of adult mortality.

One study uses a longitudinal dataset from a district under demographic surveillance in the KwaZulu-Natal Province of South Africa and finds that the death of a father is not associated with lower enrollment, grade attainment, or expenditures on schooling, once the fact that paternal deaths occur in poorer households is taken into account (father's survival status was missing for 41 percent of the sample; Case and Ardington 2006). Enrollment is about three percentage points lower for maternal orphans (relative to an average of 96 percent for children whose mothers are alive), and they have about one-third of a year less schooling (relative to 4.2 years of schooling for children whose mothers are alive).

The impact of parental deaths on school participation has also been studied in a five-year panel dataset of 17,000 children in Busia District in western Kenya (Evans and Miguel 2007). Baseline school participation among non-orphans in their sample was 87 percent. The authors find that participation declines for children who will become orphans up to two years before the parent's death, consistent with a period of AIDS-related morbidity. They find that school participation among maternal orphans after the death of a parent is about 10 percentage points lower than that of non-orphans, whereas that of paternal orphans is about 4 percentage points lower (although this estimate is not statistically significant). They do not find a statistically significant additional impact of being a two-parent orphan, although a few observations in their data allow identifying such an impact with precision. A striking result is that children with lower baseline pre-death academic test scores experience significantly larger decreases in school participation after a parent's death than children with high test scores, which suggests that households decide to focus their resources on more promising students. The tendency of parents to invest more in high-ability children within a family has been confirmed beyond orphan studies, for example, in data recently collected in Burkina Faso using objective measures of a child's ability (Akresh and others 2010).

An analysis of a sample of initially non-orphaned children in 1991–94 estimates the impact of observed orphanhood shocks on height and educational attainment in 2004, controlling for a wide range of household and child conditions before orphanhood and for community fixed effects (Beegle and others 2006). By further restricting the sample to those already reaching adulthood in 2004, the study provides evidence on the persistent impacts of becoming orphaned from ages 7 to 15, from which little or no recovery is possible. The sample was split into those aged 11–18 in 2004 and 19–28 in 2004. The latter sample focused on final adult height as well as years of education at an age where there is unlikely to be catch-up in schooling attainment. Because of the time frame of the panel (10–13 years), this second sample by design includes only children orphaned by age seven or older. Thus, the second sample reflects permanent orphanhood effects for those orphaned after age six, whereas the 11- to 18-year-olds are those orphaned at young ages, on average, with possibility of recovery. Twenty-three percent of children in the full sample lost at least one parent between the baseline survey and reinterview in 2004. The most common shock was losing a father, experienced by about 18 percent; few lost both parents in this period. The loss of a parent at very young ages (under three) is very rare in the data. The analysis finds strong effects of maternal and paternal orphanhood on education. Maternal orphans permanently lose on average close to one year of schooling. Maternal orphanhood is associated with height deficiencies for those 11–18 years old in 2004. Children not enrolled at the time of the loss of a parent lose significantly more schooling compared with non-orphans or orphans already in school when their parent dies. The authors find some evidence that schooling is protected for orphans from wealthier households.

Although the results from cross-sectional studies point to a large heterogeneity in the orphan/non-orphan differential across countries, longitudinal studies that can contrast the situation of the child before and after the death of the adult generally conclude that orphans are at a disadvantage in terms of schooling outcomes, even if it is not always in terms of enrollment. Interventions targeted at facilitating grade progression, for example, by offering remediation services for children struggling in school, might be beneficial for orphans' schooling achievements. It also appears that the loss of a mother has a stronger negative impact and that children from poorer households are more affected if they lose one of their parents.

Living Arrangements of Orphans and School Enrollment Outcomes

The literature has shown how the presence of parents or caregivers is a very important factor in ECD and in the way children respond to trauma (Gertler and others 2003; Perry and others 1995; Shonkoff and Phillips 2000) An important question is therefore, in the event of the loss of one or both parents, what is the best living arrangement to attempt, as far as possible, to replace the lost caregiver?

Using household survey data from 21 countries in Africa, one study investigates the extent to which rising orphan rates are placing pressure on the extended family (Beegle and others 2009). The authors examine trends in orphanhood and living arrangements and systematically document differences in the distribution of living arrangements across countries and time. They explore broad patterns in living arrangements for orphans and non-orphans, and changes in care-giving patterns are explored. Their findings confirm that orphanhood is increasing, although not all countries are experiencing rapid rises. In many countries, a shift has been toward grandparents taking on increased child care responsibility, especially where orphan rates are growing rapidly. This suggests some merit to the claim that the extended network is narrowing, focusing on grandparents who are older and may be less able to financially support orphans than working-age adults. However, changes are also seen in child care patterns in countries with stable orphan rates or low HIV prevalence. This suggests that future work on living arrangements should not exclude low-HIV/AIDS-prevalence countries, and explanations for changes should include a broader set of factors.

An analysis of the schooling outcomes of orphans in Rwanda suggests that the education of the adoptive parents, especially mothers, has a strong effect on the adopted children's schooling outcomes (de Walque 2009). Even after controlling for nonrandom placement by including the schooling of the biological parents and the type of relationship linking the child and the head of his or her new household, the education of the most educated female adult in the new household has a positive and significant effect on the schooling of the child fostered in the household. The magnitude of the effect is similar to the effect in a biological mother-child relationship. The effect of the education of the most educated male in the relationship is smaller than in a biological father-child relationship but remains positive and significant. When boys and girls are analyzed separately, it appears that the mother's education matters more for girls, whereas the father's education has a stronger effect on boys' educational achievement. The analysis of interaction terms indicates that the positive effects of the education of the adoptive parents are present only for children related to the head of their new household (grandchildren and other relatives). The study suggests that placing orphans in households where they have relatives minimizes their educational losses and favors the intergenerational transmission of human capital. Another study in Lesotho assesses the association between living arrangement and school achievement among orphans (Corno and de Walque 2010). Their analysis shows that 46 percent of orphans do not live with either parent. Among these, 27 percent live with grandparents, 11 percent live with other relatives, and 2 percent are not living with relatives. Data on orphans show that 13 percent have lost their mother, 69 percent have lost their father, and 18 percent have lost both biological parents. At ages 14–17, orphans have a 3 percent lower chance of being enrolled than non-orphans. Losing both parents has a major negative impact on years of education; losing a mother seems to have a greater impact on girls than losing a father. Orphans who lived with a surviving parent or close relative (such as grandparents) were able to complete more years of school in 2004 than otherwise, so there is some evidence of a protective effect. This protective effect of being placed with close relatives is also found in KwaZulu-Natal, where orphans in households headed by more distant relatives had lower educational outcomes relative to children of the head of household (Case and others 2004).

The study of the long-term impact of orphanhood in Tanzania shows that fostering arrangements have mixed effects in terms of mitigating the negative impact of the death of a parent. Children who are not fostered out before their mother or father passes have lower schooling attainment, but those orphaned at younger ages grow to a taller height (Beegle and others 2006).

Although the conclusion that orphans are likely to be better off if they are placed with close relatives is common to many studies using household survey data, that type of data is unlikely to allow a comparison with placement in institutions because institutions are usually not included in household surveys. In the study of Romanian adoptees, results indicated no measurable effect of institutional deprivation that did not extend beyond six months of age, but a substantial decrement in IQ is associated with any duration of institutional deprivation above that age (Beckett and others 2006). It is interesting to contrast these findings with results from Rwanda immediately after the 1994 genocide showing that although children living in shelters were exposed to more traumas, they demonstrated fewer post-traumatic reactions. The authors argued that this initially surprising finding could be explained by the unique circumstances in Rwandan society in the aftermath of the genocide, when communities might have been less able than institutions to care for children in the immediate aftermath of a wide-spread disaster (Dyregrov and others 2000).

Conclusion

Research on the consequences of conflicts and epidemics is an emerging and active field, with diverse contributions from psychology, medicine, demography, and economics, which is remarkable because this is also a challenging field. Conflicts and disasters are disruptive and generally unpredictable. As a consequence, very often data are available only after a disaster, sometimes several years after the events, and longitudinal studies are hard to conduct. Large and representative samples are diffi-cult to assemble (Masten and Osofsky 2010). However, the evidence points to severe consequences for the long-term well-being of children in terms of their psychological development and their health and educa-tional outcomes. This suggests that, as soon as possible after the trau-matic events, instruments specifically designed to measure ECD be included in the surveys conducted by statistical agencies at the national level and by international agencies. The studies reviewed in this chapter offer several examples of instruments well designed to capture the shocks experienced by children. Both to cover a larger spectrum of traumas and to allow a better understanding of the mechanism by which children are affected, it would be useful if researchers could go beyond years of school-ing and anthropometric measurements, even if those are useful indicators. In this respect, the use of biological indicators of stress, for example, mea-sures of cortisol levels in saliva, as was done in one study in the aftermath of Hurricane Katrina in the United States (Vigil and others 2010), would offer an additional objective level of analysis.

The findings from the literature on the impact of conflicts and epidemics highlight the severe impacts on children's well-being. The consequences of these shocks are likely to persist even into adulthood (Beegle and others 2006) and will have a long-run welfare impact on individuals as well as on society, through an adverse effect on future adult wages and productivity. The research also points to wide variety in the range of negative impacts, with some groups displaying strong resilience to the shocks tested (Blattman and Annan 2010; Klasen and others 2010). Understanding the specific mechanisms by which violence and disasters impact children's lives and welfare, as well as understanding the factors that facilitate resilience, is critical for developing adequate policy responses to protect children from negative conflict effects. Several findings also suggest that the same shocks have a stronger and more durable impact on children from initially poorer economic or educational backgrounds (Evans and Miguel 2007; Yamano and Jayne 2005).

From a policy perspective, the obvious recommendation would be to avoid conflicts and epidemics. Such a recommendation, although obvious, is unfortunately beyond the power of specialists on childhood development. Nevertheless, the findings from the literature offer more concrete and practical recommendations (Norris and others 2002, Norris, Friedman, and Watson 2002). Best practices for the care and protection of children affected by conflicts and other disasters have been assembled and defined by practitioners from humanitarian agencies (Ager and others 2010). Despite the specificities of each conflict or disaster, some consistency is seen in the findings that can help to improve preparedness in the event of futures crises (Masten and Osofsky 2010). The recommendations can be summarized as follows: First, it is important to protect and restore as quickly as possible children's relationship with their caregivers. For children who have lost their parents, it is crucial to provide nurturing caregivers. Orphans usually fare better if placed with close family members. Second, training first responders in the range of traumas that can be experienced by children and including, when possible, parents and teachers among the first responders help to give an appropriate response to children in the wake of disasters and conflicts. Finally, children's traumas are also mitigated when routines and opportunities to learn and play are maintained and supported. The restoration of school activities is a priority, as well as other activities that strengthen communities. Although school reopenings should be a priority, efforts to mitigate the impact of extreme events on children should go further; for example, offering remediation services could help traumatized children progress normally through school. Non–school-based programs could give a second chance to youth who have dropped out of school because of traumas experienced early in their childhood.

It is important to stress, however, that few of these practical recommendations have been rigorously tested and evaluated. Although in the case of sudden conflicts or disasters such rigorous impact evaluations might be unpractical, interventions supporting orphans or HIV-affected children should be more frequently evaluated for their efficiency and effectiveness (Schenk 2009).

References

Ager, A., L. Stark, B. Akesson, and N. Boothby. 2010. "Defining Best Practice in Care and Protection of Children in Crisis-Affected Settings: A Delphi Study." *Child Development* 81 (4): 1271–86.

Ainsworth, M., K. Beegle, and G. Koda. 2005. "The Impact of Adult Mortality and Parental Deaths on Primary Schooling in North-Western Tanzania." *Journal of Development Studies* 41: 412–39.

Ainsworth, M., and D. Filmer. 2006. "Inequalities in Children's Schooling: AIDS, Orphanhood, Poverty, and Gender." *World Development* 34 (6): 1099–128.

Ainsworth, M., and I. Semali. 2000. "The Impact of Adult Deaths on Children's Health in Northwestern Tanzania." Policy Research Working Paper No. 2266, World Bank, Washington, DC.

Akresh, R., E. Bagby, D. de Walque, and H. Kazianga. 2010. "Child Ability and Household Human Capital Investment Decisions in Burkina Faso." World Bank Policy Research Working Paper No. 5370. World Bank, Washington, DC.

Akresh, R., and D. de Walque. 2008. "Armed Conflict and Schooling: Evidence from the 1994 Rwandan Genocide." World Bank Policy Research Working Paper No. 4606, World Bank, Washington, DC.

Akresh, R., P. Verwimp, and T. Bundervoet. 2007. "Civil War, Crop Failure and Child Stunting in Rwanda." World Bank Policy Research Working Paper No. 4208, World Bank, Washington, DC.

Alderman, H., J. Hoddinott, and B. Kinsey. 2006. "Long Term Consequences of Early Childhood Malnutrition." *Oxford Economic Papers* 58 (3): 450–74.

Baillieu, N. M., and J. P. Potterton. 2008. "The Extent of Delay of Language, Motor, and Cognitive Development in HIV-Positive Infants." *Journal of Neurologic Physical Therapy* 32 (3): 118–21.

Beasley, N. M. R., A. Hall, A. M. Tomkins, C. Donnelly, P. Ntimbwa, J. Kivuga, C. M. Kihamia, W. Lorri, and D. A. P. Bundy. 2000. "The Health of Enrolled and Non Enrolled Children of School Age in Tanga, Tanzania." *Acta Tropica* 76 (3): 223–29.

Beckett, C., B. Maughan, M. Rutter, J. Castle, E. Colvert, C. Groothues, J. Kreppner, S. Stevens, T. G. O'Connor, and E. J. S. Sonuga-Barke. 2006. "Do the Effects of Early Severe Deprivation on Cognition Persist into Early Adolescence? Findings from the English and Romanian Adoptees Study." *Child Development* 77: 696–711.

Beegle, K., J. De Weerdt, and S. Dercon. 2006. "Orphanhood and the Long-Run Impact on Children." *American Journal of Agricultural Economics* 88 (5): 1266–72.

Beegle, K., D. Filmer, A. Stokes, and L. Tiereova. 2009. "Orphanhood and Living Arrangements of Children in Sub-Saharan Africa." World Bank Policy Research Working Paper 4889. World Bank, Washington, DC.

Bennell, P. 2005. "The Impact of the AIDS Epidemic on the Schooling of Orphans and Other Directly Affected Children in Sub-Saharan Africa." *Journal of Development Studies* 41: 467–88.

Betancourt, T. S., I. I. Borisova, T. P. Williams, R. T. Brennan, T. H. Whitfield, M. De La Soudiere, J. Williamson, and S. E. Gilman. 2010. "Sierra Leone's Former Child Soldiers: A Follow-Up Study of Psychosocial Adjustment and Community Reintegration." *Child Development* 81 (4): 1077–95.

Bhargava, A. 2005. "AIDS Epidemic and the Psychological Well-Being and School Participation of Ethiopian Orphans." *Psychology, Health & Medicine* 10: 263–75.

Bicego, G., S. Rutstein, and K. Johnson. 2003. "Dimensions of the Emerging Orphan Crisis in Sub-Saharan Africa." *Social Science & Medicine* 56 (6): 1235–47.

Blattman, C., and J. Annan. 2010. "The Consequences of Child Soldiering." *Review of Economics and Statistics* 92 (4): 882–98.

Case, A., and C. Ardington. 2006. "The Impact of Parental Death on School Outcomes: Longitudinal Evidence from South Africa." *Demography* 43 (3): 401–20.

Case, A., C. Paxson, and J. Ableidinger. 2004. "Orphans in Africa: Parental Death, Poverty and School Enrollment." *Demography* 41: 483–508.

Catani, C., A. H. Gewirtz, E. Wieling, E. Schauer, T. Elbert, and F. Neuner. 2010. "Tsunami, War, and Cumulative Risk in the Lives of Sri Lankan Schoolchildren." *Child Development* 81 (4): 1176–91.

Celebi Oncu, E., and A. Metindogan Wise. 2010. "The Effects of the 1999 Turkish Earthquake on Young Children: Analyzing Traumatized Children's Completion of Short Stories." *Child Development* 81 (4): 1161–75.

Corno, L., and D. de Walque. 2010. "Orphanhood, Living Arrangements and Schooling: Evidence from Lesotho." Unpublished manuscript, World Bank, Washington, DC.

Daniels, M. C., and L. S. Adair. 2004. "Growth in Young Filipino Children Predicts Schooling Trajectories through High School." *Journal of Nutrition* 134 (6): 1439–46.

de Walque, D. 2006. "The Socio-Demographic Legacy of the Khmer Rouge Period in Cambodia." *Population Studies* 60 (2): 223–31.

———. 2009. "Parental Education and Children's Schooling Outcomes: Evidence from Recomposed Families in Rwanda." *Economic Development and Cultural Change* 57 (4): 723–46.

Dyregrov, A., R. Gjestad, and M. Raundalen. 2002. "Children Exposed to Warfare: A Longitudinal Study." *Journal of Traumatic Stress* 15: 59–68.

Dyregrov, A., L. Gupta, R. Gjestad, and E. Mukanoheli. 2000. "Trauma Exposure and Psychological Reactions to Genocide among Rwandan Children." *Journal of Traumatic Stress* 13: 3–21.

Eisenberg, N., C. Hofer, and J. Vaughan. 2007. "Effortful Control and Its Socioemotional Consequences." In *Handbook of Emotion Regulation,* ed. J. J. Gross, 287–306. New York: Guilford.

Engle, P. L., L. Fernald, H. Alderman, J. Behrman, C. O'Gara, A. Yousafzai, M. Cabral de Mello, M. Hidrabo, N. Ulker, I. Ertem, and S. Iltus. 2010. "Strategies for

Improving Outcomes for Young Children in Developing Countries." Unpublished manuscript.

Evans, D. K., and E. Miguel. 2007. "Orphans and Schooling in Africa: A Longitudinal Analysis." *Demography* 44: 35–57.

Ferguson, G., and J. Jelsma. 2009. "The Prevalence of Motor Delay among HIV Infected Children Living in Cape Town, South Africa." *International Journal of Rehabilitation Research* 32 (2): 108–14.

Fernando, G. A., K. E. Miller, and others. 2010. "Growing Pains: The Impact of Disaster-Related and Daily Stressors on the Psychological and Psychosocial Functioning of Youth in Sri Lanka." *Child Development* 81 (4): 1192–210.

Gertler, P., D. I. Levine, S. Martinez, and S. Bertozzi. 2003. "Losing the Presence and Presents of Parents: How Parental Death Affects Children." Unpublished manuscript.

Gertler, P., D. I. Levine, and M. Ames. 2004. "Schooling and Parental Death." *Review of Economics & Statistics* 86: 211–25.

Glewwe, P., H. G. Jacoby, and E. M. King. 2001. "Early Childhood Nutrition and Academic Achievement: A Longitudinal Analysis." *Journal of Public Economics* 81 (3): 345–68.

Hall, A. 2001. "An Association between Chronic Undernutrition and Educational Test Scores in Vietnamese Children." *European Journal of Clinical Nutrition* 55 (9): 801–4.

Hutchinson, S. E., and C. A. Powell. 1997. "Nutrition, Anaemia, Geohelminth Infection and School Achievement in Rural Jamaican Primary School Children." *European Journal of Clinical Nutrition* 51 (11): 729–35.

Isanaka, S., C. Duggan, and W. W. Fawzi. 2009. "Patterns of Postnatal Growth in HIV-Infected and HIV-Exposed Children." *Nutrition Reviews* 67 (6): 343–59.

Jamison, D. T. 1986. "Child Malnutrition and School Performance in China." *Journal of Development Economics* 20 (2): 299–309.

Kithakye, M., A. S. Morris, A. M. Terranova, and S. S. Myers. 2010. "The Kenyan Political Conflict and Children's Adjustment." *Child Development* 81 (4): 1114–28.

Klasen, F., G. Oettingen, J. Daniels, M. Post, C. Hoyer, and H. Adam. 2010. "Posttraumatic Resilience in Former Ugandan Child Soldiers." *Child Development* 81 (4): 1096–113.

Kreppner, J., M. Rutter, M. Rutter, C. Beckett, J. Castle, E. Colvert, C. Groothues, A. Hawkins, T. G. O'Connor, S. Stevens, and E. J. S. Sonuga-Barke. 2007. "Normality and Impairment Following Profound Early Institutional Deprivation: A Longitudinal Follow-Up into Early Adolescence." *Journal of Abnormal Child Psychology* 43 (4): 931–46.

Kronenberg, M. E., T. C. Hansel, A. M. Brennan, H. J. Osofsky, J. D. Osofsky, and B. Lawrason. 2010. "Children of Katrina: Lessons Learned about Postdisaster Symptoms and Recovery Patterns." *Child Development* 81 (4): 1241–59.

Kuterovac, G., A. Dyregrove, and R. Stuvland. 1994. "Children in War: A Silent Majority under Stress." *British Journal of Medical Psychology* 67: 363–75.

Lloyd, C. B., and A. K. Blanc. 1996. "Children's Schooling in Sub-Saharan Africa: The Role of Fathers, Mothers, and Others." *Population and Development Review* 22 (2): 265–98.

Macksoud, M. S., and J. L. Aber. 1996. "The War Experiences and Psychosocial Development of Children in Lebanon." *Child Development* 67 (1): 70–88.

Makame, V., and S. Grantham-McGregor. 2002. "Psychological Well-Being of Orphans in Dar Es Salaam, Tanzania." *Acta Paediatrica* 91: 459–65.

Masten, A. S., and J. D. Osofsky. 2010. "Disasters and Their Impact on Child Development: Introduction to the Special Section." *Child Development* 81 (4): 1029–39.

Moock, P. R., and J. Leslie. 1986. "Childhood Malnutrition and Schooling in the Terai Region of Nepal." *Journal of Development Economics* 20 (1): 33–52.

National Scientific Council on the Developing Child. 2005. "Excessive Stress Disrupts the Architecture of the Developing Brain." Working Paper, Center on the Developing Child, Harvard University, Cambridge, MA.

Norris, F., M. Friedman, P. J. Watson, C. M. Byrne, E. Diaz, and K. Kaniasty. 2002. "60,000 Disaster Victims Speak. Part I. An Empirical Review of the Empirical Literature, 1981–2001." *Psychiatry* 65 (3): 207–39.

Norris, F., M. Friedman, and P. J. Watson. 2002. "60,000 Disaster Victims Speak. Part II. Summary and Implications of the Disaster Mental Health Research." *Psychiatry* 65 (3): 240–60.

Perry, B. D., R. A. Pollard, T. L. Blakley, W. L. Baker, and D. Vigilante. 1995. "Childhood Trauma, the Neurobiology of Adaptation, and 'Use-Dependent' Development of the Brain: How 'States' Become 'Traits.'" *Infant Mental Health Journal* 16: 271–91.

Potterton, J., A. Stewart, P. Cooper, and P. Becker. 2010. "The Effect of a Basic Home Stimulation Programme on the Development of Young Children Infected with HIV." *Developmental Medicine & Child Neurology* 52 (6): 547–51.

Rothbart, M. K., and J. E. Bates. 2006. "Temperament." In *Social, Emotional, and Personality Development,* ed. N. Eisenberg, vol. 3, 99–166. New York: Wiley.

Sack, W. H., G. Clarke, C. Him, D. Dickason, B. Goff, K. Lanham, and J. D. Kinzie. 1993. "A 6-Year Follow-up Study of Cambodian Refugee Adolescents Traumatized as Children." *Journal of the American Academy of Child and Adolescent Psychiatry* 32 (2): 431–37.

Schenk, K. 2009. "Community Interventions Providing Care and Support to Orphans and Vulnerable Children: A Review of Evaluation Evidence." *AIDS Care* 21 (7): 918–42.

Sharrif, Z., J. Bond, and N. E. Johnson. 2009. "Nutrition and Educational Achievement of Urban Primary Schoolchildren in Malaysia." *Asia Pacific Journal of Clinical Nutrition* 9: 264–73.

Shaw, J. A. 2003. "Children Exposed to War/Terrorism." *Clinical Child & Family Psychology Review* 6: 237–46.

Shemyakina, O. Forthcoming. "The Effect of Armed Conflict on Accumulation of Schooling: Results from Tajikistan." *Journal of Development Economics.* DOI: 10.1016/j.jdeveco.2010.05.002.

Sherr, L., J. Mueller, and R. Varrall. 2009. "A Systematic Review of Cognitive Development and Child Human Immunodeficiency Virus Infection." *Psychology, Health & Medicine* 14: 387–404.

Shonkoff, J. P., W. T. Boyce, and B. S. McEwen. 2009. "Neuroscience, Molecular Biology, and the Childhood Roots of Health Disparities: Building a New

Framework for Health Promotion and Disease Prevention." *JAMA* 301 (21): 2252–59.

Shonkoff, J. P., and D. Phillips, eds. 2000. *From Neurons to Neighborhoods: The Science of Early Childhood Development.* Washington, DC: National Academy Press.

Sigman, M., C. Neumann, A. A. J. Jansen, and N. Bwibo. 1989. "Cognitive Abilities of Kenyan Children in Relation to Nutrition, Family Characteristics, and Education." *Child Development* 60: 1463–74.

Stevens, S., E. J. S. Sonuga-Barke, J. Kreppner, C. Beckett, J. Castle, E. Colvert, C. Groothues, A. Hawkin, and M. Rutter. 2008. "Inattention/Overactivity Following Early Severe Institutional Deprivation: Presentation and Associations in Early Adolescence." *Journal of Abnormal Child Psychology* 36 (3): 385–98.

Subbarao, K., Angel Mattimore, and Kathrin Plangemann. 2001. "Social Protection of Africa's Orphans and Other Vulnerable Children." Africa Region Human Development Working Paper, World Bank, Washington, DC.

UNAIDS. 2009. "AIDS Epidemic Update: November 2009." UNAIDS, Geneva.

Van Rie, A., P. R. Harrington, A. Dow A, and K. Robertson. 2007. "Neurologic and Neurodevelopmental Manifestations of Pediatric HIV/AIDS: A Global Perspective." *European Journal of Paediatric Neurology* 11: 1–9.

Van Rie, A., A. Mupuala, and A. Dow. 2008. "Impact of the HIV/AIDS Epidemic on the Neurodevelopment of Preschool-Aged Children in Kinshasa, Democratic Republic of the Congo." *Pediatrics* 122 (1): e123–e28.

Vigil, J. M., D. C. Geary, D. A. Granger, and M. V. Flinn. 2010. "Sex Differences in Salivary Cortisol, Alpha-Amylase, and Psychological Functioning Following Hurricane Katrina." *Child Development* 81 (4): 1228–40.

WHO/UNAIDS/UNICEF. 2010. "Towards Universal Access. Scaling Up Priority HIV/AIDS Interventions in the Health Sector." Progress Report 2010, World Health Organization, Geneva.

Yamano, T., and T. S. Jayne. 2005. "Working-Age Adult Mortality and Primary School Attendance in Rural Kenya." *Economic Development & Cultural Change* 53 (3): 619–53.

Yamauchi, F. 2008. "Early Childhood Nutrition, Schooling, and Sibling Inequality in a Dynamic Context: Evidence from South Africa." *Economic Development & Cultural Change* 56 (3): 657–82.

4

Promoting Equity through Early Child Development Interventions for Children from Birth through Three Years of Age

Susan Walker

Early childhood is a critical period for development, and early experiences can have long-term effects on brain function and cognitive and psychosocial functioning. Brain development is affected by the quality of the environment, including nutrition, infection, and stimulation. Synapse formation is experience dependent, and lack of stimulation and social interaction can have lasting cognitive and emotional effects (National Research Council and Institute of Medicine 2000; Thompson and Nelson 2001).

Lack of appropriate early experiences places children at a disadvantage on school entry and at risk of poor school progress and lower educational attainment. Longitudinal studies in low- and middle-income (LAMI) countries have shown that children with lower ability on school entry have poorer scores on achievement tests, are more likely to repeat grades and drop out of school, and leave school at a lower grade level (Grantham-McGregor and others 2007). Lower educational attainment is associated with subsequent lower adult earning. In addition, lower levels of parental education affect child care and are associated with poorer parenting practices (Ertem and others 2007; Paxson and Schady 2007). The impact of early child development (ECD) on adult cognition, behavior, and earnings continues the poverty cycle. Thus, early childhood interventions to promote cognitive and social-emotional development will facilitate later gains from educational and societal opportunities and are a critical strategy to promote equity.

Several long-term studies of early childhood intervention for disadvantaged children in the United States have shown benefits for adult educational outcomes, behavior, and employment. Some of the key studies are summarized in table 4.1 (Campbell and others 2002; Eckenrode and others 2010; McCormick and others 2006; Reynolds and others 2007; Schweinhart and others 2005). The interventions have provided high-quality preschool experiences (Reynolds and others 2007; Schweinhart and others 2005), center-based care from infancy to five years of age (Campbell and others 2002), home visits during pregnancy and up to age two (Eckenrode and others 2010), and a comprehensive strategy of home- and center-based services up to age three (McCormick and others 2006). The most consistent benefits are for educational outcomes, whereas findings for employment and earnings, antisocial behavior, and other risk behaviors are more varied. Although these studies demonstrate the potential of early childhood interventions to modify outcomes over a lifetime, the interventions have generally been high intensity and high quality and involved human and financial resources not typical of large-scale programs in the United States and well beyond the reach of most LAMI countries.

In developing countries expansion of ECD programs has focused on children three years of age and older through expansion of access to preschools and efforts to improve the quality of preschools (EFA Global Monitoring Report Team 2006). Attention to this age group is facilitated by consensus on preschool attendance as the most appropriate strategy to promote young child development in this age range.

The focus of this chapter is on the newborn to three years of age group, for whom less information is available to guide policy on effective large-scale programs. ECD programs for this group have primarily concerned nutrition and health. This age is a critical period for nutrition (Lozoff and others 2006; Martorell and others 2010), and recent attention has been given to the potential impact of improvements in health and nutrition, not just for physical growth and development, but for gains in human capital as well (Hoddinott and others 2008; Victora and others 2008). However, substantial gains in cognitive and social-emotional development are unlikely without attention to ensuring quality interaction and stimulation, which is essential for optimal brain and behavioral development (M. M. Black and others 2008). The first part of this chapter reviews the evidence for the impact of interventions aimed at improving early stimulation for children from birth to age three in LAMI countries comparing various strategies

Table 4.1 Summary of Long-Term Effects of U.S. ECD Programs

Study and follow-up age and sample	Intervention	Cognitive/ Educational	Employment	Violence	Risk behaviors
Abecedarian: 111 high-risk infants randomly assigned to experimental or control groups, 104 measured at age 21 Campbell and others 2002	Full-day educational day care infancy to age 5	Significant benefits to IQ (4.4 points). Benefits to reading and math (1.8 and 1.3 grade-level equivalent). More likely to be in college	No difference in whether employed but higher level of employment	No difference in self-reported weapon-carrying, violent behavior, convictions	Decline in teen pregnancy and marijuana, cigarettes, and alcohol not significant
Perry Preschool: 123 low-income African American children randomly assigned to preschool or no preschool, follow-up at ages 19, 27, and 40 Schweinhart and others 2005	High-quality preschool from ages 3–4	More high school graduation. Higher literacy at age 27, better attitudes toward school at age 19	More likely to be employed, higher earnings at age 40	Fewer arrests, less time in prison	Decline in drug use (marijuana, pills)
Chicago Child Parent Centre: Matched comparison of children attending intervention preschools and kindergarten with alternative kindergarten (no preschool), 1,389 of 1,539 followed up at age 24 Reynolds and others 2007	High-quality preschool and kindergarten compared with no preschool and regular kindergarten	Higher grade level, more school completion. More likely to attend 4-year college	No effects on employment, income, welfare	Fewer incarcerations, felony arrests, and convictions	No difference in drug use, smoking, teenage pregnancy

(continued next page)

Table 4.1 Summary of Long-Term Effects of U.S. ECD Programs (continued)

Study and follow-up age and sample	Intervention	Cognitive/ Educational	Employment	Violence	Risk behaviors
Nurse Home Visitation Program: 400 pregnant women enrolled, randomly assigned to comparison, visits in pregnancy, or visits in pregnancy and up to age 2, 310 followed up at age 19 Eckenrode and others 2010	Average of 9 home visits during pregnancy and 23 up to age 2 aimed at improving health-related behaviors and child health and development through better care and maternal life choices	No effect on high school graduation	No effect on economic productivity (currently employed, or in school or job training). No effect on reliance on welfare.	Girls only, fewer arrests and convictions. No effect on self-reported criminal behavior.	No effect on drug use, use of family planning, or teen pregnancy
Infant Health and Development Program: 985 LBW preterm infants in 8 sites randomized to intervention or follow-up only, 636 measured at age 18 McCormick and others 2006	Educational program through weekly home visits in first year and fortnightly in years 2 and 3. Daily center-based education began at 12 months as well as parent support groups every other month	No benefits for birth weight ≤ 2,000 grams, benefits to receptive vocabulary (PPVT) and mathematics in high LBW group (2,001-2,499 grams). No differences in school dropout rate	Not measured	No difference in arrests or incarcerations	Fewer self-reported risk behaviors in HLBW. No difference in general behavior problems by youth or caregiver report

Source: Author's compilation.

Note: Participants in the Abcedarian and Chicago studies also reported fewer depressive symptoms. HLBW = high low birth weight (2,001–2,499 grams); LBW = low birth weight; PPVT = Peabody Picture Vocabulary Test.

used to either enrich parenting practices or provide services directly to the child. Family, child, and program characteristics that influence benefits are then discussed, and opportunities for integration with health and nutrition services are identified. Finally the necessary program investments in terms of human and material resources are outlined, as well as research needs to inform expansion of programs to reach the large numbers of children affected. The focus on this age group rather than the wider age range of previous reviews (Engle and others 2007; Nores and Barnett 2009) is an attempt to draw attention to the need to find strategies to enhance learning opportunities for younger children and to begin to synthesize the existing evidence, which can inform policy development for these children.

Concurrent Benefits of ECD Interventions for Child Development

Children from birth to age three are primarily cared for in the home, although use of formal and informal day care is likely to increase with increased urbanization, fewer extended families, and increased maternal employment. Efforts to enrich environments for children in this age group have employed a variety of approaches aimed at enhancing the capacity of the mother or primary caregiver to provide stimulation and interactions. The evaluations of parent-focused interventions have mainly been efficacy trials with the interventions implemented by the research teams, although in some cases they were linked to existing programs or health services and may have involved training health service staff (Hamadani and others 2006; Potterton and others 2009; Powell and Grantham-McGregor 1989; Powell and others 2004). A few evaluations were of ongoing community or nongovernmental organization (NGO) programs (Peairson and others 2008; Powell 2004).

Parent-focused interventions are reviewed first and then provision of nonparental care through day care centers, of which there are fewer evaluations. Studies were identified by a PubMed search using several terms (for example, child development, language, and emotional development linked with terms such as early intervention, and stimulation). Citation lists in the articles retrieved were also reviewed to identify additional studies. Only evaluations that had appropriate comparison groups were included.

Promotion of Better Parenting and Mother-Child Interaction through Home Visits

Nine studies of the benefits for child development of home visits with parents to enhance their ability to facilitate their child's development were evaluated (details are summarized in table 4.2). Two studies were conducted

Table 4.2 Promotion of Better Parenting and Mother-Child Interaction through Home Visits

Authors, country	Sample and design	Intervention	Intensity: Average no. of contacts/month[a]	Type of visitor, training, and supervision	Impact on child development[b]
Hamadani and others 2006, Bangladesh	20 community nutrition centers randomized to intervention (n = 10) or control (n = 10). Undernourished children (less than −2 z-scores WAZ) aged 6–24 months were enrolled, intervention n = 104, control n = 102	Weekly group meetings at nutrition centers for 10 months, then fortnightly for 2 months. Topics included child development and play. Home visits twice weekly for 8 months, then weekly for 4 months. Aimed at promoting positive mother–child interaction and demonstrating play activities	Average number of home visits achieved: 68; duration of visits not stated. Average number of group sessions attended: 23. Average contacts per month: 7.6	Literate women from intervention villages, given 2 weeks' training. Supervisors observed visits, no information on frequency	Significant benefit for Bayley mental development index (d = 0.32) but not motor development (d = 0.17). During test session intervention children were happier, more cooperative and responsive, and vocalized more (d ranged from 0.17, responsive, to 0.45, cooperative)
Nahar and others 2009, Bangladesh	Severely malnourished children aged 6–24 months. Control group studied year before intervention group; 33/77 intervention children and 37/ 56 control children followed up	Daily half-hour group and individual sessions for mothers and children for 2 weeks in hospital. 11 home visits over a 6-month period after discharge and 7 visits to center. Using play sessions, mothers shown activities to promote child development	Duration of home visits not stated. Daily contact in hospital. Average of 3 contacts/ month after discharge	Visitors had 8 years schooling, given 2 weeks' training. Supervisors observed visits, no information on frequency	Significant benefits for Bayley mental score (d = 0.85) and motor (d = 0.50) development. No benefits for behavior during test session

Study	Design and sample	Intervention	Visit details	Visitors/training	Results
Eickmann and others 2003, Brazil	Quasi-experimental pre- and posttest. 78 infants tested at age 12 months in intervention town, 78 controls from 3 smaller towns. 66 and 70 tested at 18 months	Intervention after 12-month test. Three workshops (about 8 mothers per workshop) involving demonstration and practice to improve interaction through play. 10 home visit play sessions	Home visits 3-45 minutes' duration. Approximately 2 contacts per month	Workshop trainers were occupational therapists with child development specialization. No information on home visitors	Significant benefit for Bayley MDI ($d = 0.82$) and PDI ($d = 0.66$) at 18 months
Grantham-McGregor, Schofield, and Powell 1987, Jamaica	Severely malnourished children aged 6-24 months on enrollment. 16 children given medical care only. 18 in subsequent year also received stimulation	Daily play sessions in hospital. After discharge weekly visits for 2 years and fortnightly visits in third year. Focused on mothers and helping them promote child's development. Visitors demonstrated play techniques using homemade toys	Duration of visits 1 hour. 4 visits/month planned for first 2 years. No information on number of contacts achieved	CHWs with primary education. No information on supervision	At end of intervention (3 years after leaving hospital) large benefits for DQ ($d = 0.94$) and PPVT ($d = 0.96$)
Powell and Grantham-McGregor 1989, Jamaica	Study 1: children aged 6-30 months from poor neighborhoods randomly assigned to control, monthly, and fortnightly home visits. Study 2: children aged 16-30 months	Visits by CHWs. Objective to improve maternal-child interaction and promote development through play. Visits included combinations of language activities,	Visits lasted about 1 hour. Each CHW visited maximum of 13 families. Objective of study was to examine impact of visit frequency (weekly, fortnightly, monthly).	Most CHWs had incomplete secondary education, given 8 weeks' training in child development and intervention. Supervised by clinic	Study 1: No significant benefits from monthly visits. Moderate benefits from fortnightly visits ($d = 0.43$ after 1 year). Comparing children in the same age range from Study 1 and Study 2:

(continued next page)

Table 4.2 Promotion of Better Parenting and Mother-Child Interaction through Home Visits (continued)

Authors, country	Sample and design	Intervention	Intensity: Average no. of contacts/month[a]	Type of visitor, training, and supervision	Impact on child development[b]
	randomly assigned to control or weekly visits	games, songs, paper and crayon activities. Emphasis on praise and ensuring mother and child experienced success. Toys left in home and exchanged at next visit	No information on actual visit frequency achieved	nurse who observed 5% of visits using evaluation checklist. CHWs kept record book of visits for each child. Nurse met weekly with CHWs to discuss visits	Large benefits from weekly visits, $d = 1.11$; fortnightly, $d = 0.36$
Grantham-McGregor and others 1991, Jamaica	129 stunted children aged 9–24 months randomized to 4 groups: supplementation, stimulation, supplement and stimulation, control	Weekly home visits for 2 years to encourage positive interaction and demonstrate play activities. Homemade toys and simple picture books were provided. Mothers encouraged to play with child between visits. Supplementation: 1 kilogram milk-based formula/week. Control group weekly visits to obtain morbidity information	Home visits 1 hour duration. 4 visits/month planned; no information on amount achieved	CHWs conducted visits. Supervisor monitored 10% of visits	Significant benefit from stimulation to DQ ($d = 0.86$) and for all sub-scales. Significant benefit from supplementation with additive benefits for group receiving both interventions. In a subset of children, no impact of either intervention on behavior after 6 months of intervention (Meeks Gardner and others 2003)

Source	Sample	Intervention	Dosage	Training/supervision	Results
Powell and others 2004, Jamaica	Undernourished children aged 9–30 months attending nutrition clinics. 18 clinics randomly assigned to intervention children (n = 65) or control (n = 64)	Weekly half-hour visits for 1 year involving mother and child. Play activities demonstrated	Median number of visits achieved was 32.5 (of planned 50), about 2.7/month	CHWs given 2 weeks' training on child development and intervention. Supervisor (child development specialist) observed each CHW once/month and visited clinics fortnightly to review and discuss visits	Significant benefits for DQ (d = 0.91) and for mothers' child-rearing knowledge (d = 1.25) and practices (d = 0.65)
Powell 2004, Jamaica	Matched design 78/90 intervention and 53/70 control children aged 12–30 months on enrollment followed up after 1 year	Weekly visits included songs, action rhymes, and play activities conducted with child. Discussed what child could learn from play activities with mothers. Monthly meeting for parents at a center to discuss child-rearing practices and other topics. Parents also made toys at these meetings	No information on duration of visits or frequency of visits achieved	"Roving caregivers," recently completed secondary school, given 2 weeks' preservice training. 1-day workshops held fortnightly to discuss visits and prepare weekly work plans and toy kits. 1-week courses run every 3 months	Significant effects for DQ (d = 0.70), benefits for hand and eye and performance subscales, not for hearing and speech

(continued next page)

Table 4.2 Promotion of Better Parenting and Mother-Child Interaction through Home Visits *(continued)*

Authors, country	Sample and design	Intervention	Intensity: Average no. of contacts/ month[a]	Type of visitor, training, and supervision	Impact on child development[b]
Meeks Gardner and others 2003; Walker and others 2004, Jamaica	140 term LBW infants randomly assigned to intervention or control	Weekly 1-hour visits from birth for 8 weeks, focused on improving maternal responsiveness. Weekly half-hour visits from age 7 to 24 months similar to previous Jamaican interventions. Control group visited to obtain morbidity and infant feeding information	Median of 75% of scheduled visits achieved, 3 visits/month	CHWs received 2 weeks' training before each phase on child development and conduct of intervention. Supervisor observed visits once/month and met with CHWs weekly to review visits	Benefits of early intervention at 7 months for problem solving ($d = 0.30$) and behavior in test session (more cooperative and happy). At 24 months significant benefits of intervention for performance ($d = 0.42$) and hand and eye ($d = 0.36$) subscales of Griffiths test. Overall DQ $d = 0.27$

Source: Author's compilation.

Note: May also involve group sessions. CHW = community health worker; DQ = developmental quotient; LBW = low birth weight; MDI = mental development index; PDI = psychomotor development index; PPVT = Peabody Picture Vocabulary Test; WAZ = weight-for-age z-score.

a. Contacts include group sessions where used and are averaged per month; intensity may have varied during specific periods.

b. Effect size (Cohen's *d*) was calculated using unadjusted posttest values (Thalheimer and Cook 2002) to enable comparison among studies. Calculation of effect size using change, for those studies where information was available, showed effect sizes within the same range (small, medium, large).

in Bangladesh, one in Brazil, and the remaining six in Jamaica. In all studies the objective of the home visits was to help the parent become more effective at promoting development.

Interventions
In Jamaica, five intervention studies were led by the same research group. The studies targeted different risk groups—severely malnourished children (Grantham-McGregor, Schofield, and Powell 1987), stunted children (Grantham-McGregor and others 1991), and term low-birth-weight infants (Walker and others 2004)—and evaluated the impact of visit frequency (Powell and Grantham-McGregor 1989) and the feasibility of integrating with nutrition services (Powell and others 2004). Visits included demonstration of play activities and involving the mother, or primary caregiver if not the mother, in a play session with her child. Visits comprised various combinations of language activities, games, songs, simple jigsaw puzzles, and crayon and paper activities. Homemade toys and simple picture books were used in the play sessions and left in the home and exchanged at the next visit. Emphasis was placed on enriching verbal interaction between the mother and child; mothers were encouraged to chat with their children and to name things and actions in the house and yard. Mothers were also encouraged to use positive feedback and praise and to avoid physical punishment.

The visits were conducted by community health workers (CHWs). In Jamaica, at the time the studies were conducted, CHWs generally had between primary and incomplete secondary-level education, although in the later studies some had complete secondary education. All received eight weeks of training provided by the Ministry of Health in nutrition and health care. They were given between two and eight weeks of additional training in (1) child development; (2) the intervention program, including teaching techniques; (3) the conduct of the visits, which emphasized a friendly, supportive relationship with the mother; and (4) toy making.

A curriculum manual was developed with suggested activities by stage of development and was provided to the CHWs. Together with the supervisor the appropriate stage in the curriculum for each child was determined. The CHWs were trained to ensure that the child and the mother experienced success during the visit. Supervision was provided by a member of the research team or in one study by health clinic nurses. CHWs met with the supervisor to discuss the visits, and the supervisor also observed between 5 and 10 percent of the visits.

A further Jamaican study was an evaluation of an ongoing program implemented by an NGO (Powell 2004). Although the objectives were similar, in this case visitors were young women who had just completed secondary school. They were given two weeks of training before beginning the visits, and one-day workshops were held fortnightly to discuss the visits and prepare weekly work plans and toy kits. Observations and feedback from the mothers suggested that less emphasis was placed on including the mother in the play session. However, the program included monthly meetings for the parents at which child development, parenting, and other topics were discussed.

The two studies in Bangladesh adapted the intervention used in Jamaica for that culture, incorporating traditional games and songs. Visits were conducted by literate village women in one study and female health workers in the other. In addition to the home visits, in both studies mothers attended centers where individual play sessions (Nahar and others 2009) or group sessions on topics concerning child development and the importance of play (Hamadani and others 2006) were conducted.

The final study was implemented in Brazil (Eickmann and others 2003) and began with an initial home visit by one of the trainers (occupational therapists with specialization in child development) to introduce the program and discuss the importance of play for child development. Three half-day workshops were held for groups of about eight mothers, and 10 visits were made over six months by home visitors to reinforce the workshops through a play session with the mother and child. Workshops were conducted by the trainers and involved demonstration and practice of play activities to promote different aspects of development, toy making, interaction through everyday activities, and review and discussion of what was learned.

Benefits for Child Development
All studies of home visits demonstrated significant benefits of intervention for child development. A few had small effect sizes, but typically effects were medium to large (table 4.2).

Two studies showed large benefits for mental development for children recovering from severe malnutrition (Grantham-McGregor, Schofield, and Powell 1987; Nahar and others 2009). These both involved daily play sessions while, children were in the hospital followed by home visits for six months (Nahar and others 2009) or three years (Grantham-McGregor, Schofield, and Powell 1987). Thus, the potential for benefits for extremely disadvantaged children is clear. Three other studies focused on undernourished children. The Jamaican study of stunted children (height-for-age less than −2 standard deviations [SD] of reference values) showed a large effect on the developmental level (Grantham-McGregor and others 1991), as did another study in which children were somewhat less undernourished on enrollment (weight-for-age less than −1.5 SD, with weight-for-age less than −2 SD in the last three months; Powell and others 2004). Surprisingly, the study in Bangladesh with undernourished children (weight-for-age less than −2 SD) in the community demonstrated a relatively small although significant benefit to scores on the Bayley mental development index (MDI) and no significant benefits for motor development (Hamadani and others 2006). Another study of the benefits of psychosocial stimulation for term low-birth-weight infants who have experienced undernutrition in utero also had modest benefits (Walker and others 2004).

The remaining three studies did not focus specifically on undernourished children but targeted children in poor communities. All showed medium-to-large effects on developmental levels (Eickmann and others 2003; Powell 2004; Powell and Grantham-McGregor 1989).

Only three of the studies described attempted to measure effects on children's behavior. In all three this was by rating of behavior while the developmental tests were being conducted. Results were inconsistent. One study showed no benefits for behavior (Nahar and others 2009), two showed benefits for the children's cooperation with the tester and to their emotional tone (children were happier), and in one of these studies children vocalized more (Hamadani and others 2006; Meeks Gardner and others 2003).

Lessons from Home Visiting Interventions

One clear conclusion from the evaluations of home visit interventions is that they can be successfully implemented by women who have completed only their primary education or partially completed their secondary education. Visitors included CHWs, literate village women, and young women who had just completed secondary education. Some important caveats must be made to this. Although the CHWs (Jamaica) and female health workers (Bangladesh) generally had no more than incomplete secondary education, they had successfully gained employment in a context of high unemployment and may well have had important noncognitive skills that facilitated their effectiveness. In one study that did not use paraprofessionals as visitors but recruited literate village women, the impact of the intervention was modest, particularly given the intensity of contacts (Hamadani and others 2006). It is not clear from the study how these women were identified or what, if any, prior work experience they had.

In most studies visitors have been mature women of similar age or older than the mothers being visited. In contrast, the program of "roving caregivers" in Jamaica used young women in the National Youth Service, for many of whom this was their first working experience. Although the intervention had a significant benefit for child development, some concern was expressed that these young women were less able to engage the mothers and to ensure they participated fully in the visits and sometimes conducted the play sessions with the child alone (Christine Powell, personal communication). This may have implications for the sustainability of benefits.

Although accepting that visits can be conducted by paraprofessionals, an additional issue that needs to be considered is the important role of supervision. Supervision was usually conducted by a professional with training in child development, although in one study this role was accomplished by the clinic nurse (Powell and Grantham-McGregor 1989). Supervision involved observation of visits and regular meetings with the visitors to discuss the visits and plan for subsequent ones. This enabled the supervisor to provide guidance on the content of the visits to ensure the activities were at appropriate levels for individual children and to give feedback on both the content of the visits and the manner in which they were conducted. For example, in addition to the actual activities engaged in, a focus of the Jamaican interventions has been the empathy of the visitor and her role in supporting the mother in becoming more effective at promoting development. Supervision is an essential component of the programs that have been evaluated and is an important consideration in planning for scaling up of interventions.

The frequency of visits necessary to achieve benefits to child development is also important in determining the feasibility of implementing similar interventions on a larger scale. The study by Powell and Grantham-McGregor (1989) is the only one to formally evaluate the impact of visit frequency on the level of benefit achieved and concluded that monthly visits did not benefit development and that a minimum of fortnightly visits was necessary. However, the size of the benefits from fortnightly visits was less than half that of weekly visits (see table 4.2 for details). The frequency of contacts (home visits plus group sessions where used) in most of the interventions was two to four times per month. Thus, it is reasonable to conclude that benefits to child development can be anticipated from programs where at least two visits are achieved per month. It is interesting to note that the intervention with the highest frequency of contacts (7.6 a month) achieved only a modest impact on development. This may suggest that a visit frequency greater than weekly does not lead to additional benefits; however, other aspects of the intervention, families, and children may have contributed to the relatively small impact.

Another characteristic of the programs important for expansion is the duration of the visits. Information on this is not available for all studies but where reported has been a half hour (Powell and others 2004; Walker and others 2004), half to three-quarters of an hour (Eickmann and others 2003), or one hour (Grantham-McGregor, Schofield, and Powell 1987; Grantham-McGregor and others 1991; Powell and Grantham-McGregor 1989). The Jamaican intervention with low-birth-weight (LBW) infants (Walker and others 2004) that used a half hour visit duration had smaller benefits than other similar interventions in Jamaica where the visit duration was longer, but it is unclear whether this or other aspects of the intervention or target group led to the difference in benefits. Information is currently insufficient to determine whether visit duration could be reduced to facilitate program expansion.

Evaluations of the interventions were conducted after they had been implemented for periods ranging from six months to three years. The results suggest that benefits begin to emerge within six months of intervention. In the Jamaican study of stunted children, development was assessed after six months of intervention and then every six months thereafter up to two years, when the intervention ended. Benefits of intervention were evident at the first six-month assessment, and further gains occurred throughout the two years of intervention (Grantham-McGregor and others 1991). What remains to be answered is how the duration of intervention affects the sustainability of benefits.

In addition to intervention characteristics, it is possible that characteristics of the child or caregiver may affect the impact of the intervention. As mentioned in the preceding section, large benefits have been seen in interventions targeted to severely malnourished and to stunted and undernourished children, although in one study benefits were less. The single study with term LBW infants had smaller benefits (Walker and others 2004). Three interventions were implemented more generally with children from poor families that also demonstrated benefits (Eickmann and others 2003; Powell 2004; Powell and Grantham-McGregor 1989). Thus, it seems reasonable to conclude that the loss of developmental potential in children disadvantaged through poverty, undernutrition, or both, can be reduced or prevented through home visits that help parents learn how to promote child development.

The age at which intervention begins might also be hypothesized to affect impact, but little evidence is available from the studies reviewed to address this. In many of the evaluations children's ages on enrollment spanned an age interval of 12 to 24 months (for example, in separate studies, age on enrollment 6 to 24 months and 9 to 30 months), and no investigation has looked at whether children who were enrolled in infancy benefited more or less than those who were older on enrollment. The age at which intervention ends may have implications for sustainability.

Characteristics such as maternal education and family resources may also influence the impact of the interventions, but these have rarely been investigated as potential moderators. Mothers in the studies reviewed usually had no more than an incomplete secondary education (Eickmann and others 2003; Hamadani and others 2006; Powell and others 2004; Walker and others 2004), with many having an incomplete primary education. Although some of the analyses of intervention impact have controlled for the level of maternal education (Eickmann and others 2003; Powell and others 2004), no evaluation has been done of whether the interventions were more effective in mothers with higher or lower education levels. This is important to ensure that mothers of varying education levels are able to gain from the interventions.

Individual Counseling of Mothers at Clinics

Despite the consistent evidence that providing parenting education through home visits benefits child development and that these visits can be effectively conducted by paraprofessionals, the model remains a high-intensity one in terms of human resources. Alternate strategies to reach greater numbers of children are needed, but evidence of their impact on child development is limited. One approach has been to provide parents with counseling and training when they access health services. This model has been developed by the World Health Organization (WHO) and UNICEF as the Care for Development module to be part of the Integrated Management of Childhood Illnesses. The module provides guidelines for health professionals to counsel parents on how to promote development and includes counseling cards with age-specific messages and illustrations of activities. Counseling is done with individual mothers and can be done whenever the mother and child attend the health service for well child or sick visits. Surprisingly, given the efforts to develop the program and materials, only one published evaluation of the impact on child development was identified. This study conducted in a rural county in China demonstrated significant benefits for child development in those randomized to intervention compared with controls (Jin and others 2007; see table 4.3). Although the findings have to be interpreted with caution because the person who conducted the developmental assessments was aware of the children's group assignment, they suggest that this approach has the potential to benefit development. Differences were also seen in how this intervention was implemented and how Care for Development is likely to be implemented at scale. Counseling sessions lasted 30 to 60 minutes, which is unlikely to be achieved in routine child health clinics, and in addition to the clinic session an additional session was conducted within six months to relate the advice to the home environment using materials in the home. Sessions involved both demonstration of activities and practice by mothers. Potential obstacles to implementation were also discussed with the mothers and solutions to these suggested.

Two other studies provided intervention by training mothers of high-risk children at a clinic or hospital. One involved HIV-infected children whose mothers or caregivers were given individualized stimulation programs when they attended the clinic for the child's regular three-month visit (Potterton and others 2009). Activities centered on developmentally appropriate play that could be part of the family's usual daily routine (see table 4.3 for more

Table 4.3 Studies on Individual Counseling of Mothers at Clinics

	Study authors and year, country		
	Jin and others 2007, China	Potterton and others 2010, South Africa	Nair and others 2009, India
Sample and design	100 families with a child younger than 2 years from 7 randomly selected villages. Families randomly allocated to intervention ($n = 50$) or control condition ($n = 50$)	122 HIV-positive children aged less than 30 months randomly assigned to intervention or control groups (institutionalized children excluded)	800 infants (27% preterm, 50% LBW) admitted to special care nursery randomized to intervention or control groups. 665 infants tested at age 1 and 735 at age 2
Intervention	Two 30–60-minute counseling sessions using the WHO "Care for Development" guidelines, one on enrollment and one within 6 months. Mothers were given a card depicting age-specific messages. The card was discussed in the counseling sessions using demonstration and practice of play activities, discussion of obstacles to implementation, and help with problem solving	Caregivers given home stimulation programs individualized for children when they attended for usual clinic visit every 3 months. Structured around daily activities and developmentally appropriate play. Caregivers given a picture book and asked to spend time with child looking at and talking about pictures daily	Control group routine postnatal checkup. Intervention mothers trained individually and in groups to give stimulation and to continue at home. Compliance assessed at monthly home visits for 1 year
Type of trainer	Health professionals conducted counseling. Not clear where counseling was done. Likely that counseling at first visit was done at clinic, second at home	Intervention done by physiotherapist	Training of mothers conducted by occupational therapist. Number of training sessions and duration not given. Unclear whether training also given during home visits or just monitored compliance

(continued next page)

Table 4.3 Studies on Individual Counseling of Mothers at Clinics *(continued)*

	Study authors and year, country		
	Jin and others 2007, China	**Potterton and others 2010, South Africa**	**Nair and others 2009, India**
Impact on child development[a]	Significant benefits at end of 6 months to Gesell quotients in adaptive (*d* = 0.49), language (*d* = 0.52), and social (*d* = 0.17) development. No significant benefits for motor development.	Significant improvement after 12 months in intervention group compared with control in Bayley MDI (*d* = 0.27) and PDI (*d* = 0.19)	Intervention infants had higher Bayley MDI (*d* = 0.38) and PDI (*d* = 0.40) scores. Benefits for VLBW, LBW, and NBW infants.
Comments	Tester not blind to children's group	Severe developmental delay in both groups. Despite improvement in intervention group, children remained severely delayed. Moderate to severe growth retardation. 16% on HAART at baseline, 86% at end of year	Benefits at age 2, half that at end of intervention

Source: Author's compilation.

Note: HAART = highly active antiretroviral treatment; LBW = low birth weight; MDI = mental development index; NBW = normal birth weight; PDI = psychomotor development index; VLBW = very low birth weight; WHO = World Health Organization.

a. Effect size (Cohen's *d*) was calculated using unadjusted posttest values (Thalheimer and Cook 2002) to enable comparison among studies. Calculation of effect size using change, for those studies where information was available, showed effect sizes within the same range (small, medium, large).

intervention details). After one year, significant benefits to mental and motor development were seen from intervention, although both intervention and control groups remained severely delayed. In the other study mothers of high-risk neonates received individual and group training in a hospital in early stimulation, which they were to continue at home (Nair and others 2009). Monthly home visits were made for one year to assess whether mothers were implementing the program; it is unclear whether these visits were also used for further training. Benefits at the end of the intervention year were small to moderate, and one year later the size of the benefits was cut in half, suggesting benefits may not be sustained.

These studies are insufficient to reach conclusions on the benefits of strategies using counseling attached to health services but suggest that the approach has potential and needs further evaluation. In these studies interventions were conducted by health professionals and in two of the three studies were individualized for the mother and child. It is also likely that counseling sessions need to be long enough to allow time for demonstration of activities and for mothers to practice.

Parent Training at Group Sessions

The numbers of parents and children reached by interventions to improve parenting behaviors could also be increased by delivering interventions through group sessions. Again, relatively few evaluations of this approach have been done (table 4.4). In India, mothers and children who attended a village crèche (nursery) were compared with those in a village without a crèche (Sharma and Nagar 2009). At the crèche, age-appropriate toys and play materials and activities to promote development were provided. Information on providing a good home environment such as stimulation, parental involvement, and play materials was given to mothers and discussed. After 18 months a large benefit for motor development was seen; mental development was not reported. It is unclear from the report of the study who was responsible for implementing the crèche, how often mothers and children attended, the duration of the sessions, and the extent of child-directed activities.

In a parenting program in Bangladesh, groups of about 20 mothers attended 90-minute educational sessions on health, nutrition, and promotion of child development (Aboud 2007). Sessions were conducted by women with some secondary education who were given training and supervision. Mothers attended an average of 16 sessions. No benefits were seen for children's receptive vocabulary, which was the only measure of child development, or mother-child verbal interaction. Small-to-moderate effects on mothers' knowledge and stimulation in the home were seen. Within the sessions emphasis was placed on encouraging

Table 4.4 Parent Training at Group Sessions

	Study authors and date, country		
	Aboud 2007, Bangladesh	**Sharma and Nagar 2009, India**	**Peairson and others 2008, Paraguay**
Sample and design	Mothers recruited from 22 villages that had received a parenting intervention in the previous year ($n = 170$) and 22 villages with no intervention ($n = 159$). Children aged 2–3 years during intervention. Post-test comparison of intervention and control	Infants <18 months, 69 infants from intervention village and 76 infants from a control village	Infants 0–24 months. From remote rural areas. 46 no intervention and 60 had participated in Pastoral del Niño. Intervention and no intervention families from same areas but different communities. No significant differences between intervention and no intervention in parental education, employment and income
Intervention	90-minute weekly education sessions to groups of about 20 mothers. Topics included nutrition and health as well as child development. Mothers attended an average of 16 sessions over the year. Emphasis was on positive behaviors, but only 20% were demonstrated and few materials used	Mothers and infants attended crèche in village for 18 months and were given age appropriate toys and activities to enhance development and information on child development and providing a good home environment	Monthly meetings at community centre. Parents encouraged to promote development through play and to converse with child. Intervention also focused on health and nutrition. Attendance at meetings from pregnancy to age 5 years

Type of trainer and supervision	Facilitators had some secondary education and received 17 days' training and a manual of topics. Supervision was done on 4 days/month – not clear what this involved or by whom	No information on how often mothers attended crèche or who conducted the sessions or duration of sessions.	Meetings conducted by volunteer community leaders who served 10–20 families and received training from regional leaders (no details). Volunteers also did home visits but not stated how often. No information on how often mothers attended meetings
Impact on child development[a]	Significant benefits to mothers child-rearing knowledge (effect size $d = 0.31$) and stimulation in the home ($d = 0.34$). No benefits to verbal interaction or child receptive vocabulary	No differences between villages on pre-test. At post-test infants in intervention village had significantly higher Bayley motor score ($d = 1.72$) and HOME score.	Intervention significantly higher Bayley MDI ($d = 0.62$) PDI not done. Significantly higher HOME ($d = 1.16$). Mothers more likely to report setting aside time to teach child ($p = 0.009$) and playing with child daily ($p = 0.051$)
Comments	Benefits to stimulation greater if mothers had at least some education (one year or more)	Bayley MDI not reported. No investigation of any village level differences which may have affected results	No information on why some communities had program and others did not or on community level differences that might affect outcome

Source: Author's compilation.

Note: HAART = highly active antiretroviral treatment; LBW = low birth weight; MDI = mental development index; NBW = normal birth weight; PDI = psychomotor development index; VLBW = very low birth weight; WHO = World Health.

a. Effect size (Cohen's *d*) was calculated using unadjusted posttest values (Thalheimer and Cook 2002) to enable comparison among studies. Calculation of effect size using change, for those studies where information was available, showed effect sizes within the same range (small, medium, large).

positive behaviors and attempts were made to engage the mothers in discussion and problem solving, but use of demonstration was limited and very few materials were used.

A community-based group parenting program in Paraguay, run as an outreach program of the Roman Catholic Church, using volunteer leaders, had significant benefits on children's mental development (Peairson and others 2008). Parents attended monthly meetings at which they were encouraged to promote development by playing and chatting with their children. Volunteers also conducted home visits, but little information is available on what these involved or their frequency.

The conclusions that can be reached from these studies are limited. Again, evidence seems to suggest the need for demonstration and practice, given the lack of child benefits in the Bangladesh program. The choice of trainers may also be important. In the Paraguay study the volunteer leaders were from the same communities, which may have facilitated understanding and rapport with the parents and contributed to program benefits.

In these, and in the individual parenting sessions described in the previous section, mothers' education ranged from an average of two to three years in Bangladesh to five to eight years in Paraguay. About one-third of the mothers in the study in China were described as illiterate, whereas in the South African study about 25 percent of the mothers had completed secondary school. Mothers with limited education, therefore, seem to benefit from these interventions. Only the study by Aboud (2007) specifically examined whether maternal education moderated benefits and found that benefits for stimulation were less in mothers who did not have at least a minimum of exposure to formal education (one year).

Center-Based Strategies

Provision of early childhood stimulation for children less than three years of age at centers has not been a frequent strategy in LAMI countries, where most of the attention for this age group has been on working through parents. However, as increasing numbers of mothers work, and in urban areas do not always have the support of family members, use of informal day care arrangements is likely to increase. Low-income women are unlikely to be able to afford formal day care; therefore, attention to the quality of care provided in these informal settings will be an essential component in ensuring adequate care for young children.

Two large-scale examples of community-based day care from Latin America have been evaluated. In Bolivia, the Proyecto Integral de Desarrollo Infantil (PIDI: Integrated Child Development program) provided care for children aged six months to six years in homes of women within the community. Children were cared for in groups of up to 15 children by two to three caregivers. Caregivers were from a social background similar to that of the children's parents and received training in child development. The goal of the program was to provide an integrated program of health, nutrition, and education. Meals were provided, and caregivers were trained to provide a stimulating environment. The program served poor children mainly in urban areas.

An evaluation of the program used two rounds of survey data collected in 1995–96 and 1997–98 (Behrman, Cheng, and Todd 2004). Comparisons were made with children from areas without the program and with children from areas with the program who had not been enrolled in day care, and these comparisons indicated benefits from the program for motor, language, and psychosocial development. We focus on the results for younger children and on the comparison that used only children enrolled in the program, comparing those who had been enrolled for one month or less with those enrolled for 13–18 months. For children aged 6–24 months, those who had been in the program for 13–18 months had benefits in all areas of development; children aged 25–36 months showed benefits for gross motor but not fine motor development and benefits for language and psychosocial skills. Finally, children aged 37–41 months (who would have been younger than age three for the majority of their time in the program) showed improved psychosocial skills but not significant benefits for motor or language development. The size of the increases in scores ranged from 3 to 10 percent. Based on assumptions of the link between improved cognitive skills and nutrition and adult earnings, the benefit-to-cost ratio of the program was estimated at 1.4–3.7.

The Colombia Programa Hogares Communitarios de Bienestar (Program for Home-Based Community Day Care) uses a similar approach to that of PIDI. Begun in 1987, it targets children up to age six from families in the lowest income groups. Although delivered throughout the country, it has been reported to be best suited for urban areas. Up to 15 children are cared for by a mother from the community and an assistant. Both attend a 40-hour training workshop and are supervised by staff from the Colombia Family Welfare Institute, an agency of the Ministry of Health. Parent associations are also involved in organization and supervision of centers, and parents pay 25–37 percent of a daily minimum wage per month. Children are provided with meals and snacks to provide 50–70 percent of daily requirements, and activities to foster social maturity and development are conducted, such as supervised free play, creative activities, language activities, and a variety of new experiences. In later years, concerns that children under age two were not adequately cared for when mixed with older children led to a similar but separate program for younger children, the Child and Family Care program.

The Colombia program was evaluated in 2007 (Bernal and others 2009), at which time over 61,000 day care centers were serving approximately 780,000 children. We again focus on the results for younger children that compare those exposed to the program for 16 months or more with those enrolled for less than two months. Children aged 36–48 months (the youngest age group evaluated) who had been in the program for at least 16 months had better verbal comprehension and better scores in verbal ability, mathematical reasoning, and general knowledge than those recently enrolled, although no significant differences were seen in overall intellectual ability. Effect sizes were generally small but probably important at the population level. Benefits were also seen for children's social development with better interaction and fewer problems with social isolation in those with greater exposure to the program. However, exposure to the program was associated with higher levels of aggression.

The longer-term benefits of the program were also investigated in children who were eligible for the program from birth to six years of age, comparing 943 children who had participated with 947 nonparticipants by means of their scores on a national test administered in grade 5 of primary school. Controlling for potential confounders such as parental education and home characteristics, children who had been exposed to the program had higher scores. The gain in scores was mainly due to benefits to language.

An integrated program was conducted in the Philippines that included provision of health and nutrition services as well as parent education and home-based day care. Parent education seminars were implemented in all the program areas, and 44 percent had day care compared with none in the nonprogram areas. However, day care was predominantly for children three to five years of age because there was little uptake of the "Day Care Mom" program for those under age three. Although it is not possible to identify the impact of the individual components of the program, among children less than age three at the final survey those with at least 12 months of exposure to the program had better motor, cognitive, language, and socioemotional skills than those with less than four months' exposure (Armecin and others 2006).

Impact of Parental Enrichment on Parenting Knowledge and Behavior

The objective of the parental enrichment programs (and, to a lesser extent, center-based programs, which have outreach for parents or involve them in the running of the centers) is to enhance parents' knowledge of child development and enable them to provide the stimulation and experiences in the home necessary to promote their children's development. These changes in parental behavior are then expected to be part of the mechanism through which the child's development and behavior benefit (for home-visits programs, more direct benefits from the visits themselves may also be seen). Thus, benefits to parental outcomes have also been used as indicators of the success of interventions (table 4.5). Several home-visits interventions have demonstrated benefits for mothers' knowledge (Hamadani and others 2006; Powell 2004; Powell and others 2004; Rahman and others 2008), and, more important, some have shown benefits for the level of stimulation provided in the home (Powell and others 2004; Walker and others 2004), although where measured, this has not always been found (for example, roving caregivers in Jamaica; Powell 2004). Improvements in maternal sensitivity and responsiveness have also been shown (Cooper and others 2009). Parent training using group sessions has also benefited home stimulation, with effects varying from small to large (Aboud 2007; Peairson and others 2008; Sharma and Nagar 2009). Only one study using individual counseling of the mother measured effects on stimulation and showed modest benefits (Ertem and others 2006).

Whether change in parental behavior mediates the benefits for child development from early intervention programs has been examined on only a few occasions. In the intervention with term LBW infants in Jamaica, improvements in the level of stimulation in the home mediated some of the intervention benefits for developmental quotient (DQ; Walker and others 2004); however, recent analysis of the trial with stunted Jamaican children showed that change in home stimulation contributed to a relatively small proportion of intervention benefits for development (unpublished results).

Only three studies were identified that have examined whether changes to parental behavior from early childhood programs are sustained. In one, with follow-up conducted when children were aged 9 to 11, home stimulation and provision of play materials were not different, but mothers in the intervention group provided more school books and had sent the children to preschool earlier (children in the intervention group attended preschool for approximately twice as long as control children; Grantham-McGregor and others 1994). In the study of stunted children, follow-up when children were seven years of age showed no intervention differences in parental behavior (Grantham-McGregor and others 1997); however, at age 11 mothers who participated in the stimulation intervention provided their children with more reading materials but not more toys and games than mothers in nonstimulation groups. They were also more likely to support the child in homework and provide a variety of activities (trips, visits to public library). Among mothers of term LBW infants, no intervention benefits for stimulation were seen at age six years, measured with the Middle Childhood Home Observation for

Table 4.5 Impact of Interventions on Parenting Knowledge and Stimulation

Study	Parenting outcomes
Home visits	
Hamadani and others 2006, Bangladesh[a]	Knowledge of child rearing, $d = 1.02$
Grantham-McGregor and others 1991, Jamaica[a]	Stimulation (HOME), $d = 0.49$
Powell and others 2004, Jamaica[a]	Child-rearing knowledge ($d = 1.25$) and practices ($d = 0.65$)
Powell 2004, Jamaica[a]	Benefits for child-rearing knowledge ($d = 0.64$), no benefits for HOME
Walker and others 2004, Jamaica[a]	Stimulation (HOME), $d = 0.37$
Cooper and others 2009, South Africa Intervention to promote sensitive and responsive parenting. Visits by local women given 4 months of training. Mothers randomized to intervention or control. Intervention comprised 16 visits beginning antenatally to age 5 months. Control routine fortnightly visits to monitor health and growth	Mother-child interactions at 6 and 12 months more sensitive ($d = 0.24, 0.26$) and less intrusive ($d = 0.26, 0.24$)
Rahman and others 2008, Pakistan Cluster randomized trial of "learning through play" program with focus on mother-child interaction. Mothers enrolled in third trimester. Community health workers conducted half-day workshop for groups of about 8 mothers on age 2-month developmental stage. During routine fortnightly visits, spent 15–20 minutes discussing infants' development	At 3 months, knowledge of early infant development increased, $d = 2.23$
Group training	
Sharma and Nagar 2009, India[b]	Stimulation (HOME), $d = 3.51$
Aboud 2007, Bangladesh[b]	Stimulation (HOME) ($d = 0.34$), knowledge ($d = 0.31$), no benefits for verbal interaction
Peairson and others 2008, Paraguay	Significantly higher HOME, $d = 1.16$
Clinic-based counseling	
Ertem and others 2006, Turkey Children aged 24 months or less. Controls provided standard care. Subsequently, after training of pediatricians, intervention group counseled during sick child visits using Care for Development intervention	Stimulation (HOME) 1 month after visit, median scores not different, but greater proportion of intervention group had "optimal" scores (equal to 38 or above)

Source: Author's compilation.

Note: HOME = Home Observation for Measurement of the Environment.

a. See table 4.2 for details.

b. See table 4.4 for details.

Measurement of the Environment (HOME; Walker and others 2010). The limited information available suggests that any long-term benefits to parental behavior may be mainly related to decisions about schooling and provision of support for schooling. It is possible that intervention alters parents' perception of their child's potential, with subsequent changes to decisions related to investments in education. More evidence is needed in this area because this could be a significant additional benefit from early intervention, which would in turn increase the long-term gains for children's educational outcomes.

Evidence for Long-Term Benefits for Child Cognition and Behavior

The studies reviewed in this chapter provide consistent evidence that interventions to provide stimulation and learning opportunities for children from birth to age three through a variety of approaches can be successful in preventing the loss of developmental potential in children from poor families in LAMI countries. The evidence base is strongest for home-visits programs where trained paraprofessionals work with the mother and child. Children who receive early intervention are therefore likely to benefit more from preschool and then from formal schooling. Findings from at least five LAMI countries demonstrate that early cognitive ability predicts school outcomes such as achievement levels and grade level attained (Grantham-McGregor and others 2007). It is therefore reasonable to anticipate that gains in early development will be associated with long-term gains in education to the benefit of both the individual and society.

Medium- and long-term follow-up has been performed for children who received early intervention. In Jamaica, a home-visits program to improve mother-child interaction benefited development of term LBW infants at age two when the intervention ended. Children were reassessed at age six when the majority of them had just started primary school. Significant benefits were seen from the intervention for their performance IQ and memory, and they had significantly fewer behavioral difficulties (Walker and others 2010). No benefits for language were found. The effect sizes for benefits to cognition at age six were moderate and similar to those seen in early childhood and slightly greater (0.58 SD) for behavior. The reduction in behavior difficulties may be particularly important for these children at a time when they are making the transition to primary school.

Sustained benefits in primary-school–aged children were also reported in an evaluation of the Colombian home day care program, where benefits were found for achievement in language (described earlier; Bernal and others 2009), and in an earlier Colombian study home visits up to age three were associated with better reading readiness at age seven in boys only (Super and Herrera 1991).

Two small groups of children, severely malnourished between 6 and 24 months of age, were followed up to late adolescence. One group received stimulation in the hospital followed by home visits to help mothers promote development through play and better interaction. Visits were weekly for two years and then fortnightly for the third year. The stimulation group had higher scores on the Wechsler Intelligence Scales for Children than children who had not had intervention 14 years after they left the hospital (11 years after intervention ended; Grantham-McGregor and others 1994). The effect size was large (0.92 SD) and comparable to that seen when IQ was first measured, two years after intervention ended. The participants who had received stimulation also had higher scores in reading and overall school achievement ($p < 0.1$).

The most comprehensive evidence of long-term benefits from early intervention comes from the Jamaican study of stunted children, aged 9–24 months on enrollment, who participated in a two-year randomized trial of supplementation and/or psychosocial stimulation (for details of the original study and findings, see table 4.2). The children were reassessed at ages 7, 11, and 17 (table 4.6; Grantham-McGregor and others 1997; Walker and others 2000, 2005). Benefits to cognition were seen at each follow-up, whereas benefits in tests of educational achievement started to emerge at age 11 ($p < 0.1$) and were significant for reading at age 17 years. Similarly, behavior differences were not seen when first assessed by teacher and parent report at age 11 (Chang and others 2002), but by age 17 parents reported that the participants had fewer problems with attention and tended to show less oppositional behavior (Walker and others 2006). In addition, participants self-reported fewer symptoms of depression and anxiety and better self-esteem (Walker and others 2006).

The results of this study indicate that early intervention has long-term benefits for IQ, educational achievement, and behavior and supports the hypothesized benefits for long-term outcomes for children who receive early intervention. The size of the benefits for IQ and reading ability suggests that benefits for adult employment are likely. Further, better psychological functioning seen in program participants is likely to benefit functioning in the workplace and within society.

In this Jamaican study, visits were conducted weekly for two years. The program focused on working with mothers to enable them to be more effective in promoting their child's development. Mothers were encouraged to chat with and listen to their children, to use everyday activities to teach concepts, and to integrate play activities into their daily routine. It is likely that this emphasis on reaching the child through the mother contributed to the sustainability of intervention benefits.

Table 4.6 Long-Term Effects of Psychosocial Stimulation: The Jamaica Study

Age at Follow-up (Years)	Outcome		
	Cognition	Education	Behavior
7–8 Grantham-McGregor and others 1997	Benefits for IQ (effect size 0.41 SD) and other cognitive tests not significant individually, but stimulation groups (and supplement only group) had better scores than control group on 13–14 of 15 tests (sign test $p = 0.01$). Significant benefits for perceptual motor function.	No significant benefits for school achievement	Not assessed
11–12 Chang and others 2002 Walker and others 2000	Significant benefits for IQ (effect size 0.52 SD), reasoning ability, and vocabulary compared with control group. No benefits for 2 other language tests and tests of memory and attention	Suggestive of benefits for reading, spelling, and comprehension (all $p < 0.1$) but not mathematics	No benefits for behavior by teacher and parent reports
17–18 Walker and others 2005 Walker and others 2006	Significant benefits to IQ (effect size 0.51 SD) vocabulary (analogies and PPVT) and reasoning ability compared with no stimulation groups (control and supplement only)	Significant benefits for reading and comprehension. No benefits for mathematics. Reduction in school dropout rate.	Significant reduction in participants' reports of symptoms of anxiety and depression, and parents' reports of attention problems. Participants reported higher self-esteem. No effect on antisocial behavior. Less opposi-tional behavior reported by parents ($p = 0.1$).

Source: Author's compilation.

Note: PPVT = Peabody Picture Vocabulary Test; SD = standard deviation.

As is typical for Jamaica, 99 percent of the children in the study (control and intervention) attended preschool, with 91.7 percent attending for at least two years. Thus the sustained benefits are in a context where children who received early intervention went on to center-based early education.

Long-term gains from strategies to promote optimal development in the birth to age three group are likely to be most successful where attention is also placed on ensuring continuing access to learning opportunities.

Linking Early Intervention with Health and Nutrition Programs

Recent reviews have highlighted the importance of nutrition and health issues for ECD in LAMI countries (Walker and others 2007) and have estimated the cost-effectiveness of interventions to address these (Behrman, Alderman, and Hoddinott 2004). Nutrition and health factors that contribute to poor young child development are summarized in table 4.7. These conditions affect large numbers of children in LAMI countries (for example, linear growth retardation in 32 percent of children under age

Table 4.7 Priority Nutrition and Health Risks Affecting Children from Birth to Three Years of Age in LAMI Countries

Risk	Summary of evidence
Linear growth retardation (stunting)	Cohort studies show poor cognitive and social-emotional outcomes. Supplementation trials show benefits for development (one with long-term gains)
Iodine deficiency	Meta-analyses show consistent deficits, and trials show benefits of prenatal and postnatal supplementation
Iron deficiency anemia	Cohort studies show long-term deficits. Preventive supplementation benefits motor, cognitive, and social development
Malaria	Severe malaria is associated with neurological deficits. Frequent uncomplicated attacks and asymptomatic parasitemia may lead to poor cognitive and educational outcomes
Intra-uterine growth restriction	Consistent evidence for lower developmental levels in early childhood
Environmental toxins	Most consistent evidence for lead with deficits beginning at low levels of exposure
Maternal depressive symptoms	Associated with poorer quality parenting and poor developmental outcomes
Exposure to violence	Domestic and community violence affects family functioning and young child outcomes

Source: Adapted from Walker and others 2007.

Note: LAMI = low- and middle-income countries.

five, low birth weight in 16 percent of births; R. E. Black and others 2008). Interventions to reduce the prevalence of nutrition and health risks and to treat affected children are essential for optimal child development. These interventions include promotion of exclusive breast feeding; improved young child nutrition, in particular complementary feeding; iodine fortification programs; prevention of iron deficiency anemia; and early effective treatment of malaria.

Children with health and nutrition risks are also likely to be at risk of inadequate early learning environments. Thus, linking ECD programs with those targeting children identified through nutrition and health programs is likely to be an effective way of ensuring that ECD interventions reach children in greatest need. As reviewed earlier, substantial evidence shows that children with nutrition and health risks benefit from interventions to promote increased stimulation and improve parent-child interaction. Thus, integrated programs are likely to be a cost-effective approach to achieving gains in ECD. Evidence from a meta-analysis of non-U.S. studies also shows that the impact on cognitive and social emotional development was greater when interventions included stimulation compared with interventions comprising only nutrition or financial assistance (Nores and Barnett 2009).

In many countries the health services are the main government service for children under three years of age. Thus, these services, which also provide nutrition programs, offer a potential infrastructure in which to integrate early development programs. A critical need exists for evaluation of strategies within health services to reach high-risk children and to provide more general parenting programs. However, in some countries attendance at health services decreases once the early immunization schedule is complete at 18–24 months. A further challenge is how to reach children after this and before enrollment in center-based early education.

Comparing Strategies and Investments for the Birth to Age Three Group

Early intervention leads to gains in child development with subsequent gains for educational attainment and expected benefits for adult employment. Thus, ensuring that young children have quality caregiver-child interactions and stimulation is likely to reduce inequalities in attainment through benefits for individuals and contribute to national development.

Several approaches have been used to reach the birth to age three group. These have varying impacts and differ in the investments that are required to deliver the programs, as summarized in table 4.8. In moving toward expanding the numbers of children reached, the choice of strategies would need to be based on the likelihood and size of immediate and sustainable

Table 4.8 Benefits and Investments according to Type of Early Intervention Program

Type of program	Evidence for benefits to development	Required investments	Numbers of children reached
Home visits	9 efficacy studies: All showed benefits for development, usually medium to large effect, evidence for long-term gains	Personnel: Paraprofessional home visitors Training and supervision Materials for simple toys and picture books	15–20/visitor if fully assigned to home visits; 4–5/visitor if employed in health sector with other duties
Individual counseling	3 studies: All showed benefits for development, effects small to medium	Personnel: Health professionals conducted counseling in studies reviewed. Unclear whether these could be done by paraprofessionals with training and supervision. Training for counselors Materials: counseling cards, materials for demonstration	Potential to reach large numbers of children, but feasibility not established, and impact of short counseling sessions not demonstrated
Parent training	3 studies: 1 benefit for motor development (mental development not reported), 1 benefit for mental development (motor not reported), 1 benefit for parent knowledge and stimulation, no child benefits	Personnel: Group leaders not professionals but generally with more education (at least some secondary) than home visitors. Training and supervision. Materials for demonstration	15–20 parents/ workshop, number reached depends on how many workshops each parent would need to attend and how many workshops one group leader could conduct per week
Home day care	2 evaluations of large-scale programs: Significant benefits but generally small, 1 showed benefit-cost ratio of 1.4–3.7, 1 showed gains in primary school	Personnel: Day care mothers and assistants; training and supervision. Upgrading of homes to ensure suitable for day care. Meals and play materials	15 children/center

Source: Author's compilation.

benefits and the investments required to achieve these gains. The investments will depend on personnel required and the availability of an existing infrastructure with which early childhood interventions can be integrated.

Personnel to implement the program are in most cases the largest cost, which is influenced by the level of persons required and the numbers of children who can be reached per staff member. These are compared for different approaches with delivery in table 4.8. In addition to staff who will deliver the program, a need is seen for training and supervision. This will require investment of the time of nurses or other health staff if the program is nested within the health service or the hiring of additional personnel.

Choice of strategy will also depend on the existing national and community infrastructure with which ECD programs could be integrated. Integration may require different approaches in urban and rural areas, but successful interventions in rural areas suggest the feasibility of training people within villages (Hamadani and others 2006) or building on community programs (Peairson and others 2008). Several of the interventions evaluated have been implemented as additions to existing programs (Hamadani and others 2006) or have been based within health services (Potterton and others 2009; Powell and Grantham-McGregor 1989), although few have been fully integrated with the existing services (the Philippines integrated ECD program is probably the only example; Armecin and others 2006).

Home Visits

The study by Powell and others (2004) examined the feasibility of training CHWs already employed in health centers to conduct home visits, which would be done in addition to their regular duties. The program was successful, and it was estimated that each CHW could visit about four or five children each week. Thus, the feasibility and sustainability of home-visits programs will be greater where health services already employ CHWs or a similar cadre of workers. Even where this is the case, there is a cost to other services that the CHWs may have provided. Sustainability of programs will require ownership by the health services and acceptance that promotion of ECD is a health sector activity.

Individual Parent Counseling

Evidence suggests that individual counseling of caregivers when they attend health services for regular care can benefit development and that receiving all services at one location is attractive to mothers (Potterton and others 2009). The WHO/UNICEF Care for Development program is intended to be included as a part of the health services for young children. The same issues apply, as for home-visits programs, with regard to ownership by the health sector because health staff will be expected to learn new skills and conduct counseling (5–10 minutes at each visit) in addition to ongoing activities in clinics, which are often overcrowded and where staff have limited time for each patient.

Parent Groups

Training of parents in group sessions has received only limited evaluation but has the potential to reach large numbers of families. Sessions could be linked with community infrastructure, such as community centers and schools. However, further evidence is necessary for benefits for child development and the essential components of training before large-scale expansion of this approach.

Day Care

Home day care centers utilize existing community homes that may require upgrading to be suitable. The programs also require funds to pay the day care mother and provide meals and play materials for the children. Some level of cost sharing with parents may be possible. This type of intervention has been found to be more suited to urban areas where working mothers are less likely to have other family members to rely on for child care. Unlike other strategies, examples are found of large-scale programs that have been shown to benefit child development.

Research Needs for Program Expansion

Making choices for which strategy or a combination of strategies will best serve the needs of families and children in a country or region can begin to be made based on the evidence available. Additional information would facilitate this process (box 4.1). Probably the most urgent is the identification of the modifications to programs that are necessary for scaling up and evaluation of the effect of these changes on program impact. Limited evidence is available on the benefits of improving parenting through individual parent counseling or parent groups. Further evaluations of these approaches and others that can be implemented at scale are urgently needed.

BOX 4.1

Research Needs for Expansion of ECD Programs for Children Less than Three Years Old

- Modification of programs to facilitate large-scale implementation and evaluation of programs at scale.
- Evaluation of health systems to identify any changes needed to ensure capacity to accommodate ECD programs.
- Routine collection within efficacy trials of information needed to inform scaling up.
- Further evidence of sustainability of benefits and factors that influence sustainability.
- Assessment of cost-benefit ratio.

Programs are more likely to be sustainable if they are integrated with an existing infrastructure. This presents challenges where staff employed are expected to conduct additional activities in situations where human resources are already stretched. Understanding of the health system (or other service with which ECD could be integrated) will be essential to determine the barriers to scaling up and identify solutions to facilitate successful integration of ECD. For example, evaluation of the acceptability of Care for Development for health center staff and the fidelity with which it is implemented will be critical to successful expansion.

The conclusions that could be reached from existing research would be greater if information needed to inform scaling up was routinely included. Efforts to encourage researchers to report data, such as qualifications of personnel, training and supervision given, numbers of parents and children reached per staff member, and other materials and supplies needed, would facilitate the evaluation of the cost and feasibility of programs and their potential for scaling up.

Evidence for long-term benefits of intervention comes from relatively few studies, most of which were conducted in Jamaica. Further follow-up studies would enable stronger conclusions on the minimum duration and intensity of intervention necessary for long-term gains. In the Jamaican study of stunted children, benefits in early childhood were large and medium in late adolescence. Additional information is needed on whether the size of impact in early childhood predicts long-term gains.

Although the types of investments needed were summarized in table 4.8, few assessments are available of the ratio of benefits to costs, which would facilitate both advocacy and decision making for programs to be used.

Conclusions

Promoting optimal development among children from birth to three years of age requires attention to nutrition, health, and ensuring quality caregiver-child interaction and stimulation. Early stimulation interventions prevent the loss in developmental potential experienced by large numbers of children in LAMI countries; the evidence for benefits is strongest for strategies that provide parental enrichment through home visits. Sustained benefits for cognitive and psychological functioning and educational achievement have been demonstrated. These are likely to benefit adult earning, functioning in society, and parenting of the next generation and thus promote equity.

A need is seen for agreement on strategies or sets of strategies, based on this evidence and on the investments required, so that consistent recommendations can be given to governments and other agencies. A clear strategy or set of strategies needs to be developed to provide comprehensive ECD programs for children between birth and age three. This is likely to require investment in evaluations of the effectiveness of a variety of approaches to delivery that can be implemented at scale.

A critical need is also seen for continued advocacy for expansion of early stimulation programs for children between birth and age three. Opportunities for integrating stimulation with existing services for children need to be identified, and provision of stimulation needs to be included as part of the core set of services provided for children under three years of age.

References

Aboud, F. E. 2007. "Evaluation of an Early Childhood Parenting Programme in Rural Bangladesh." *Journal of Health Population and Nutrition* 25: 3–13.

Armecin, G., J. R. Behrman, P. Duazo, S. Ghuman, S. Gultiano, E. King, and N. Lee. 2006. "Early Childhood Development through an Integrated Program: Evidence from the Philippines." World Bank Policy Research Working Paper No. 3922. World Bank, Washington, DC.

Behrman, J. R., H. Alderman, and J. Hoddinott. 2004. "Copenhagen Consensus—Challenges and Opportunities: Hunger and Malnutrition." In *Global Crises, Global Solutions,* ed. B. Lomborg. Cambridge: Cambridge University Press.

Behrman, J. R., Y. Cheng, and P. E. Todd. 2004b. "Evaluating Preschool Programs When Length of Exposure to the Program Varies: A Nonparametric Approach." *Review of Economics and Statistics* 86: 108–32.

Bernal, R., C., Fernandez, C. E. Florez, A. Gaviria, P. R. Ocampo, B. Samper, and F. Sanchez. 2009. "Evaluation of the Early Childhood Program Hogares Comunitarios de Bienestar in Colombia (2009–16)." Documentos CEDE, Universidade de los Andes, Bogota, Colombia.

Black, M. M., S. P. Walker, T. D. Wachs, N. Ulkuer, J. M. Gardner, S. Grantham-McGregor, B. Lozoff, P. L. Engle, and M. C. de Mello. 2008. "Policies to Reduce Undernutrition Include Child Development." *Lancet* 371: 454–55.

Black, R. E., L. H. Allen, Z. A. Bhutta, L. E. Caulfield, M. de Onis, M. Ezzati, C. Mathers, and J. Rivera. 2008. "Maternal and Child Undernutrition: Global and Regional Exposures and Health Consequences." *Lancet* 371: 243–60.

Campbell, F. A., C. T. Ramey, E. Pungello, J. Sparling, and S. Miller-Johnson. 2002. "Early Childhood Education: Young Adult Outcomes from the Abcedarian Project." *Applied Developmental Science* 6: 42–57.

Chang, S. M., S. P. Walker, S. Grantham-McGregor, and C. A. Powell. 2002. "Early Childhood Stunting and Later Behaviour and School Achievement." *Journal of Child Psychology and Psychiatry* 43: 775–83.

Cooper, P. J., M. Tomlinson, L. Swartz, M. Landman, C. Molteno, A. Stein, K. McPherson, and L. Murray. 2009. "Improving Quality of Mother-Infant Relationship and Infant Attachment in Socioeconomically Deprived Community in South Africa: Randomised Controlled Trial." *British Medical Journal* 338: b974 doi:10.1136/bmj.b974.

Eckenrode, J., M. Campa, D. W. Luckey, C. R. Henderson, Jr., R. Cole, H. Kitzman, E. Anson, K. Sidora-Arcoleo, J. Powers, and D. Olds. 2010. "Long-Term Effects of Prenatal and Infancy Nurse Home Visitation on the Life Course of Youths: 19-Year Follow-up of a Randomized Trial." *Archives of Pediatric and Adolescent Medicine* 164: 9–15.

EFA Global Monitoring Report Team. 2006. "Worldwide Progress in Early Childhood Care and Education." In *EFA Global Monitoring Report 2007: Strong Foundations*, 117–51. Paris: UNESCO.

Eickmann, S. H., A. C. Lima, M. Q. Guerra, M. C. Lima, P. I. Lira, S. R. Huttly, and A. Ashworth. 2003. "Improved Cognitive and Motor Development in a Community-Based Intervention of Psychosocial Stimulation in Northeast Brazil." *Developmental Medicine and Child Neurology* 45: 536–41.

Engle, P. L., M. M. Black, J. R. Behrman, M. Cabral de Mello, P. J. Gertler, L. Kapiriri, R. Martorell, M. E. Young, and the International Child Development Steering Group. 2007. "Strategies to Avoid the Loss of Developmental Potential in More Than 200 Million Children in the Developing World." *Lancet* 369 (9557): 229–42.

Ertem, I. O., G. Atay, B. E. Bingoler, D. G. Dogan, A. Bayhan, and D. Sarica. 2006. "Promoting Child Development at Sick-Child Visits: A Controlled Trial." *Pediatrics* 118: e124–e131.

Ertem, I. O., G. Atay, D. G. Dogan, A. Bayhan, B. E. Bingoler, C. G. Gok, S. Ozbas, D. Haznedaroglu, and S. Isikli. 2007. "Mothers' Knowledge of Young Child Development in a Developing Country." *Child: Care, Health and Development* 33: 728–37.

Grantham-McGregor, S., Y. B. Cheung, S. Cueto, P. Glewwe, L. Richter, B. Strupp, and International Child Development Steering Group. 2007. "Child Development in Developing Countries: Developmental Potential in the First Five Years for Children in Developing Countries." *Lancet* 369 (9555): 60–70.

Grantham-McGregor, S., C. Powell, S. Walker, S. Chang, and P. Fletcher. 1994. "The Long-Term Follow-up of Severely Malnourished Children Who Participated in an Intervention Program." *Child Development* 65: 428–39.

Grantham-McGregor, S. M., C. A. Powell, S. P. Walker, and J. H. Himes. 1991. "Nutritional Supplementation, Psychosocial Stimulation, and Mental Development of Stunted Children: The Jamaican Study." *Lancet* 338: 1–5.

Grantham-McGregor, S., W. Schofield, and C. Powell. 1987. "Development of Severely Malnourished Children Who Received Psychosocial Stimulation: Six-Year Follow-Up." *Pediatrics* 79: 247–54.

Grantham-McGregor, S. M., S. P. Walker, S. M. Chang, and C. A. Powell. 1997. "Effects of Early Childhood Supplementation with and without Stimulation on Later Development in Stunted Jamaican Children." *American Journal of Clinical Nutrition* 66 (2): 247–543.

Hamadani, J. D., S. N. Huda, F. Khatun, and S. M. Grantham-McGregor. 2006. "Psychosocial Stimulation Improves the Development of Undernourished Children in Rural Bangladesh." *Journal of Nutrition* 136: 2645–52.

Hoddinott, J., J. A. Maluccio, J. R. Behrman, R. Flores, and R. Martorell. 2008. "Effect of a Nutrition Intervention during Early Childhood on Economic Productivity in Guatemalan Adults." *Lancet* 371: 411–16.

Jin, X., Y. Sun, F. Jiang, J. Ma, C. Morgan, and X. Shen. 2007. "'Care for Development'" Intervention in Rural China: A Prospective Follow-up Study." *Journal of Developmental and Behavioral Pediatrics* 28: 213–18.

Lozoff, B., J. Beard, J. Connor, F. Barbara, M. Georgieff, and T. Schallert. 2006. "Long-Lasting Neural and Behavioral Effects of Iron Deficiency in Infancy." *Nutrition Reviews* 64: S34–S43.

Martorell, R., B. L. Horta, L. S. Adair, A. D. Stein, L. Richter, C. H. Fall, S. K. Bhargava, S. K. Biswas, L. Perez, F. C. Barros, and C. G. Victora. 2010. "Weight Gain in the First Two Years of Life Is an Important Predictor of Schooling Outcomes in Pooled Analyses from Five Birth Cohorts from Low- and Middle-Income Countries." *Journal of Nutrition* 140: 348–54.

McCormick, M. C., J. Brooks-Gunn, S. L. Buka, J. Goldman, J. Yu, M. Salganik, D. T. Scott, F. C. Bennett, L. L. Kay, J. C. Bernbaum, C. R. Bauer, C. Martin, E. R. Woods, A. Martin, and P. H. Casey. 2006. "Early Intervention in Low Birth Weight Premature Infants: Results at 18 Years of Age for the Infant Health and Development Program." *Pediatrics* 117: 771–80.

Meeks Gardner, J. S. P. Walker, C. A. Powell, and S. Grantham-McGregor. 2003. "A Randomized Controlled Trial of a Home-Visiting Intervention on Cognition and Behavior in Term Low Birth Weight Infants." *Journal of Pediatrics* 143: 634–39.

Nahar, B., J. D. Hamadani, T. Ahmed, F. Tofail, A. Rahman, S. N. Huda, and S. M. Grantham-McGregor. 2009. "Effects of Psychosocial Stimulation on Growth and Development of Severely Malnourished Children in a Nutrition Unit in Bangladesh." *European Journal of Clinical Nutrition* 63: 725–31.

Nair, M. K., E. Philip, L. Jeyaseelan, B. George, S. Mathews, and K. Padma. 2009. "Effect of Child Development Centre Model Early Stimulation among at Risk Babies—A Randomized Controlled Trial." *Indian Pediatrics* 46: S20–S26.

National Research Council and Institute of Medicine. 2000. *From Neurons to Neighborhoods: The Science of Early Childhood Development.* Washington, DC: National Academy Press.

Nores, M., and W. S. Barnett. 2009. "Benefits of Early Childhood Interventions across the World: (Under) Investing in the Very Young." *Economics of Education Review* 29 (2): 271–82.

Paxson, C., and N. Schady. 2007. "Cognitive Development among Young Children in Ecuador: The Roles of Wealth, Health, and Parenting." *Journal of Human Resources* 42 (1): 49–84.

Peairson, S., A. M. Berghout Austin, C. Nielsen de Aquino, and E. Urbieta de Burro. 2008. "Cognitive Development and Home Environment of Rural Paraguayan Infants and Toddlers Participating in Pastoral Del Niño, an Early Child Development Program." *Journal of Research in Childhood Education* 22: 343–62.

Potterton, J., A. Stewart, P. Cooper, and P. Becker. 2010. "The Effect of a Basic Home Stimulation Programme on the Development of Young Children Infected with HIV." *Developmental Medicine and Child Neurology* 52 (6): 547–51.

Powell, C. 2004. "An Evaluation of the Roving Caregivers Programme of the Rural Family Support Organization, May Pen, Clarendon, Jamaica." UNICEF, Kingston, Jamaica.

Powell, C., H. Baker-Henningham, S. Walker, J. Gernay, and S. Grantham-McGregor. 2004. "Feasibility of Integrating Early Stimulation into Primary Care for Undernourished Jamaican Children: Cluster Randomised Controlled Trial." *British Medical Journal* 329: 89–92.

Powell, C., and S. Grantham-McGregor. 1989. "Home Visiting of Varying Frequency and Child Development." *Pediatrics* 84: 157–64.

Rahman, A., Z. Iqbal, C. Roberts, and N. Husain. 2008. "Cluster Randomized Trial of a Parent-Based Intervention to Support Early Development of Children in a Low-Income Country." *Child: Care, Health and Development* 35: 56–62.

Reynolds, A. J., J. A. Temple, S. R. Ou, D. L. Robertson, J. P. Mersky, J. W. Topitzes, and M. D. Niles. 2007. "Effects of a School-Based, Early Childhood Intervention on Adult Health and Well-being: A 19-Year Follow-up of Low-Income Families." *Archives of Pediatric and Adolescent Medicine* 161: 730–39.

Schweinhart, L. J., J. Montie, Z. Xiang, W. S. Barnett, C. R. Belfield, and M. Nores. 2005. *Lifetime Effects: The High/Scope Perry Preschool Study through Age 40. Monographs of the High/Scope Educational Research Foundation* 14. Ypsilanti, MI: High/Scope Press.

Sharma, S., and S. Nagar. 2009. "Influence of Home Environment on Psychomotor Development of Infants in Kangra District of Himachal Pradesh." *Journal of Social Science* 21: 225–29.

Super, C., and M. G. Herrera. 1991. "Cognitive Outcomes of Early Nutritional Intervention in the Bogota Study." Conference abstract, Society for Research in Child Development.

Thalheimer, W., and S. Cook. 2002. "How to Calculate Effect Sizes from Published Research Articles: A Simplified Methodology." http://www.docstoc.com/docs/47860289/How-to-calculate-effect-sizes-from-published-research-A-simplified-methodology.

Thompson, R. A., and C. A. Nelson. 2001. "Developmental Science and the Media. Early Brain Development." *American Psychologist* 56: 5–15.

Victora, C. G., L. Adair, C. Fall, P. C. Hallal, R. Martorell, L. Richter, and H. S. Sachdev. 2008. "Maternal and Child Undernutrition: Consequences for Adult Health and Human Capital." *Lancet* 371: 340–57.

Walker, S. P., S. M. Chang, C. A. Powell, and S. M. Grantham-McGregor. 2004. "Psychosocial Intervention Improves the Development of Term Low-Birth-Weight Infants." *Journal of Nutrition* 134 (6): 1417–23.

———. 2005. "Effects of Early Childhood Psychosocial Stimulation and Nutritional Supplementation on Cognition and Education in Growth-Stunted Jamaican Children: Prospective Cohort Study." *Lancet* 366: 1804–7.

Walker, S. P., S. M. Chang, C. A. Powell, E. Simonoff, and S. M. Grantham-McGregor. 2006. "Effects of Psychosocial Stimulation and Dietary Supplementation in Early Childhood on Psychosocial Functioning in Late Adolescence: Follow-up of Randomised Controlled Trial." *British Medical Journal* 333: 472–74.

Walker, S. P., S. M. Chang, N. Younger, and S. M. Grantham-McGregor. 2010. "The Effect of Psychosocial Stimulation on Cognition and Behaviour at 6 Years in a Cohort of Term, Low-Birthweight Jamaican Children." *Developmental Medicine & Child Neurology* 52: E148–E154.

Walker, S. P., S. M. Grantham-McGregor, C. A. Powell, and S. M. Chang. 2000. "Effects of Growth Restriction in Early Childhood on Growth, IQ, and Cognition at Age 11 to 12 Years and the Benefits of Nutritional Supplementation and Psychosocial Stimulation." *Journal of Pediatrics* 137: 36–41.

Walker, S. P., T. D. Wachs, J. M. Gardner, B. Lozoff, G. A. Wasserman, E. Pollitt, and J. A. Carter. 2007. "Child Development: Risk Factors for Adverse Outcomes in Developing Countries." *Lancet* 369 (9556): 145–57.

5

The Convergence of Equity and Efficiency in ECD Programs

Harold Alderman and Emiliana Vegas

There are numerous examples of the limited impact of years of schooling on learning (see Glewwe and Kremer 2006; Hanushek and Woessmann 2008). Often these studies conclude that the school system, including teachers, comes up short in preparing students with the skills needed to succeed. Without exonerating schools and teachers, it can *also* be the case that the students, or a subset of them, come to schools with enormous disadvantages that could be offset through interventions in early childhood. One illustration of this possibility is provided in a study by Filmer and Schady (2009), which found that a scholarship program for lower secondary schools in Cambodia revealed no evidence that recipient children did any better on mathematics and vocabulary tests, despite an increase in enrollment and attendance of approximately 25 percentage points. The tests were administered 18 months after the program's implementation, and so it is unlikely that the absence of a response reflects a premature assessment of a cumulative result (King and Behrman 2009). Moreover, the data provide no support to the possibility that overcrowding of classrooms accounts for the absence of a learning response. More likely, the results reflect the fact that by lowering the cost of schooling, the intervention induced students with lower-than-average expected economic returns to schooling to enroll.

This point is more general. As illustrated in figure 5.1, in many school systems, a large proportion of children do not even reach basic literacy until well into their primary school years, if ever. For example, 60 percent of Malian youth are not able to read a simple sentence until their sixth year of schooling. In three of the four countries illustrated, half the children have not reached this minimum competence until their fourth year of classes. Similarly, more children in a sample of children who had completed third grade in the Punjab of Pakistan could not add or subtract than could perform these basic math skills (Andrabi and others 2007). Clearly this indicates wasted resources as well as a likely contribution to early dropout rates of discouraged children.

These examples provide an entry to the theme of this chapter. Clearly, the absence of a tangible learning outcome implies an inefficient education investment. Moreover, although Filmer and Schady (2009) studied only lower-income students who were eligible for a scholarship, and, thus, they could not assess learning of children from prosperous families who enroll at the margin in response to other inducements, the results reported

Figure 5.1 Proportion of 15- to 19-Year-Olds Who Can Read a Simple Sentence, by Highest Grade Completed

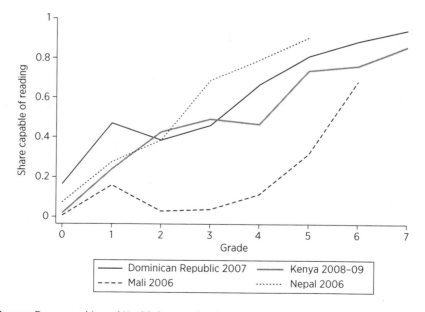

Source: Demographic and Health Surveys for the respective countries and years.

by Naudeau and colleagues in chapter 1 point to the possibility that cognitive capacity and income are correlated by the time a child reaches school age.

To the degree that this is the case, attempts to address the demand gap in access to and quality of primary or secondary schooling with programs such as conditional transfer programs will be hindered by the absence of effective interventions to preempt the loss of potential before preschool. This is consistent with theoretical expectations on the demand for schooling that, as is standard, presume that an unconstrained household will set marginal expected benefits from schooling to equal the costs. Phrased as such, however, the cognitive capacity perspective provides an additional dimension to the often debated and difficult-to-measure question of the relative returns to investing in demand-side interventions compared with supply-side approaches (Orazem, Glewwe, and Patrinos 2009). Although improving the quality of schools and teachers can be expected to have an impact on the demand for education, as will, in other circumstances, addressing imperfect information and credit markets, this chapter argues that a third and complementary approach to improving schooling outcomes is through improving the learning potential of students before they enroll in the first year of formal schooling.

The argument is presented, first, by briefly introducing a model of school outcomes that includes both the quality of schooling and the abilities of the child. These abilities may include those that are malleable as well as those that are less amenable to parental decisions or public interventions. Then this chapter discusses the link between the demand for basic schooling and the likely vulnerability of children before entering primary school. The discussion includes salient points in the literature on the relation of income to the demand for education. This is followed by a look at how nutrition may influence school readiness, and the following sections review how preschool programs may have a similar preparatory role for primary and subsequent education and the placement and demand for preschool programs. The final section concludes.

How Might Early Childhood Development Influence the Demand for Education and Student Quality?

The economic benefits of education are usually measured in terms of adult outcomes. These are often specified in earning functions or wage equations, although it is generally accepted that nonpecuniary benefits including improved health, reduced fertility, stronger citizenship, and an improved ability to care for children are also outcomes of educational investments. In the most basic models, wages or similar outcomes are considered functions of years of schooling (S). As Hanushek and Woessmann (2008) discuss in their review, a key empirical question is how to distinguish the impact of schooling itself from ability, either by including measures of ability (A) or by comparing siblings as well as using similar econometric approaches. Ability can be measured in many ways and can include noncognitive and cognitive skills. The noncognitive skills include a range of socioemotional behavioral factors such as conduct, motivation, persistence, team work, and attitudes toward risk. Equation 5.1 summarizes this simple relation, indicating that wages increase proportionally as a function of years of school as well as ability:

$$\ln(\text{Wages}) = f[\,S,\,A\,]. \tag{5.1}$$

Taking this one step further, it is useful to consider learning per se (L) as distinct from schooling and to add various schooling inputs (I) that increase learning to the basic model:[1]

$$\ln(\text{Wages}) = f[\,S(A,\,I),\,L(A,\,I),\,A\,]. \tag{5.2}$$

Expressed in words, equation (5.2) states the same dependence of wages on ability and years of schooling as equation (5.1) but also indicates that both years of school completed and learning are themselves dependent on the ability of the student as well as the inputs into the teaching process. It also emphasizes that ability affects earnings not only through learning but also through a range of behaviors and preferences that influence personality (Cunha and Heckman 2009).

Hanushek and Woessmann (2008) make two empirical observations that are relevant to this chapter. First, they report that the measured impact of years of schooling declines appreciably when learning is included in an estimate of wages at the individual level; in cross-country regressions of gross national product and schooling, measures of learning pick up virtually all the total impact of years of schooling. Second, ability affects both years of schooling and what is learned in school. Indeed, Heckman and Vytlacil (2001) maintain that it is not possible, over a wide range of variation in schooling and ability, to estimate the separate impacts of years of schooling obtained and that of ability in wage estimates.

The majority of models and of attempts to estimate the impact of ability, however, take ability as exogenous. To address the question of early childhood development (ECD), however, one needs a multiperiod model in which investments made in period 1 (preschool) affect the learning that occurs in school in period 2. Most of the returns to education accrue in a third period, postschool.[2]

Such a multiperiod model can be used to investigate the impact of programs in the initial period (E_1) and household characteristics (X_1) on ability before entrance into school. As expressed in equation (5.3), ability is assumed to respond to these programs:

$$\delta A_1/\delta X_1 > 0 \text{ and } \delta A_1/\delta E_1 > 0. \tag{5.3}$$

Furthermore, household characteristics are generally defined such that ability increases in response to these characteristics. For numerous practical applications, ability may be assessed in terms of school readiness, although this is not always how ability is defined.

A multiperiod approach is also needed to study whether outcomes in the initial period influence the amount of learning in school, as well as any tendency to drop out early. Equation (5.4) shows this relation of learning and skills to ability in the initial period:

$$\delta L_2/\delta A_1 > 0 \text{ and } \delta S_2/\delta A_1 > 0. \tag{5.4}$$

If positive, as illustrated here, equation (5.4) implies that gaps in skills widen over time. Moderately sized delays in school readiness, then, would lead to major differences in school outcomes over the years of primary and secondary education and would be consistent with what Cunha and Heckman (2009) call self-productivity.

Moreover, a multiperiod model of schooling could be used to determine if programs in primary and secondary schools offset initial cognitive development delays or, alternatively, whether the children entering school with higher ability benefit more from the quality of the school: That is, how does the contribution of different investments in education depend on the ability of the student? This is shown in equation (5.5), which measures whether the impact of an investment in the second period is higher for more able students:

$$\delta_2 L_2/\delta I_2 \delta A_1 > 0 \text{ and } \delta_2 S_2/\delta I_2 \delta A_1 > 0. \tag{5.5}$$

If the relationships in equation (5.5) are positive, as shown here, then investments in a later period have a larger return for higher-ability students than for children with lower ability. Cunha and Heckman (2009) refer to this as dynamic complementarity. As economic efficiency implies larger investments where the returns are highest, complementarity implies allocating more resources to the higher-performing students.

Moreover, if ability is itself responsive to earlier investments, then earlier investments increase the return to later ones, through self-productivity. However, whether dynamic complementarity will magnify inequality is an empirical question. Conceptually, there may also be inputs in schooling that substitute for early child investments and, thus, compensate for limited amounts of inputs earlier. Indeed, researchers have found positive impacts of compensatory interventions in primary education in Latin American countries (see, for example, McEwan 2008; Shapiro and Trevino 2004).

In such a case, equation (5.5) will imply that as ability increases, the returns to some current inputs are actually smaller than they are for lower-ability students, and the relationship in the equation would be negative.

Thus, under quite plausible assumptions and in keeping with much of the current evidence, complementarity and self-productivity imply that early investments can address both equity and efficiency: that is, if programs are effective at addressing the loss of potential that occurs early in childhood, these programs may both increase the returns to schooling and deliver most of the benefits to households with lower-than-average endowments. If, however, these investments are neglected and ability gaps occur in early childhood, then investments in schooling will generally involve a trade-off between equity and efficiency. With early gaps in ability, complementarity and self-productivity imply that the most productive investments in schools will be aimed at the higher-ability students; addressing the needs of the students with lower ability will lower average returns.

Any estimation of the impact of endogenous ability on either schooling outcomes in period two or outcomes for adults in period 3 (for example, wages) must confront the challenge of identifying the inputs in the separate stages. For example, it is clearly difficult to separate causes of malnutrition and early cognitive impairment from other causes of poor basic schooling that will also affect lifetime productivity; stimulation of preschoolers and subsequent educational attainments *both* reflect household decisions regarding investments in children. Generally, to control for such behavioral determinants it is necessary that the data from earlier periods of heightened vulnerability contain information on programs that are not correlated with subsequent household schooling choices yet have a measurable influence on early cognitive development. Alternatively, such identification requires economic- or weather-related shocks in the initial period that are of sufficient magnitude and persistence to affect a child's development yet are sufficiently transitory *not* to affect subsequent schooling decisions directly.

Although randomized experiments can provide the identification for specific interventions,[3] the data requirements are intimidating. Moreover, in many cases one is interested in understanding a finer breakdown than the three-period model mentioned above. For example, one might want to distinguish whether a preschool program for children four and five years of age can compensate for cognitive development delays in a child during the first three years of life. Whether or not this compensation occurs, it is then important to indicate how such preschool programs prepare a child for later schooling. Although the value of such a research program is readily apparent, its execution is stymied by the fact that analyses of preschool-aged populations are often unable to follow children through their school years, never mind into long-term (adult) outcomes. Conversely, adult attainments usually have limited data on childhood conditions.

Thus, the development of the knowledge base on long-term outcomes of ECD interventions is still in its early stages. However, an increasing body of research is explaining how gaps in skills manifest in different settings (as summarized in equation [5.3]). Evidence for how much ability, widely defined, responds to specific programs as well as to household characteristics is discussed in Naudeau and colleagues (chapter 1) and Walker (chapter 4). Less evidence is at hand for self-productivity and complementarity. The latter is a particular focus of this chapter, which explores the role of preschool programs in low-income settings.

A few relatively small studies carry a large weight in the literature, with developed countries dominating the evidence. Most noteworthy are the studies of programs in the United States reviewed and elaborated upon in Cunha and others (2006). This literature attempts to delineate the age patterns of skills formation and responses to interventions. Research from psychology and neurology indicates that critical periods of formation exist very early in a child's life.[4] For some skills, the window of opportunity for full development is in the first three years of life (Shaklee and Fletcher 2002; Shonkoff and Phillips 2000); other abilities, including noncognitive skills, may be relatively malleable later in an individual's life (Cunha and Heckman 2009). One key stylized fact from this literature is the observation that income matters in the sense that children are not able to purchase a favorable family environment but, further, that it is possible to partially compensate for adverse family conditions (Cunha and others 2006). However, the later the remediation, the less effective it is.

Nevertheless, although this knowledge base is building upon interdisciplinary foundations, its application to a wide range of social and economic settings is still problematic. Recent reviews have increased the understanding of early interventions in low-income (Engle and others 2007) and middle-income (Vegas and Santibáñez 2010) settings, but the data and analytical challenges remain daunting. For example, relatively few full-scale programs reveal both what works in a systematic manner and what it might cost to achieve such results. Of course, costs matter in two related ways.

First, the relative efficiency of investments in early interventions depends not only on the responsiveness of the child to an intervention—that is, the magnitude of equation (5.3)—but also on the cost of providing the necessary inputs. For example, although the longitudinal study of the Perry preschool program in the United States has contributed greatly to our understanding that the returns to human capital investments decline with the age of the individual, that program cost $9,785 in 2004 dollars per child per year (Cunha and others 2006).

Second, even with a favorable benefit-to-cost ratio, the fiscal envelope for a country may make a full-scale investment problematic. This is illustrated by the experience of Bolivia's Proyecto Integral de Desarrollo

Infantil (PIDI; Integrated Project of Child Development). That program was found to have a benefit-to-cost ratio between 1.7 and 3.7 (Behrman, Cheng, and Todd 2004). The program, however, was discontinued earlier than planned and a portion of the World Bank credit returned unspent. Although a few institutional reasons contributed to this decision, fiscal concerns also played a role. At the time of the evaluation, the cost of the PIDI program was approximately $43 per month per child for a combination of full-time day care, nutritional inputs, and systematic learning environments for low-income children aged 6–72 months. Although this was clearly less than the cost for the Perry program, these costs were incurred at a time when the country's annual gross domestic product per capita was approximately $800.

How Do Initial Household Resources Influence the Benefits of Subsequent Schooling? The Role of Income

Numerous studies have looked at the demand for education. For example, Behrman and Knowles (1999) review 42 studies and find only a modest relation of income and schooling attainment, but they also maintain that many of the results reported in the literature likely underestimate the association of income and schooling.[5] Behrman and Knowles also point out that on theoretical grounds demand for education is not necessarily expected to be determined by income. They review the conditions under which one might expect the demand for education to be neutral with respect to income. As is often the case, these conditions include the assumption that markets—in particular, markets for credit—function perfectly. Additionally, for there to be no income gradient in demand, it is generally assumed that prices and quality do not differ by wealth. However, such an income gradient in prices or quality might be present if policies lead to better schools in more wealthy neighborhoods. It is also assumed that access to information is costless or otherwise distributed so that wealth is not a factor in its dissemination. If these assumptions do not hold (and several empirical studies suggest they do not), an income gradient may be present in investments in schooling even if the benefits of schooling are uncorrelated with income.

Additionally, in general it is assumed that for schooling to be uncorrelated with income it should be a pure investment: that is, if a current consumption element is influencing the demand for education, then the demand for schooling will resemble the demand for any other component of household utility rather than a pure investment. Many other reasons explain, however, why the pure investment returns to schooling would differ by household wealth that reflects neither the price of schooling nor the utility derived directly. In particular, if the actual average returns from schooling are correlated with income, then demand will reflect these differences. This takes the discussion back to the likelihood that the knowledge obtained in school (hence the economic returns) differs according to the ability of the student and, furthermore, that an income gradient is found in capacity to benefit from school that occurs before primary school. Taken together, these features will result in lower expected returns to schooling for children in settings where cognitive capacity is also low. This will be manifest in a lower demand for schooling in these settings.

Indeed, a comparison of scores from the Programme for International Student Assessment for 14 countries indicates the poorest quintile of students in each country scored lower than the wealthiest quintile of students (World Bank 2006). Only 15-year-old students participate in this assessment. Because many students drop out of school before age 15, the results may reflect a selection bias over the full population. However, this would not introduce a bias among the test takers. Thus, the difference across income groups does not reflect differences in ability that lead to dropping out at an earlier age. Instead, under the assumption that there is an income gradient in school dropout rates in many of the countries studied (though some countries successfully enforce mandatory schooling), these scores are likely to underestimate the achievement gap.

The proposition that household inputs might complement the resources provided by a school is not controversial, although it is hard to isolate the effects of household wealth on schooling. Suppose that more able parents both earn more and have children that inherit their ability; then, on average, children from wealthier households will do better in school. In this case, however, it is innate ability per se, and not wealth, that accounts for the higher returns from schooling and, ultimately, more schooling demand. If, however, a portion of the impact of wealth on schooling is through an input that is purchased rather than inherited, then one would like to identify the input and provide it—or a close substitute—to lower-income students.

What inputs that may be purchased influence the returns from schooling? Can certain interventions affect what has been traditionally considered as inherited ability? Clearly interventions in early childhood, including nutrition, cognitive stimulation, and preschool education, can preempt the cognitive delays experienced on average by children born into socioeconomically disadvantaged households (Engle and others 2010). However, before elaborating on a range of such interventions, it is worthwhile to discuss one alternative to preventing such delays: the possibility of offsetting them within the formal primary and secondary school system. In other words, if, instead of self-productivity, convergence is observed or if there are substitutes for preschool ability instead of dynamic complementarity, then the decision whether to invest early or later is a different economic argument than if the preschool period is critical.

Are differences in cognitive development between children of wealthy and poor households at the time of preschool entry sustained throughout the school years and beyond? Empirical research suggests that providing extra resources to schools enrolling disadvantaged students can help compensate for students' early disadvantages (Cook and Evans 2000; McEwan 2008). Compensatory education programs that provide extra resources, such as materials, infrastructure, grants, teacher training, or pedagogical support, to schools enrolling disadvantaged children do exist. In the United States, programs such as Chapter 1 of the Elementary and Secondary Education Act of 1965 and Head Start, a preschool program targeted to socioeconomically disadvantaged children, have provided resources to disadvantaged students early in their school careers. Although evaluations of Chapter 1 programs showed immediate improvement in student test scores, the effects lasted only a year. In the case of Head Start, students showed noticeable improvement in test scores and dropout and repetition rates, but again, the effects dissipated by the third grade, and Head Start students were no more likely than other students to complete high school. These findings suggest that compensatory programs such as Head Start may need to stay in place for longer periods to produce long-term effects (Shapiro and Trevino 2004).

Evidence from Latin America also indicates that compensatory programs and extended school days can improve student learning, reducing failure, repetition, and dropout rates and are especially effective for indigenous students. Compensatory programs provide targeted resources, such as didactic materials, small grants, or special support to teachers, to poor or struggling schools. Mexico's Consejo Nacional de Fomento Educativo (CONAFE; National Council of Education Promotion) provides extra resources to disadvantaged schools and supports rural secondary students in *telesecundaria* (distance learning) education. Shapiro and Trevino's (2004) evaluation of the CONAFE program and its impact on student test scores shows that the program is most effective in improving primary school math learning and secondary school Spanish learning. In Chile, indigenous students obtain lower test scores, on average, than nonindigenous students. McEwan (2008) studied the changes in the test score gap between two cohorts of Chilean eighth graders in the late 1990s and found that the gap declined by 0.1 to 0.2 standard deviation. His analysis suggests that the most plausible explanation is related to Chile's large-scale school reforms that were targeted at low-achieving schools and students. Mexico's CONAFE program and Chile's school reforms both appear to have had positive effects on indigenous student learning. Because schools appear to play the largest role in the test score gap between indigenous and nonindigenous children, it is no surprise that school-based compensatory programs would help to reduce this gap. To the degree that this is the case, the preschool period is sensitive but not the only means to close ability gaps. However, it remains likely that the costs of compensatory programs—when they can be found— exceed those for preschool programs.

In general, moreover, economists and education specialists have found isolating the inputs that contribute to learning in school to be challenging. Banerjee and others (2007) suggest that one reason for this is that the effectiveness of inputs depends on the background of the student. For example, Glewwe, Kremer, and Moulin (2009) observe that the provision of textbooks in rural Kenya did not raise scores on average, although this intervention did have a favorable impact for those students with the highest initial test scores. This, then, is consistent with dynamic complementarity, which exacerbates initial inequality of skills.

In contrast, Banerjee and others (2007) find that specific remedial interventions aimed at children scoring lowest in basic skills can close performance gaps. Their examples of tutoring by community-based instructors and of computer-assisted training in India, then, provide relatively unique examples of programs at the primary level that substitute for earlier inputs into learning. Moreover, these examples appear inexpensive. The data are not yet sufficient to assess whether such programs are cost-effective relative to preschool programs. Indeed, given the novelty of this particular finding, the evidence can more likely be considered a second-chance approach rather than a preferred strategy.

To summarize the main points of this section: Although theory posits that investments in schooling may be neutral to income, the assumptions required for this to hold are unlikely to prevail. One key issue is that the returns to schooling may differ by income as reflected in equation (5.4); as verified by the evidence in chapter 1, ability or preschool readiness differs appreciably by asset levels. Thus, one explanation for differences in demand for schooling by income is the lagged effect of differences in ECD. Therefore, in the absence of effective preschool programs or a wide range of inputs in primary school that would offset this absence or both, schooling achievement will track a child's initial environment.

How Do Initial Household Resources Influence the Benefits of Subsequent Schooling? The Role of Nutrition

With a few notable exceptions, the evidence for the contribution of child nutrition on economic productivity as mediated through cognitive capacity is based on indirect inferences, albeit with fair consistency and regularity of these results. For example, extensive evidence exists that nutrition affects cognitive capacity of children as well as little doubt that cognitive (and noncognitive) ability contributes to school performance, and through this channel, one can infer the impact of nutrition on wages.[6]

The understanding of the role of health on schooling has been bolstered by a growing body of longitudinal studies that confirm the hypothesis that nutritional shocks in early childhood affect subsequent schooling. This section briefly discusses some of this evidence that relates nutritional status of young children to school outcomes later in life. For example, during droughts in Zimbabwe in 1982–83 and 1983–84, infants less than two years old—the period a child is most vulnerable to heath shocks—had higher undernutrition (or stunting rates) attributable to the deficient rainfall. By 2000, these children had completed fewer grades of school. In this case, the economic costs of childhood stunting were estimated as a 14 percent reduction in lifetime earnings (Alderman, Hoddinott, and Kinsey 2006). Similar results have been reported from droughts in Tanzania (Alderman, Hoogeveen, and Rossi 2009) and from changes in health policy in South Africa (Yamauchi 2008).

Families may use assessments of children's cognitive capacity when determining whether to start or continue investing in schooling (Akresh and others 2010). Such schooling decisions may be mediated, in part, by schools or caregivers using the child's size as a marker for school readiness. Additionally, or alternatively, a child's stature relative to his or her age may be an observable (both to the researcher and to the household) indicator of cognitive capacity. However, even longitudinal studies indicating the impact of early childhood malnutrition stemming from economic and weather shocks on subsequent schooling do not directly address the question of whether nutrition interventions delivered to a broader population outside a short-term crisis situation will have a similar favorable impact on cognitive capacity and schooling. Many subtle differences are found in the range of impacts of malnutrition, in regard to both the nature and timing of nutritional shocks; for example, the trimester in which a pregnant woman is affected by a nutrient deficiency will influence the consequences for the child when he or she is an adult. Thus, inferences about malnutrition stemming from one of many possible causal pathways are only partial predictors of the impact on cognitive development of different interventions aimed at improving a child's nutritional status.[7] A pair of studies followed children who received nutritional supplements as children to adulthood and followed a randomly selected control group for a quarter century (Hoddinott and others 2008; Maluccio and others 2009). The studies provide some verification that the indirect inferences of the impact of nutrition on schooling and earnings based on economic and weather shocks are not misleading in regard to potential programmatic impacts. When the treated individuals were between 25 and 42 years old, both women and men had higher scores on cognitive tests than did their peers in the control group. Moreover, those men who had received the supplements before the age of three earned on average 44 percent higher wages. This is on the higher end of the range derived indirectly or from studies that compare twins with different birth weights. A significant increase of wages for women in this cohort was not seen—perhaps because of limited wage opportunities in the communities— but increases in schooling attainment for women were identified.

Field, Robles, and Torero (2009) provide another study that confirms that predictions based on inference going from nutrition to schooling via an intermediate result on the correlates of cognitive capacity are borne out in tracking studies. A number of cross-sectional studies have shown that iodine deficiency can affect brain development. For example, a meta-analysis indicates that individuals with an iodine deficiency had, on average, IQs that were 13.5 points lower than comparison groups (Grantham-McGregor, Fernald, and Sethuraman 1999). Consistent with this evidence, Field, Robles, and Torero (2009) show that a decade and a half after mothers in Tanzania received iodine supplementation their children had, on average, 0.35–0.56 years of additional schooling, and the impact was greater for girls. Although this study was not a randomized experiment, the authors constructed a counterfactual by comparing sibling and age cohorts in the context of a rollout of a discrete program. This study provides evidence of inputs in the first early childhood period that increase school investments and presumably (though not measured in the cited paper) learning. It also is relevant to the distinction of periods that are critical or sensitive for inputs. To summarize, newly available data confirm that malnutrition stemming from both chronic poverty as well as acute crises can have serious implications for subsequent schooling. This is regularly shown in cross-sectional studies, only a few of which have been referenced here. Thus, investments in nutrition can have major economic returns, even in environments in which improvements in health care reduce the worrisome link between malnutrition and the risk of child mortality.

How Do Initial Household Investments Condition the Benefits of Subsequent Schooling? The Role of Early Childhood Education Programs

The research discussed above and in chapter 1 has shown that the cognitive development pathways of children differ by household income and nutrition. Elsewhere in this volume, Walker (chapter 4) discusses how few programs have managed to prevent a growing gap in cognitive potential in the first few years of life. Moreover, this chapter references limited evidence that targeted programs in school can partially offset this gap. However, a key question for this study is the extent to which educational interventions in the years immediately *before* primary school entry can help reduce these gaps so that socioeconomically advantaged and disadvantaged children have equal opportunity to reap the returns from schooling. The evidence base for this includes numerous studies of the long-term benefits of preschool programs aimed at disadvantaged children, albeit generally from developed countries. For example, Chetty and others (2010) tracked a cohort of children who were randomized to different preschool (kindergarten) classrooms and concluded that they benefited from smaller classes and more experienced teachers. Although grades improved according to the quality of the program when tested in early years, this gain attenuated over time. However, earnings, home ownership, and similar outcomes at age 27 were strongly related to these initial test scores. The authors conclude that the higher earnings associated with early school quality reflect changes in social and emotional behavior, changes that economists often refer to as improved noncognitive skills.

The phenomenon reported in Chetty and others (2010) that early education programs lead to improved scores on tests designed to measure cognitive development that last for only a few years is commonly observed and contributes to the emphasis on noncognitive skills. Even with such attenuation, however, because learning is cumulative—that is, it is a product of time and ability integrated over time—even a temporary gain in cognitive ability will lead to increased learning. Plausibly, the gap in reading illustrated in figure 5.1 would be smaller, even with a short-term boost in cognitive capacity.

Looking at a younger cohort, Currie and Thomas (2000) found that children who participated in Head Start did better later in school than their siblings who did not benefit from the preschool intervention. Deming (2009) as well as Carneiro and Ginha (2009) replicated the Currie and Thomas study using more recent data for the same children. Employing different identification strategies, the two recent studies found positive effects of the preschool intervention on outcomes measured during the adolescence years (Almond and Currie 2010).

Less is known, however, about broad-based preschool programs in middle- and low-income settings. In part, this reflects the difficulty in identification of the impact of program specifics from the impact of self-selection. For example, comparisons of subsequent school achievement for those who went to preschool with those who did not often merely show that if a family values education—reflecting unobserved household characteristics—subsequent school performance generally improves.[8]

Recent papers from Latin America address the problem of self-selection by comparing cohorts of children during periods of expansion of services. For example, Berlinski, Galiani, and Manacorda (2008) use the fact that as Uruguay expanded its preschool provision, attendance in such programs increased, to identify the impact of such programs on school achievement. By comparing siblings and cohorts, the authors find that by the time a child reached age 15, those who attended preschool accumulated 0.8 years more education. Given concern for selection bias, it is noteworthy that this result is robust to alternative methods of estimation whether using ordinary least squares regressions, intrafamily fixed effects, or instrumental variables regressions. However, little difference was seen in overall impact whether a child attended a single year of preschool or more. From a standpoint of offsetting early cognitive gaps, it is noteworthy that the impact of preschool attendance was largest for those children from households with less education. The authors also indicate that those who did not attend preschool had a higher rate of grade repetition. Finally, the authors venture a range for an estimate of the benefit-to-cost ratio for preschool education. The lowest of these—that for the highest assumed discount rate of future earnings—is 3.2.[9] Thus, for every dollar spent on preschool education an increase is estimated in the stream of future earnings of at least $3. When the discount of future earnings is less, the benefit-to-cost ratio was estimated at 19.1.

Another study used a similar strategy of an exogenous increase of supply to identify an increase in demand for participation in preschool in Argentina (Berlinski, Galiani, and Gertler 2009). Baseline preschool enrollment in the initial years of the time period studied was less than 50 percent (compared with more than 80 percent in the Uruguay study) and increased to 65 percent by the end of the period. The authors use the expansion of preschool classrooms, rather than a direct measure of the participation in the opportunity,[10] to indicate the impact of preschool programs. They find that an increase of one preschool place per child increases test scores in mathematics and Spanish by 0.23 standard deviation, an increase they compare to the reported impact in the literature for a decrease of 10 students per primary classroom.

Bernal and others (2009) provide similar evidence using the capacity of early childhood care and education programs at the municipal level as an instrument to understand participation in a preschool program that improved school achievement in the fifth grade. This study of the income-targeted program for children from birth to age six in Colombia, Hogares Comunitarios de Bienestar Familiar (Community Homes of the Institute of Family Welfare), also noted that children who were in the program and had at least 16 months of participation had better nutritional status and psychosocial development and performed higher on tests of cognitive development than a control group matched using propensity score matching. Similar results were found using the length of exposure to identify program impact. Whether or not the childcare provider (the "community mother") had received training on ECD was also found to be a significant determinant of the observed program effects.

Rodrigues, Pinto, and Santos (2010) also use the supply of day care and preschool (kindergarten) facilities in municipalities in Brazil, as well as the average incidence of contagious diseases among children at preschool age, as instruments to explain the decision to send children to preschool institutions. As with the studies reported above, they find that preschool attendance led to higher school performance, in this case as revealed by math test scores. Indeed, they find their results to be directly comparable to those from Argentina (Berlinski, Galiani, and Gertler 2009). Moreover, the results are robust to an alternative approach using a panel of schools and inferring causality based on the variation of the proportion of children starting school after either kindergarten or preschool.

Of course, a wider range of studies have assessed the impact of preschool programs using plausible identification strategies (Engle and others 2010; Nores and Barnett 2010). Many of these papers measure significant outputs in terms of changes in indicators of cognitive or noncognitive ability. Most of these studies contrast, however, with the four studies from Latin America discussed above in that they generally do not directly address the question of how investments in preschool affect subsequent schooling outcomes. The output measured in most studies of preschool programs is reported in effect sizes of developmental scores. Such indicators may provide insight into the program effectiveness for outcomes in early childhood, in keeping with equation (5.3), but they often do not have the data to determine the impact of these changes in ability on schooling outcomes (equations [5.4] and [5.5]), which in turn can be used to calculate impacts on future earnings in keeping with equation (5.2).

One recent study that addresses equations (5.4) and (5.5), albeit not in a manner that can easily be mapped to school outcomes, looks at self-productivity of skills in India using a panel covering children in Andhra Pradesh (Helmers and Patnam 2010). The skills measured in this study are latent variables based on indicators of both cognitive and noncognitive (personality) ability, and the model is identified through a recursive structure using parental investments rather than by an experimental design. The study shows that cognitive ability in one period (age eight in this study) both is responsive to parental investments and has a positive impact on cognitive ability four years later. Moreover, the analysis finds that early cognitive ability influences subsequent noncognitive ability, an indication of self-productivity. As Cunha and Heckman (2010) explain, self-productivity occurs when the skills acquired in one period persist into future periods, which suggests that skills are both self-reinforcing and cross-fertilizing.

Another benefit-to-cost study of early child education is based on a long-term panel from Turkey (Kaytaz 2005), which looked at the beneficiaries of an intervention that differed from conventional preschool programs in which teachers or caregivers worked with the children who attended the center. Instead, the program trained parents to improve the home learning environment for their children. The benefit-to-cost estimates reported in this study for center-based parental training using plausible discount rates of 10 and 6 percent were 4.25 and 6.37, respectively. The benefit-to-cost estimates for the home-based parental training using the same discount rates of 10 and 6 percent were 5.91 and 8.74, respectively. These benefits are based on the increase in schooling (and reduced dropout rates) and the expected increase of earnings that can be inferred from these levels of schooling; the earnings of the beneficiaries were not collected. These estimates do not include any increased learning per year of school, and, thus, as Kaytaz indicates, they are lower-bound estimates.

As indicated in this section, recent studies from middle-income settings have replicated results from a few U.S. programs that show enduring impacts of preschool programs. These studies move beyond evidence of contemporary changes in measures of cognitive capacity. With data for the impact on increased schooling or earning, it is possible to venture benefit-to-cost estimates of investments in preschool programs. These prove to be quite favorable.

Equity in Access to Early Childhood Education

Although preschool programs may improve subsequent school performance, in many settings those who are most likely to receive it are those who need it least. It is clear that attendance in preschool programs is associated with the education and wealth levels of the household and especially the mother's education. For example, a study of Maternal Infant Child and Demographic and Health Surveys from 52 countries covering the period between 1999 and 2003 found a consistent wealth gradient (Nonoyama-Tarumia, Loaiza, and Engle 2009). The study found that, for children three and four years old, 33 counrty-specific coefficient estimates of the impact of wealth on preschool attendance are significantly positive and only 2 are negative, whereas 12 are not significantly different from zero. The estimates for children 5 and 6 years old[11] have 25 significantly positive coefficients, with no coefficients that have negative signs, and 5 that were not significant. Maternal education is even more consistently positively associated with participation in organized learning for young children; for the younger cohort, in 18 data sets primary education of the mother was positively associated with preschool program, and only 1 had a negative association. No significantly negative coefficient estimates were found for secondary or higher education and 36 positive ones. A similar strong pattern favoring enrollment in urban areas and for girls was noted.

Nonoyama-Tarumia, Loaiza, and Engle (2009) acknowledge certain challenges to assessing reported preschool participation in cross-country settings. For example, the age of primary schooling, and hence the age of preschool, differs, as does the duration of programs. Even the concept of organized preschool programs relative to day care is not uniform across countries. Finally, as with many school databases, the information in public records may exclude private schools, a major component of preschool programs. Nevertheless, the patterns in the study by Nonoyama-Tarumia, Loaiza, and Engle are confirmed with other data. For example, more recent data from Latin America and the Caribbean indicate that, in a large group of countries, substantial differences by socioeconomic background in access to preschool persist (figure 5.2).

Although this pattern is in keeping with what is known about schooling at all levels, the income or wealth disparity in preschool education is often substantially greater than the gap in primary enrollments. Figure 5.3 presents the ratio of school enrollments in preprimary to primary education by developing world regions for 2007, the most recent year for which data are available. Were the gaps in access equal for preschool and primary education, these ratios would equal 1. As figure 5.3 shows, however, the disparity

Figure 5.2 Ratio of Preprimary School Enrollment Rates, First to Fifth Quintile of Household Income, Latin America and the Caribbean, 2007

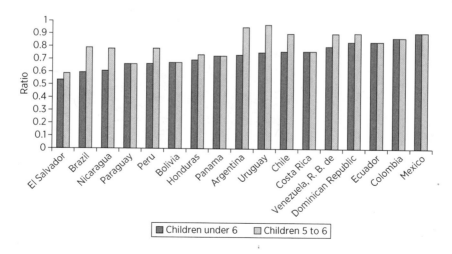

Source: World Bank estimates using 2007 CEDLAS data, as presented in Vegas and Santibáñez 2010.

Figure 5.3 Ratio of Gross Enrollment Rates in Preprimary and Primary School, by Region, 2007

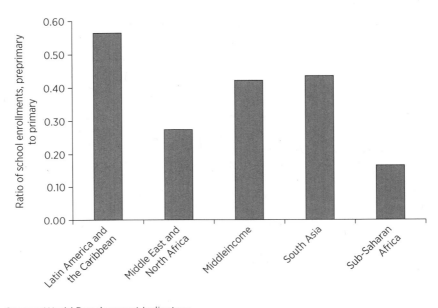

Source: World Development Indicators.

in access to preprimary education is much greater than access to primary, especially in Sub-Saharan Africa and the Middle East and North Africa.

This pattern is confirmed with an analysis of data from 2005 covering 27 low- and middle-income countries. In only four of those countries was the ratio of preprimary wealth gap to primary greater than 0.5. The closer this ratio is to one, the more preprimary enrollment patterns resemble those in primary. For three of those countries—Bangladesh, Belarus, and Thailand—this was because the poorest quintile had preschool enrollment rates at least 70 percent of that for the wealthiest, whereas in Ghana the poor had preschool enrollments less than a third those of the wealthiest but also relatively low primary enrollments compared with the more prosperous households. For 21 of these 27 countries, the poor had preschool enrollment rates less than a third those of the wealthiest, although for 16 of these countries the poor were at or nearly at universal primary school initiation (that is, more than 95 percent of the poor were reported as having enrolled in primary school).

Although preschool enrollments currently favor the relatively well-off, it is not necessarily the case that increased public investment in preschool will follow this pattern. For one thing, globally, much of the demand for preschool is addressed by the private sector. Moreover, Lanjouw and Ravallion (1999) argue that even when the average benefit incidence favors the nonpoor, marginal investments may favor low-income households. The distribution of the benefits of such marginal incidence depends, in part, on whether the public investments are focused primarily on increasing the quality of existing services and lowering their price or whether the investments are aimed primarily at expanding coverage (Younger 2003). As preschool enrollments saturate for the well off—that is, at some point there can be no increase in attendance rates—expansion of enrollments generally favors the initially excluded group. The distribution of expenditures on increased quality is less predictable.

Berlinski, Galiani, and Manacorda (2008) present evidence for the expansion of enrollments over more than a decade of investments. They indicate that as the supply of preschool services in Uruguay increased between 1989 and 2000, participation in preschools increased by 12 percentage points so that well over 90 percent of all children attended preschool by the end of the period. Because the majority of children excluded from preschool at the start of the period studied came from low socioeconomic households, the expansion narrowed the participation gap. Similarly, the placement of the 3,754 new preschool classrooms that Argentina constructed between 1993 and 1999 was disproportionately where preschool enrollment was lowest (Berlinski, Galiani, and Gertler 2009).

Noteworthy, these two countries have the ratios of preschool enrollments for children aged five to six that are closest to 1 in figure 5.2. Although it is tempting to interpret the investments in preschool as a form of dynamic substitutability—in contrast with the dynamic complementarity discussed above—in fact, the gap is closed not by inputs in basic schooling (as in equation [5.5]) but by programs in the preschool period. Thus, the results are a step toward supporting the premise of this study: that preschool investments can contribute to intergenerational equity by increasing the returns to formal schooling.

Many countries aim at the universal provision of preschools, often motivated by a human rights–based perspective. South Africa, for example, explicitly references the Declaration of the Rights of Children in its ECD policy (Biersteker 2010). The rollout, however, has been more rapid in the provinces with higher capacity, thus delaying the potential impact on equity. In partial contrast, Chile has introduced a national ECD policy, Chile Crece Contigo (Grow Together), that is also motivated by a rights-based approach but that aims at focused or priority access to services for children in the most vulnerable 40 percent of the population (Valderrama and Raczynski 2010). Although the program seeks to foster comprehensive development of children by guaranteeing universal support for biological, cognitive, and psychosocial development for all children, the focused nature of the strategy is designed to prioritize expenditures. Thus, the focusing of services differs from targeting—which often seeks to exclude a relatively well-off population from a program or from state subsidies—but nevertheless has a poverty orientation in its conceptualization.

Two final points are relevant to the question of whether preschool programs can close gaps in learning. First, although the current evidence documenting dynamic complementarity or substitutes is too limited to allow a firm statement as to what is needed at the primary school level to make the most of preschool inputs, the observation by Currie and Thomas (2000) that the benefits of Head Start depend, in part, on the quality of the school system in which the child subsequently enrolls can almost surely be generalized to other countries.[12]

Second, although it is similarly the case that the evidence base remains limited, the generalization that the quality of the preschool experience is more relevant than mere attendance is intuitive. The challenge is to ascertain what constitutes a quality program. Nores and Barnett (2010, 279), for example, conclude their meta-analysis with the observation that "program design matters but there is a lack of clarity about what dimensions matter how much and for what reasons." Most studies that inquire into the question indicate that formal schools do better than nonformal ones, although even the latter have positive benefits (Engle and others 2010). Seldom, however, do the available studies control for self-selection into programs; far more common are value-added studies that look at changes in skills over time as in the study by Malmberg, Mwaura, and Sylva (2011), which assessed madrasas in East Africa relative to other preschools, or Rao and Person's (2007) appraisal of formal and informal preschools in Cambodia. In contrast, Rolla and others (2006) were able to randomly assign kindergarten children to different interventions designed for lagging students. As with the Banerjee and others (2007) study for slightly older students, this study found that tutoring improved scores and was more beneficial than providing classroom teachers with more materials.

In addition to more studies of this nature, studies that assess the cost of different programs and help guide interventions can be instructive, particularly in settings where budgets are so limited that primary classrooms have upwards of 50 students.[13] Current data for preschool programs in very low-income countries are limited. One study, by Jaramillo and Mingat (2008), presents estimates from four African countries with the caveat that the sample cannot be considered representative. In these four countries—Benin, Cameroon, Côte d'Ivoire, and Niger—the cost per preschool child ranged from 20 percent higher than the cost per primary pupil to twice as much. Jaramillo and Mingat estimate that the ratio of preschool to primary school cost for all of Africa is 1.37. Because the average preschool pupil-to-teacher ratio in Africa was reported at 27.2 and the comparable ratio was

44.6 in primary school, the cost per preschool teacher must be lower than the salary for primary teachers to reach this ratio of costs. Jaramillo and Mingat also report that the cost per pupil in public preschool programs in four other African countries ranges from twice the cost in community programs to five times as much.[14] Both the differences in community cost and the differences in costs per teacher may also be indicative of differences in service quality, but it is likely that reliable estimates of the relationship between costs and quality for preschools will not be available for quite some time.

One other statistic from Jaramillo and Mingat (2008) is noteworthy: The cost per preschool student in Africa was reported to be 17 percent of per capita GNP. This is quite close to the ratio of the Perry preschool program to the GNP in the United States. The unit costs of preschool as a percentage of average income reported in either the Perry preprogram or Jaramillo and Mingat, however, are higher than that in Uruguay, as can be inferred from the Berlinski, Galiani, and Manacorda (2008) calculations of the benefit-to-cost ratio for preschool investments. The costs in that program are in the range of only 5 percent of per capita GNP, although, of course, they are higher in absolute value than the unit costs in Africa.

Three key observations are found in this section. First, income disparities in enrollments in preschool exceed the remaining divergence in primary school enrollments. Second, although there is relatively little information on the degree to which this gap reflects supply of placements or demand for the programs, concerted efforts to expand public availability of preschool can close this gap appreciably. Finally, the section notes the paucity of information on what is needed to increase the quality of preschools, especially where public resources are highly constrained.

Conclusions

In their recent research review, Cunha and Heckman (2010) posit that there is no equity-efficiency trade-off for investments in early childhood, although it often does hold for schooling investments later in life. Preschool investments focused on the poor not only help to offset the handicap of the limited assets at their disposal, but also turn out to have higher rates of return than other plausible programs. These investments include an array of programs to improve the nutrition of pregnant women and children in the first three years of the latter's lives, as well as to promote a stimulating environment for these children. Programs to expand preschool availability may have a somewhat lower rate of return than these earliest investments; although the evidence base is too thin to comfortably state this as a widespread pattern, the available data point to high rates of return for investments aimed at this age group as well.

Although there are a wide range of studies on the demand for primary and secondary school, less is known about the degree to which this demand reflects a failure to reach full potential in the preschool period. Nor have programs designed to stimulate demand for preschool services received the level of attention that has been devoted to demand for primary education. Plausibly, transfer programs linked to preschool enrollment will have an impact similar to what has been noted for transfer programs and fee waivers for primary enrollment. Indeed, given the overall positive impact of preschool programs studied and the remaining gap in preschool participation, it appears that efficiency and equity could simultaneously be promoted by shifting the focus of conditional cash transfer (CCT) programs from primary school attendance to preschool attendance. Demand-side programs aimed at primary school participation (where the rates of school initiation are often greater than 90 percent) may be less effective than similar transfers with a requirement of preschool participation. This is particularly relevant in Latin America, where CCT programs are present in virtually every country and where preschool programs are similarly well established. Such a shift is unlikely to have any negative consequences for the educational objectives of CCT programs; it is hard to picture a child attending preschool and not going on to primary school even if the cash incentive is greater for the former.

However, cash transfers are not the sole way to promote the natural link of equity and efficiency that early child education presents. As indicated, if gaps in cognitive and noncognitive skills are related to household resources and if they persist into school-age years under very plausible assumptions about educational systems, these gaps will remain, and perhaps widen, throughout the child's youth. Although remedial education programs may reduce such gaps, the limited data for the costs of such programs in developed countries imply that it is far more efficient to address the gaps at an early age. In the poorest countries, increasing investments in early childhood education will be critical to improving the learning outcomes and completion rates of students in basic and secondary education. In this sense, it is promising that in the recent meetings of the Education for All-Fast Track Initiative, it was recommended to increase funding to expand early childhood education in the poorest countries in the world, those that qualify for grants from the International Development Agency.

In many countries preschool education is mainly provided by the private sector and nongovernmental organization providers. This is changing in many middle-income countries, but it is still common that the expansion of services first reaches those children who require such programs the least. Thus, prioritization of public support can also promote equity of outcomes of the full education system. This implies a continuum of programs from transfers to focused investments in parenting education and preschool programs that link education policy with other sectors, including health and social protection. Because many preschool programs that include health interventions are targeted partially on the basis of nutritional status, this serves as a reminder that ECD is inherently cross-sectoral.

A final observation on such preschool programs is that the recognition of their role in increasing school readiness is only a first step. Preschool programs are unlikely to be effective if they are merely bringing primary school curriculum to younger children; they are unlikely to be affordable and sustainable in very low-income settings if they use the same resources as those currently devoted to primary and secondary schooling. This is a particular concern where trained teachers are scarce and where such training is often geared toward rote learning and a narrow set of skills.

Thus, having both technical and financial resources for measuring the quality of ECD interventions is a priority for developing countries. Similarly, evidence-based guidance for countries as to the institutional and governance arrangements that are most effective in ensuring access to quality ECD programs is needed. These two challenges should be at the top of the development agenda for ECD.

In many countries ECD is promoted as a rights-based service (with universal coverage as an objective), rather than as a program designed to compensate a subpopulation for gaps in the child's home environment or to offset consequences of early malnutrition. This chapter has explored the overlap of equity and efficiency by reviewing the coverage of ECD programs in various countries throughout the world using household surveys. The chapter also has presented evidence about the variation in responses to ECD programs by households from different income or wealth groups. In low-income countries both demand for, and supply of, ECD programs are limited, and direct competition is seen for limited human resources in education and health systems. In middle-income countries, more programs exist, but gaps remain in access between children from different socioeconomic, ethnic, or racial backgrounds. This chapter has considered the degree to which ECD—already considered an element of education and health strategies in many countries—can also be viewed as a component of poverty reduction and social protection strategies.

Notes

1. Hanushek and Woessmann (2008) refer to this learning as cognitive skills, but it is a very different concept of cognitive skills than is used in this volume. Nor is it necessary that learning refer to cognitive skills alone (even if most measurement focuses on these); noncognitive ability is regularly shown to have a significant impact on earnings and other outcomes.

2. This is the flavor of the oft-cited model of Cunha and Heckman (2007). See also Behrman, Glewwe, and Miguel (2007).
3. Cunha and Heckman (2009) use a different approach to uncover the time frame of family inputs into cognitive and noncognitive development utilizing cross-equation restrictions and a set of proxy measurements for latent skills.
4. Cunha and Heckman (2009) call a period critical if after the period an input has no measurable impact. A sensitive period for a skill is when that period has the highest response to an input, but at a later date some increase of the skill is nevertheless possible.
5. The point is also made by Filmer and Pritchett (2001), who use a wealth index as an alternative to measures of income or expenditures and, thus, avoid the bias toward zero from measure errors in these variables.
6. Behrman, Alderman, and Hoddinott (2004) present a review of this evidence.
7. This is in keeping with the observation that identification using natural experiments provides local treatment effects (Angrist and Imbrens 1994). In this example, the causal inference from such estimates pertains to those individuals who were directly affected by the shocks rather than to the larger population.
8. See Almond and Currie (2010) for an analysis of the methodological challenges to separating preferences from program impacts and how recent research has addressed them.
9. Discounted future benefits are used because a dollar now—which can be invested and thus earn a positive rate of return—is worth more than a dollar at a later date. Economists generally agree on the need for such a discount, but there is no universally accepted rate for making such an adjustment; hence, a range of estimates are commonly reported.
10. However, they also argue that they cannot reject the hypothesis that each new place increases preschool enrollment by one student.
11. The study excluded cases in which primary school begins by age 6.
12. Equation (5.5) can be viewed as the impact of school readiness on the returns to school inputs or, equally, the impact of school inputs on the returns to preschool ability. Mathematically these two interpretations of the second derivative of a learning production function cannot be distinguished.
13. Randomized trials of preschool programs in Cambodia and Mozambique supported by the Spanish Impact Evaluation Trust and the U.K.'s Department for International Development are currently in the field.
14. It is not clear in the tables why the data for these four countries are not included with the information on the costs for the other four countries.

References

Akresh, Richard, Emilie Bagby, Damien de Walque, and Harounan Kazianga. 2010. "Child Ability and Household Human Capital Investment Decisions in Burkina Faso." Policy Research Working Paper No. 5370, World Bank, Washington, DC.

Alderman, Harold, John Hoddinott, and William Kinsey. 2006. "Long Term Consequences of Early Childhood Malnutrition." *Oxford Economic Papers* 58 (3): 450–74.

Alderman, Harold, Hans Hoogeveen, and Mariacristina Rossi. 2009. "Preschool Nutrition and Subsequent Schooling Attainment: Longitudinal Evidence from Tanzania." *Economic Development and Cultural Change* 57 (2): 239–60.

Almond, Douglas, and Janet Currie. 2010. "Human Capital Development before Age Five." NBER Working Paper No. 15827, National Bureau of Economic Research, Cambridge, MA.

Andrabi, T., J. Das, A. Khwaja, T. Vishwanath, and T. Zajonc. 2007. *The Learning and Educational Achievement in Punjab Schools (LEAPS) Report.* Washington, DC: World Bank.

Angrist, J., and G. Imbens. 1994. "Identification and Estimation of Local Average Treatment Effects." *Econometrica* 62: 467–76.

Banerjee, Abhijit, Shawn Cole, Esther Duflo, and Leigh Linden. 2007. "Remedying Education: Evidence from Two Randomized Experiments in India." *Quarterly Journal of Economics* 122 (3): 1235–64.

Behrman, Jere, Harold Alderman, and John Hoddinott. 2004. "Hunger and Malnutrition." In *Global Crises, Global Solutions,* ed. Bjorn Lomborg, 363–442. Cambridge: Cambridge University Press.

Behrman, J., Y. Cheng, and P. Todd. 2004. "Evaluating Preschool Programs When Length of Exposure to the Program Varies: A Nonparametric Approach." *Review of Economics and Statistics* 86 (1): 108–32.

Behrman, Jere, Paul Glewwe, and Edward Miguel. 2007. "Methodologies to Evaluate Early Childhood Development Programs." Doing Impact Evaluation Paper No. 9, World Bank, Washington, DC.

Behrman, Jere, and James Knowles. 1999. "Household Income and Child Schooling in Vietnam." *World Bank Economic Review* 13 (2): 211–56.

Berlinski, S., S. Galiani, and P. J. Gertler. 2009. "The Effect of Pre-Primary Education on Primary School Performance." *Journal of Public Economics* 93: 219–34.

Berlinski, S., S. Galiani, and M. Manacorda. 2008. "Giving Children a Better Start: Preschool Attendance and School-Age Profiles." *Journal of Public Economics* 92: 1416–40.

Bernal, Raquel, Camila Fernández, Carmen Elisa Flórez, Alejandro Gaviria, Paul René Ocampo, Belén Samper, and Fabio Sánchez. 2009. "Evaluación de impacto del Programa Hogares Comunitarios de Bienestar del ICBF." Working Paper, Centro de Estudio sobre Dessollo Econmico, Universidad de los Andes, Bogota.

Biersteker, Linda. 2010. "Scaling-Up Early Child Development in South Africa." Working Paper No. 16, Wolfensohn Center for Development–Brookings Institution, Washington, DC. http://www.brookings.edu/papers/2010/04 _child_development_south_africa_biersteker.aspx.

Carneiro, Pedro, and Rita Ginha. 2009. "Preventing Behavior Problems in Childhood and Adolescence: Evidence from Head Start." University College London, London. https://docs.google.com/leaf?id=0BxhB_zZedpE8NWJmZGM5ZmM tMjlhNy00MzQ1LTg2ODYtODc0NGRmYTUwMzc5&hl=en&authkey=CLyn17 kE&pli=1.

Chetty, Raj, John N. Friedman, Nathaniel Hilger, Emmanuel Saez, Diane Whitmore Schanzenbach, and Danny Yagan. 2010. "How Does Your Kindergarten Classroom Affect Your Earnings? Evidence from Project STAR." NBER Working Paper No. 16381, National Bureau of Economic Research, Cambridge, MA.

Cook, Michael D., and William N. Evans. 2000. "Families or Schools? Explaining the Convergence in White and Black Academic Performance." *Journal of Labor Economics* 18 (4): 729–54.

Cunha, Flavio, and James Heckman. 2007. "The Technology of Skills Formation." *American Economic Review* 97 (2): 31–47.

———. 2009. "The Economics and Psychology of Inequality and Human Development." *Journal of the European Economic Association* 7 (2–3): 320–64.

———. 2010 "Investing in Our Young People." NBER Working Paper No. 16201, National Bureau of Economic Research, Cambridge, MA.

Cunha, Flavio, Jame Heckman, Lance Lochner, and Dimitriy Masterov. 2006. "Interpreting the Evidence on Life Cycle Skill Formation." In *Handbook of the Economics of Education,* ed. Eric A. Hanushek and Finis Welch, vol. 1, 697–812. Amsterdam: New Holland–Elsevier.

Currie, Janet, and Duncan Thomas. 2000. "School Quality and the Longer-Term Effects of Head Start." *Journal of Human Resources* 35 (4): 755–74.

Deming, David. 2009. "Early Childhood Intervention and Life-Cycle Skill Development: Evidence from Head Start." *American Economic Journal: Applied Economics* 1 (3): 111–34.

Engle, Patrice L., Maureen M. Black, Jere R. Behrman, Meena Cabral de Mello, Paul J. Gertler, Lydia Kapiriri, Reynaldo Martorell, Mary Eming Young, and the International Child Development Steering Group. 2007. "Strategies to Avoid the Loss of Developmental Potential in More Than 200 Million Children in the Developing World." *Lancet* 369 (9557): 229–42.

Engle, P. L., L. C. H. Fernald, H. Alderman, J. Behrman, C. O'Gara, A. Yousafzai, M. Cabral de Mello, M. Hidrobo, N. Ulkuer, I. Ertem, and S. Iltus. 2010. "Strategies for Reducing Inequalities and Improving Developmental Outcomes for Young Children in Low and Middle Income Countries." Working paper.

Field. Erica, Omar Robles, and Maximo Torero. 2009. "Iodine Deficiency and Schooling Attainment in Tanzania." *American Economic Journal: Applied Economics* 1 (4): 140–69.

Filmer, Deon, and Lant Pritchett. 2001. "Estimating Wealth Effects without Expenditure Data—Or Tears: An Application to Educational Enrollments in States of India." *Demography* 38 (1): 115–32.

Filmer, Deon, and Norbert Schady. 2009. "School Enrollment, Selection and Test Scores." Policy Research Working Paper No. 4998, World Bank, Washington, DC.

Fiszbein, Ariel, and Norbert Schady. 2009. "Conditional Cash Transfers: Reducing Present and Future Poverty." Policy Research Report, World Bank, Washington, DC.

Glewwe, Paul, and Michael Kremer. 2006. "Schools, Teachers, and Education Outcomes in Developing Countries." In *Handbook of the Economics of Education,* ed. Eric A. Hanushek and Finis Welch, vol. 2, 945–1017. Amsterdam: New Holland–Elsevier.

Glewwe, Paul, Michael Kremer, and Sylvie Moulin. 2009. "Many Children Left Behind? Textbooks and Test Scores in Kenya." *American Economic Journal: Applied Economics* 1 (1): 112–35.

Grantham-McGregor, S., L. Fernald, and K. Sethuraman. 1999. "Effects of Health and Nutrition on Cognitive and Behavioural Development in Children in the First Three Years of Life. Part 2. Infections and Micronutrient Deficiencies: Iodine, Iron and Zinc." *Food and Nutrition Bulletin* 20 (1): 76–99.

Hanushek, Eric, and Ludger Woessmann. 2008. "The Role of Cognitive Skills in Economic Development." *Journal of Economic Literature* 46 (3): 607–68.

Heckman, James, and Edward Vytlacil. 2001. "Identifying the Role of Cognitive Ability in Explaining the Level of and Change in the Return of Schooling." *Review of Economics and Statistics* 83 (1): 1–12.

Helmers, Christian, and Manasa Patnam. Forthcoming. "The Formation and Evolution of Childhood Skill Acquisition: Evidence from India." *Journal of Development Economics.* In press. doi:10.1016/j.jdeveco.2010.03.001.

Hoddinott, J., J. A. Maluccio, J. R. Behrman, R. Flores, and R. Martorell. 2008. "Effect of a Nutrition Intervention during Early Childhood on Economic Productivity in Guatemalan Adults." *Lancet* 371: 411–16.

Jaramillo, Adriana, and Alain Mingat. 2008. "Can Early Childhood Programs Be Financially Sustainable in Africa?" In *Africa's Future—Africa's Challenge: Early Childhood Care and Development (ECCD) in Sub-Saharan Africa,* ed. Marito Garcia, Alan Pence, and Judith Evans, 459–85. Washington, DC: World Bank.

Kaytaz, Mehmet. 2005. *A Cost Benefit Analysis of Preschool Education in Turkey.* Istanbul: ACEV, Mother Child Education Foundation.

King, Elizabeth, and Jere Behrman. 2009. "Timing and Duration of Exposure in Evaluations of Social Programs." *World Bank Research Observer* 24 (1): 55–82.

Lanjouw, Peter, and Martin Ravallion. 1999. "Benefit Incidence, Public Spending Reforms and the Timing of Program Capture." *World Bank Economic Review* 13 (2): 257–71.

Malmberg, Lars-Erik, Peter Mwaura, and Kathy Sylva. 2011. "Effects of a Preschool Intervention on Cognitive Development among East-African Preschool Children: A Flexibility Time Coded Growth Model." *Early Childhood Research Quarterly* 26 (1): 124–33.

Maluccio, J. A., J. Hoddinott, J. R. Behrman R. Martorell, A. R. Quisumbing, and A. D. Stein. 2009. "The Impact of Improving Nutrition during Early Childhood on Education among Guatemalan Adults." *Economic Journal* 119 (537): 734–63.

McEwan, Patrick. 2008. "Can Schools Reduce the Indigenous Test Score Gap? Evidence from Chile." *Journal of Development Studies* 44 (10): 1506–30.

Nonoyama-Tarumia, Yuko, Edilberto Loaiza, and Patrice Engle. 2009. "Inequalities in Attendance in Organized Early Learning Programmes in Developing Societies: Findings from Household Surveys." *Compare* 39 (3): 385–409.

Nores, Milagros, and W. Steven Barnett. 2010. "Benefits of Early Childhood Interventions across the World: (Under) Investing in the Very Young." *Economics of Education Review* 29 (2): 271–82.

Orazem, Peter, Paul Glewwe, and Harry Patrinos. 2009. "Education." In *Global Crises, Global Solutions: Costs and Benefits,* ed. Bjorn Lomborg, 180–214. Cambridge: Cambridge University Press.

Rao, Nirmala, and Emma Pearson. 2007. "An Evaluation of Early Childhood Care and Education Programmes in Cambodia." UNICEF, Geneva. http://www.unicef.org/evaldatabase/files/CBD_early_childhoodcare_evaluation.pdf.

Rodrigues, Clarissa, Cristine Pinto, and Daniel Santos. 2010. "The Impact of Daycare Attendance on Math Test Scores for a Cohort of 4th Graders in Brazil." Inter-American Development Bank, Washington, DC.

Rolla, S. F., M. Arias, R. Villers, and C. Snow. 2006. "Evaluating the Impact of Different Early Literacy Interventions on Low-Income Costa Rican Kindergarteners." *International Journal of Educational Research* 45 (3): 188–201.

Shaklee, H., and J. Fletcher. 2002. "Key Studies That Rocked the Cradle: How Research Changed the Way We Care for Infants and Toddlers." In *Research Applications in Family and Consumer Sciences,* ed. B. Stewart, R. Lovingood, and R. Purcell. Alexandria, VA: American Association of Family and Consumer Sciences.

Shapiro, Joseph, and Jorge Moreno Trevino. 2004. "Compensatory Education for Disadvantaged Mexican Students: An Impact Evaluation Using Propensity Score Matching." Policy Research Working Paper 3334, World Bank, Washington, DC.

Shonkoff, J. P. and D. A. Phillips. 2000. *From Neurons to Neighborhoods: The Science of Early Childhood Development.* Washington, DC: National Academy Press.

Valderrama, Consuelo, and Dagmar Raczynski. 2010. "Creche Contigo: A Scaling Up Case Study." Wolfensohn Center for Development–Brookings Institution, Washington, DC.

Vegas, Emiliana, and Lucrecia Santibáñez. 2010. *The Promise of Early Child Development in Latin America and the Caribbean.* Washington, DC: World Bank.

World Bank. 2006. *World Development Report 2007: Development for the Next Generation.* Washington, DC: World Bank.

World Development Indicators (database). World Bank, Washington, DC. http://data.worldbank.org/data-catalog/world-development-indicators.

Yamauchi, F. 2008. "Early Childhood Nutrition, Schooling and Sibling Inequality in a Dynamic Context: Evidence from South Africa." *Economic Development and Cultural Change* 56: 657–82.

Younger, Stephen. 2003. "Benefits on the Margin: Observations on Marginal Benefit Incidence." *World Bank Economic Review* 17 (1): 89–106.

Zimmermann, M. B., K. J. Connolly, M. Bozo, J. Bridson, F. Rohner, and L. Grimci. 2006. "Iodine Supplementation Improves Cognition in Iodine-Deficient Schoolchildren in Albania: A Randomized, Controlled, Double-Blind Study." *American Journal of Clinical Nutrition* 83 (1): 108–14.